D1316715

NO ILLUSIONS

NO ILLUSIONS

THE VOICES OF RUSSIA'S FUTURE LEADERS

ELLEN MICKIEWICZ

OXFORD
UNIVERSITY PRESS

OXFORD
UNIVERSITY PRESS

Oxford University Press is a department of the University of Oxford.
It furthers the University's objective of excellence in research, scholarship,
and education by publishing worldwide.

Oxford   New York
Auckland   Cape Town   Dar es Salaam   Hong Kong   Karachi
Kuala Lumpur   Madrid   Melbourne   Mexico City   Nairobi
New Delhi   Shanghai   Taipei   Toronto

With offices in
Argentina   Austria   Brazil   Chile   Czech Republic   France   Greece
Guatemala   Hungary   Italy   Japan   Poland   Portugal   Singapore
South Korea   Switzerland   Thailand   Turkey   Ukraine   Vietnam

Oxford is a registered trademark of Oxford University Press in the UK and
certain other countries.

Published in the United States of America by
Oxford University Press
198 Madison Avenue, New York, NY 10016

Library of Congress Cataloging-in-Publication Data
Mickiewicz, Ellen Propper
No illusions : the voices of Russia's future leaders / Ellen Mickiewicz.
pages cm
ISBN 978-0-19-997783-3 (hardback)
1. Political leadership—Russia (Federation)   2. Political culture—Russia
(Federation)   3. Democracy—Russia (Federation)   4. Russia (Federation)—Politics
and government—1991–   5. College students—Russia (Federation)—Attitudes.
6. College students—Russia (Federation)—Interviews.   I. Title.
JN6695.M528 2014
320.947—dc23
2014003750

1 3 5 7 9 8 6 4 2
Printed in the United States of America
on acid-free paper

CONTENTS

Introduction *1*

CHAPTER 1 America Refracted *12*

CHAPTER 2 Russian Leaders *44*

CHAPTER 3 Should I Take a Chance on Trust? *80*

CHAPTER 4 Life on the Russian Internet *110*

CHAPTER 5 Megademonstrations *140*

CHAPTER 6 Game-Changers, Reprisals, and
Political Competition *173*

CHAPTER 7 Future Tense *208*

*Appendix A: Profiles of the Three Elite
Universities in Russia* *229*
Appendix B: Characterizing the Countries *231*
Notes *235*
Index *249*

NO ILLUSIONS

INTRODUCTION

America is refracted in all directions. In the international arena what comes from America is split—just the way light is split through a prism—into all kinds of directions and colors. So, foreign policy moves and statements go out to other countries, but they are bent upon reception in their own ways. It is just a fact of trying to communicate; what gets to the receiver is subject to all of the receiver's ways of looking at things and the deep, deep roots of history and culture. New communications technologies connect world "players" faster and also rapidly put on the agenda an unheard of range of issues to solve. Any way to gain information first or earlier than others is an inestimable asset, for we cannot simply assume we have reached our goals when we do not know the degrees of refraction. All the players seek advantages and defense at the same time; often future plans collide unexpectedly on a very crowded international stage.

To reduce overextension, the United States decided to concentrate on a few areas of central interest and pivot to the East. And, in the process, it downgraded attention to Russia, by a lot. Former U.S. Ambassador to Russia James F. Collins warned that "Anybody who suggests we are going to disengage and let them stew just doesn't get it."[1] We and they fought a protracted "Cold War," and then came, not the "peace dividend," not a state of friendship, and maybe not even a state of neutral tolerance. As we shall see in the pages that follow, the view of United States foreign policy that Russia needed no serious attention has whipped around to world-wide crisis, with Russia at the center.

Before too long, when the next generation of Russian leaders takes its turn, America should know what kind of refraction is operating. What should the United States expect? What are the new people like?

They are mightily different, largely because they have been "living" in the internet, and the way they think and the conclusions they draw are not at all like those of the present leaders, President Vladimir Putin included.

Leaders of Russia's future are critical not only of the United States, but of the way it practices democracy. Young elite Russian students in the particular universities that almost completely monopolize the supply of leaders of the future are highly critical of the growing income disparities in America and the endless greed and brutal competition that they identify with American democracy. Where once there was unalloyed respect and affection, there is now criticism—not for democracy (they look with favor on the Scandinavian model)—of the world's most powerful country.

The internet has made a powerful difference among today's and tomorrow's leaders. These two generations do not know each other in Russia, where one government supporter accused the country's future leaders of hiding behind their internet screens.

The future leaders spend so much time learning and socializing on the internet that the way they think has moved from a vertical space to a horizontal one. As we shall see in chapter 2, the "internet way" for these young Russians is summed up by one of them as "on the internet, it's unimportant how important someone is." Actually he said this about then–Prime Minister Medvedev's blog and his much-touted entry into the world of tekkies. For this book I designed focus groups (with a Russian moderator) for some 108 students in the three universities that prepare most of the nation's leaders. Most of them thought Medvedev was coming late to the game, unaware of the great strengths and penetration of the internet. And unaware of how critical they, as heavy users of the internet, have become of their leaders.

———

This book lays out the way that Russia's future leaders view their own leaders, democracy, the larger world, and the most intense focus of their international outlook: the United States. The information about Russia's future leaders in this book was drawn from focus groups

2

with students at the three most elite universities in the country, from the end of March through the beginning of April 2011. During the time of these sessions, demonstrations were going on to save the last area of the forest that once surrounded Moscow. The demonstrations brought out neo-Nazis, anarchists, nationalists—all of them provided the horrific muscle, maiming and beating the ordinary people who wanted to save the forest, while the police looked on. More and bigger demonstrations protesting vote fraud in the winter of 2011–12 were extraordinary for their orderliness, solidarity, and range of beliefs and groups. In this book these events serve as a backdrop for understanding the trajectory of Russia's future leadership and their orientation toward democracy. We will look carefully at exactly how the several protests of this size were put together. They were not merely "flash mobs," and one demonstration in particular resulted in an internet voting system to transfer sovereignty from the Moscow organizers to voters themselves. Demonstrations do not end with that amazing feat. The following May a large one turned violent, and a long list of seriously repressive laws followed, spurred on afterward by the case of Edward Snowden. Now, it seemed, there was a rationale for just about any kind of restriction.

ALEKSEI NAVALNY

During the period of mass protests in Moscow, Aleksei Navalny, who used to be a lawyer, rose to prominence more and more decisively: young, tall, charismatic, he was fearless in confrontations with riot police and articulate with the masses to whom he spoke over the loud speaker. Navalny was also known in many of the focus groups as the blogger who went after state corruption and, in a new way, provided facsimiles of all the documents involved: the signatures and ranks of the officials who ordered luxury cars and devised schemes to cheat on orders of small office equipment. The government, in turn, retried him on charges of embezzlement from a case decided in his favor several years prior. Judged guilty the second time, he was given a suspended sentence. In the midst of these weighty legal maneuvers,

Navalny entered the race for Moscow's mayor. Though he lost the race, he swept by all the other well-known parties and was a hair short of forcing a runoff. Navalny managed this in part by the force of his personality, as he went everywhere he could to reach out to voters. He ran an effective internet campaign, overseen by his internet-savvy campaign manager, and he met with a wide range of groups and published his platform. The internet was vital; the traditional mass media, under state direction, froze him out totally.

THOSE WHO WILL BECOME LEADERS: WHO THEY ARE AND HOW DIFFERENT FROM THE PRESENT

Navalny has his own distinctive way of seeking leadership, and, as we will see later, he is also a figure bearing many contradictions. Different are the ways chosen by these young people from the three elite Moscow universities that are the traditional suppliers of the nation's leaders in government, business, and law. They quote nineteenth-century Russian novels; they are sometimes amused and passionate, and when it comes to discussion of the United States, they can become angry and rancorous—and at their own leaders, too. In their focus groups of ten each, they speak animatedly, but their speech can be heavy with sarcasm and sardonic comments. They bring to this table, as they will bring to the table of their professions—and to the negotiating table—a great deal of knowledge, partly from university, partly culled from the internet. They search widely there. They speak English without an accent and usually two other languages. One of the universities offers courses in fifty-three languages. Quite a few have visited the United States. While some might work abroad for a period of time, they intend to return to Russia. On the internet, they are always seeking to expand their knowledge. Because of their low level of trust in people offline and online, they use various shortcuts as clues to the character and behavior of whom and what they meet online. But they also depend on time; they know that time is the test for making decisions and trusting.

This book is the first time we have a window onto Russia's future leaders. The students come from many different specialties, and in focus groups they spontaneously contributed their ideas, thoughts, prejudices, affect, and humor. What values do they hold? What angers these skeptical and brilliant minds? What do they think of America and other countries with which they deal? We must always keep in mind that these deep roots are in minds living somewhere else—in the internet—and absorbing new ways of treating authority, status, cosmopolitanism, and trust. They are very different people from the Russian leaders we are used to seeing at international conferences and negotiations. We need to know them to be able to sit across from them at the table and to understand the shape of the refractions they have absorbed.

The World They Enter

Context is always important. Sometimes it is surprising. For example, those in the focus groups more often brought up Tolstoy and Gogol in their conversations than events of the three-quarters of a century under Soviet rule. They also display a mental dilemma when considering assembled masses in Moscow clashing in the square or instead, trying to cope with their dissatisfaction, at having a constant "revolution inside the head," as one focus-group participant put it. I examine the attitudes of these students with reference to broader areas of current and past Russian political life to provide a larger picture that participants might only refer to in abbreviated allusions.

In addition to the environmental demonstrations the focus groups lived through, there was one of another kind: a spontaneous and vicious race riot in the center of Moscow at the time, propelled by right-wing extremist groups. The few police present were totally unprepared to deal with it. This 2010 event, recalled by all in each of the focus groups, was a "Russia for Russians" explosion of brutality. Nothing of this scale had ever happened before, but in the fall of 2013, it happened again, in a district of Moscow. A Russian was knifed by a migrant worker; within days, a burst of ordinary Russian people (this time, with women prominent), backed up by the serious muscle of neo-Nazi organizations, set upon the Caucasian and Central Asian migrant workers. Thousands were taken in and slowly let go by the police.[2]

THE INTERNET AND FUTURE LEADERS

Much has been written about the internet generally and the internet in Russia, but it has not been possible to get a representative sample of the content of this exploding galaxy, where even 10,000 sites or 15 billion Twitter messages are but small pieces. Equally, it is a methodological problem to interview or survey a population: is it the right population? Whom do they represent (as a random sample frame might assure)? As Mark Blumfield has written about the United States: "Pollsters lack a 'sample frame' for the internet. In other words, there is no comprehensive list of internet users and no mechanism comparable to 10-digit telephone numbers that allows us to select online Americans at random. Even if such a mechanism were available, most e-mail providers ban unsolicited e-mail, and most of us routinely delete those messages from unknown addresses that manage to slip through our spam filters."[3] Although with the advent of biometrics, psychometrics, sentiment analysis, and much behavioral and demographic information, all of it contributing to Big Data, the pollster's vision is not as restricted as in years past, randomness is still elusive on the Web.

This book suffers neither from a necessarily restrictive content analysis of particular convenient sites, nor from problematic survey methods. By including the universities that dominate the education of Russian leaders, we have the universe of individuals who will one day determine the course of the country's international and national policies, business, and economy, and in chapter 4, we shall explore this at greater length. It is their internet worlds which are of significance, owing to the roles they will very shortly play. As in some other countries, higher education has traditionally been considered open to a small stratum of the population and, even though more universities have come online, the gateway to leadership is narrow and dominated by very few institutions of higher education: Oxford and Cambridge, for example, in Britain or Les Grandes Ecoles in France. The United States is something of an exception; the principle of universal access to higher education broadens the field of leadership recruitment, though in the early days of the Republic, a very small number of eastern universities were overwhelmingly prominent as incubators of presidents. Imperial Russia had its few suppliers of leaders, and then the Soviet Union reversed course and, in addition, raised functional literacy rates dramatically throughout the country. It created large numbers of specialized institutes, which soon outnumbered universities by a large margin. Institutes were associated with a particular branch of the economy, such as aviation or railroads or mining or medicine. The "big two" universities in Moscow still supplied the leadership. Moscow State University and the Moscow State Institute of Foreign Affairs—later designated a university—were joined, after the Soviet era, by The Higher Economic School Research University. Profiles of each of these universities appear in Appendix A. These three have dominated paths of entry into political and economic leadership positions. There are also increasing numbers of Russians who seek part of their education in Europe and America. Some of the future leaders in my study noted that a master's level degree from a United States university counts as an added value when looking for professional advancement in Russia.

These universities' influence is strongly enhanced by their reputation throughout the country, as well as by long lists of highly placed, well-known alumni, many of whom are patrons of the schools: taking on adjunct teaching duties, serving on boards, providing prime opportunities for internships in their organizations and government ministries. Internships tend to be mandatory toward the end of a student's course of study, and very often a student will, upon leaving university, return to the internship institution for full-time work. Elite alumni have elite expectations for their children's placement. All three universities have a wide range of departments, from science to social science to the humanities to schools of law. The students who participated in these focus groups fully expect to move smoothly forward—as has been the case for generations. What is strikingly different for this upcoming generation of leaders as opposed to their predecessors is their absorption in the internet; they live there and that shift has profound consequences for cognitive tools and norms.

All of the universities cooperated, offering space for the groups and technical equipment when necessary. None of the universities was involved in the slightest degree with the operation of the groups or at any preparatory stage. A well-known Moscow public opinion polling agency provided a facilitator, who recruited focus-group participants from a wide variety of disciplines. This facilitator moderated the groups in all the universities and arranged space and technical assistance.

It is true that the focus group lacks the advantage of representativeness that only the mass public opinion survey can provide. But the mass survey would yield vastly less information than the focus groups did. To be able to evaluate emotion as an important variable and how it triggers what flows to the rational mind is another advantage of focus groups. On the other hand, a mass, randomly chosen public opinion survey does have the advantage of representativeness. As William Gamson has pointed out, "[focus groups] are useful when it comes to investigating what participants think, but they excel at uncovering why participants think as they do."[4] Representativeness is not relevant here; it is replaced by a universal sample; we are working in a universe of schools. Those in the focus groups are drawn from the entire population of schools channeling the country's best students into leadership in economics, policy, and other fields. And it is from this universe, with its many faculties, that I put the focus-group participants together.

A focus group is certainly not a license to abandon the scientific method. A single facilitator led all twelve groups, thus curbing variability of atmosphere, tone, sequencing, and reaction to the person of the facilitator. Three times during the focus group, participants were given something to fill out: first, ranking countries by interest in reading about them on the internet; second, determining where a given statement, question, or call for help might be found online; and third, "mapping" their day on the internet. In the first two cases, each of the four focus groups in each university was given a different sequence or order of options. In the list of countries, the United States was never placed at the top, thus precluding the possibility of an automatic response.

Well before the groups were convened, I developed a kind of "scenario" based on the scientific research literature. It was a guide to how and in what sequence the focus groups' conversation would indirectly explore the most important research questions. The focus-group facilitator internalized the flow and purpose of the discussion and guided it tactfully so as not to bias any position or exhibit a preference. Each session lasted two hours. From the first minutes of a session, participants were engaged, lively, oftentimes emotional, and even passionate. The importance of emotion for cognitive operations should not be underestimated, and I was able to capture this in the focus group (without, of course, being present in the room).

We should also keep in mind that these young people often express attitudes and beliefs that differ depending on what was under discussion, and their comments sometimes may appear inconsistent. Yes, they are inconsistent, as all of us are. We may call it cognitive dissonance, and we all live with some form of it all the time. At a deeper level, what at first appears inconsistent is really not inconsistent at all. Cognitive studies reveal that human "mental capacities are 'modular,' that is, domain-specific and independent. We have one module for mothering, another for attending to danger, another for judging character, and so on."[5] We see domain-specific reasoning that might, on the surface, appear contradictory if we fail to realize that the domains are different. For example quite a few Russians watch State Television's First Channel's primetime news. They know that they will emerge from university as professionals needing to keep track of the state's agenda, even if the news channel reveals only part of the story. There are more comprehensive news sources, but this one source has the widest audience in Russia. At the same time, the students mainly declare the First Channel news to be propaganda and censored, and they go elsewhere to find out what is happening both at home and in the world.

Of the 108 focus-group participants, 42 came from cities outside Moscow. The groups, generally of ten each, were, in the aggregate, almost equally divided between men and women. They were second-semester students—for the most part, in their last or next to last term—during the time of the study.

Participants in the focus groups were given a questionnaire before the start of the first session. The questionnaires asked no identifying information, and each participant picked an alias for a first name. For the most part the questionnaire was about patterns of media consumption: newspapers, television, internet, blogging, and microblogging. At the end of the questionnaire I asked three questions to test their knowledge of foreign countries' leaders and also to see if they intended to vote in the upcoming parliamentary elections. It was put this way: I intend to vote____ I have not decided to vote____ I do not intend to vote____. Eighteen percent of these future leaders declared they would not vote, and another 28% said they had not decided (all were of voting age). Forty-six of 108 participants were uncertain or negative. One would think future leaders could not, by virtue of their anticipated positions of status, even think twice about showing up at the polls. The most important conclusion I draw from their uncertainty about voting is that they were certain that the legislature was not the seat of decision making. I want to underline that in the focus-group sessions, these and harsher kinds of criticisms of their present government did come up spontaneously, but not because they were prompted. What follows evolved from a series of conversations about the media, particularly the internet. If the moderator occasionally asked a question for clarification or to draw a participant into the conversation, she never favored a particular viewpoint; she presented balanced examples, favoring no side.

It is tempting to think about going back to these young people to find out what they think at a later date. Had the facilitator and I collected and retained the personal information necessary for such a follow-up study, I would have forfeited their trust and spontaneity. Instead, I destroyed evidence of real names at the conclusion of the focus-group session. Had I not done so, I could never have achieved such startling candor in the sessions. Their talk and their outbursts are so vivid and meaningful, that they leave little doubt about their values and views. In other words, it would not have been a real focus group, but a quiet, hesitant meeting of young people consenting to mouth only platitudes or formulae. The sessions were instead full of passion and anger and sarcasm and irony and laughter.

In addition to asking about media consumption and voting, the pre-questionnaire posed three political knowledge questions. It asked participants to identify the Prime Minister of Great Britain and the President of France from two lists of ten names each. Ninety-three percent were correct in naming the then–president of France, Nicolas Sarkozy; 44% could place David Cameron as prime minister of Great Britain. I also asked which party had the second highest representation in the Duma. Fifty-three percent were unable to correctly answer the Communist Party of the Soviet Union. Sarkozy had a much-publicized friendship with Putin and was always a good show: flamboyant and reveling in the speech of the *gloire* of France. Cameron did not attract attention, and, besides, the world in general, as we shall see, has very few countries that really interest these focus groups.

Working with the Results

I did not use a keyword search or algorithm for the 24 hours of discussion. Rather, as I had done in earlier research, I became thoroughly familiar with them in Russian. In that way, without translation, I was able to detect the special kind of sarcasm and gallows humor, the culturally defined pent-up emotion, as well as the short-hand, unidentified and sarcastic examples from Russian literature (especially nineteenth-century literature), and other quotations irrelevant in a keyword search, but actually expressing a great deal. It is certainly a labor-intensive method, but I did not want to dispense with any of the information or ideas expressed. And, in any case, these were most interesting young people: each one an individual, articulate and thoughtful. "Living" with these very bright, engaged, and strong-minded young people—the best in the country—has been thought-provoking and rewarding.

CHAPTER ONE

AMERICA REFRACTED

It was Christmastime in 1979. The Soviet Union suddenly invaded Afghanistan. Americans started arming the young Afghan opposition guerilla fighters called the Taliban (meaning "students"). In New York, until that incursion, which was going to go on to be a long war—as the British found out in the nineteenth century and the United States in the twenty-first—it had been the habit of the editors of *The New York Times* to relegate the least compelling, most boring foreign affairs stories to what they joked was "the Afghanistan page": the place where they had done their duty and reported a foreign story that might well be skipped by readers. The incident was too mind-numbingly far from American concerns, and readers would be hard put to connect it to their own tinsel-strewn American life.

The Taliban won the country, but the West no longer saw them as heroes, but as terrorists. The Soviet Union withdrew and began its descent into dissolution, breaking into fifteen countries, while its hold over Eastern Europe vanished and more countries sorted themselves out: Czechoslovakia split in two, while Germany coalesced into one. Yugoslavia broke out into seven and counting. Contested sovereignties are still simmering. In the United States, the challenge to superior execution of foreign policy was obviously enormous, for these unexpected upheavals were competing with the rest of the world for American attention and action.

Officials charged with responsibility for foreign policy not only want to know, but must know what appear to be the goals of all the players—on the stage and in the wings. Making foreign policy is confounded by the speed of change and the realization that so many serious issues intersect with so many others for any country playing "big politics" on the international chessboard. Emotion matters, too, whether or not it is recognized, in the "rational" development of policy. How do they in that country feel about us? How do they judge our intentions? How will they surprise us? In 1957, the Soviet Union launched the first orbiting satellite and in 1961, a Russian became the first person to orbit the Earth. The United States was working on a launcher and space vehicle, but was wholly blindsided by the Soviet accomplishment and its improvements in quick succession. Far, far, more important than the intention to explore space, the Soviet Union proved by these launches that it was able to deliver nuclear weapons to the United States, and the reverse was not true. Declassified documents in the United States National Archive show American officials trying to outdo each other in saying: How were we to know? No one suspected this. Our department can't be blamed for a monumental gap in intelligence.

In a historic proof of the law of unintended consequences, all through the seventy-four years of Soviet power, Soviet leaders used their substantial propaganda machine to make their archenemy into the single most interesting and important country in the world. Holding up the United States as their greatest threat may have helped to unify the country. So, when Nikita Khrushchev, the Soviet leader in the mid-1950s to the mid-1960s loudly proclaimed and strung banners across city streets saying "Catch up with and overtake America," it backfired. Ordinary people are much more complex than dictators could possibly understand, ruling from the heights, deaf to signals, depriving themselves of feedback. Here was the United States touted as a model. It made people curious. The United States was IT. The nuclear threat hung over both countries and it was real and terrifying, but word had come down that Soviet citizens must emulate the United States in other ways. They had to out-American the Americans, quite apart from the nuclear field.[1] Curiosity and, for many, attraction, were there to stay.

Spurned and Left Behind

When the Soviet Union dissolved after three-quarters of a century, it was an idealized America that captured Russian hopes: an America of unfettered freedom of views and a prosperous life. Russia was also preparing to have a room in "our common European home," as Mikhail Gorbachev, the last Soviet leader, kept intoning. The first post-Soviet foreign minister, Andrei Kozyrev, stood shoulder-to-shoulder with the United States in the United Nations and in bilateral matters from 1992 to 1995. He strongly supported the plan for his country to shift westward, to have allies in America and Europe. He once told an interviewer what a good thing it was that Russia dumped the "rubbish" Soviet allies (*shval'*), like Syria. As for the United States, I think Zbigniew Brzezinski summed it up well: "The logical course for the West, therefore, was to forge a long-term policy designed to draw Russia into a more binding relationship with Europe, but there is little evidence that anyone in Washington was giving the issue much constructive thought."[2]

A twenty-year record of the Russian Federation by the Russian Academy of Sciences shows stark declines in liking America, as shown in table 1.1. Note that NATO bombed Serbia in 1999, an event that roil many of the future Russian elites, whom we will meet later.[3]

Over the course of almost four decades of doing research there—talking to students, workers, creative artists, journalists, ministry officials, old and young—I found that the first reaction to a visiting American was one of warm welcome. Some of the most profound conversations

Table 1.1 Russian Federation: About the United States % respondents (national survey)

	1995	2001	2007	2011
Basically positive	78	37	37	33
Basically negative	9	39	45	48
Can't answer	13	24	18	19

Source: *Dvadtsat let reform glazami rossian (opyt mnogoletnikh sotsiologicheskikh zamerov), Analitichesky doklad* (Twenty years of reform through the eyes of Russians, Findings of multi-year sociological: Analytic Report) Moscow: Moscow Institute of Sociology of the Russian Academy of Sciences, 2011), p. 194.

I have had have been with Russians on their home turf. My interest in
Russia began early. I and my parents were born in America, and I had
no Slavic roots to help me learn Russian (my maiden name is Propper).
I studied at Wellesley College and received my Doctor's degree at Yale
University. What sealed my lasting fascination with the Soviet Union,
and then Russia, happened very early. In the summer after my freshman
year at college, I came back home to New Haven and enrolled in Yale's
intensive Russian course. Russian had become an official language of
the United Nations; Stalin had died. President Dwight Eisenhower,
who valued psychological warfare while supreme commander of Allied
forces in Europe in the Second World War, resolved to make a gigantic
entrance on the stage of cultural diplomacy: he proposed an exchange
of exhibitions. The Soviet one, housed in the Coliseum in New York,
was a relatively modest affair. The American National Exhibition in
Moscow, opening in 1959, was nothing less than a reconstruction of
American life in a park in Moscow: "a public exhibition with young
Russian-speaking Americans as guides [who did not toe any 'line' and
who were a very mixed bag of social, political, cultural, and ethnic and
racial backgrounds] countless exhibits, and brand new buildings...a
dazzling cornucopia of items for everyday use—including food, clothes,
automobiles, boats, teenage popular music, an 'affordable' Levittown
house[4], and much more, all housed in newly constructed buildings
made of modern materials."[5] The Exhibition occupied 400,000 square
feet, much more acreage than a World's Fair area. Two million seven
hundred thousand Soviet citizens came from all over that vast country.
I was one of the seventy-five Russian-speaking American guides they
would meet. It still seems incredible to me: I had had one summer of
excellent teaching at Yale and the beginning of a semester at college; I
was at the very bottom of the age range. Over a thousand Americans
competed, all older than me, and many of whom had grown up speaking Russian or were professors of Russian. We had to go through very
tough examinations in Washington, modeled on foreign service tests,
and we had to repeat our answers in Russian. Because I thought my
chances very slight, I was thoroughly relaxed and unfazed by the interview and the three men at the end of a shiny boardroom table.

Already interested in the Russian past and the Soviet present, I was changed for life by those two months in Moscow. The hundreds of people all around me were interested in my life—an American life—and somewhat less in the food preparation I was assigned to describe. I was also introduced to a state where secret police and Communist Party "agitators" were out in force; the latter were assigned to go around to all the guides to hammer away at them to "expose" untruth.

These Soviet citizens, who had seen almost nothing of the non-Communist world, were profoundly curious and, more than that, intensely and urgently seeking to understand America. It was that sense of "necessity" about bilateral enmity and their own long years of fear and suffering under Stalin and in the Second World War, that convinced us all how different and how important was this opening, this first "footprint" of the United States in Russia in the park.

I think Russia was and is so different precisely because of this sense of necessity, that it matters what happens in the world; it matters where the country is going, and it matters what America is up to. I went to the Soviet Union and then Russia many times as a scholar doing research, sometimes to give university lectures.

Once held out as the home of democracy, learning, and prosperity, the United States now appears to make a dismal showing in a Russia that on the whole had so affectionately admired America. But these depressing numbers from the Academy of Sciences' study describe post-Soviet Russia as a whole. I wanted a more urgent picture: what would future, new leaders of Russia say? To whom would American leaders be speaking in the future and what should they expect? What picture of America do the Russians have, negotiating across the table and talking economics and politics?

FOCUS-GROUP PARTICIPANTS

The 108 participants in the focus groups have acquired different modes of thinking and a limitless supply of information from all over the world. Language is no problem; almost all speak English fluently and other languages too. They can roam wherever they like on the internet and many have visited the United States for a high-school exchange, a short course, or as tourists. They are not xenophobes, but are deeply attached to Russia. Patriots, perhaps? Not for the old tsarist or Soviet empire, in which they express no interest or nostalgia.

It is life on the internet that separates this group from their own country's leaders, who have accused them of "hiding behind their screens," because today's leaders have not figured out a way to reach them. That is a new phenomenon, one that has played an impressive role in who these new leaders are.

Makers of Leaders

Historically, like most European countries, higher education was not for everyone; a small fraction would be going on to the education of the elite: Cambridge and Oxford, Les Grandes Ecoles. Today, these schools still weigh in heavily. America is different: even though the early presidents came from few schools, the notion of universal higher education became stronger and stronger as the new states were populated, and land-grants spurred the creation of many more universities.

Russia followed the European system, but after the Revolution, the Soviet government invested in narrow institutes for applied instruction: railroading, aviation, geology, textiles. There are three universities—three elite universities, all in Moscow—that prepare almost all the country's future leaders: they are Moscow State University, the Moscow State University for Foreign Affairs, and the Higher Economic School Research University. The alumni from these universities (generations, often) are outstanding in renown and achievements; they remain emotionally attached to their schools, and the schools, in turn, keep in touch, invite them to lecture, teach a course now and then, provide interns, and make contacts.

Students come from all over Russia, not just from Moscow: the schools make it a point to draw from all Russia and also include young people from former Soviet republics. These students will be the country's future leaders in economic enterprises, federal and municipal planning and administration, and certainly, the foreign service.

What I term future leaders—the young people who spoke animatedly for two hours in each focus-group session—are graduating and third year students from all three universities: 108 in all and usually ten in each small discussion group. Each group was led by a Russian facilitator with whom I had gone over and tested the blocs of issues and balanced prompts that would guide or just spark a beginning of—but not interfere with—spontaneous discussion. Each session was intimate. They came from a wide array of subject concentrations. I had permission for a professional recruiter to put together groups to meet on campus, and in no case did the university evince the slightest interest in asking what the discussion would be about or what might be covered.

Russia has, overall, a comparatively high level of post-secondary educational attainment, but of mixed types. The Institution of Higher Education (Vysshee Uchebnoe Zavedenie, VUZ) "includes all of Russia's postsecondary educational institutions; in 1995 these totaled about 500, including forty-two universities.... A college or university education is necessary for most professional and bureaucratic positions and appears to be highly desirable for a position of political power.... A high percentage of the members of Russia's parliament are university graduates.... In 1993 some 35.2 million students were enrolled in Russian schools at all levels, including...2.6 million in institutions of higher learning."[6] Not counted here—yet—are some who come out of brand-new "business" schools, where the quality varies a good deal. Many of these schools are financed by companies, such as IBM; many, by the state.

These students have been chosen by the "incubators" of future leaders, and that is a rare achievement. In Russia, overall, 54% of the population had attained some level of post-secondary education by 2012.[7] To go further students take the obligatory State standardized university entrance exam, and most have also taken exams administered by their university to winnow the numbers to the absolute top prospects. Forty-two percent of the participants do not come from Moscow, and many of them come from far away. Women make up half the total number of participants in the groups.

At the three universities many are wealthy children of prominent officials. But many are not at all privileged—they have to figure out how to pay for a subway ride or buy a book. So, they spend most of their time at the university with their computers and in the bargain cafeteria. As a whole the 108 participants who talked about their stories were definitely not representative of Russia's population. They are far more educated; expectations from their professors are much higher. One of the three universities teaches fifty-three languages and expects students to be as fluent as a native in three. Wherever they had come from, they were now Muscovites. Averages for the country-at-large are useless to describe the contours of this select population. The atmosphere in the universities is neither snobbish nor self-congratulatory: students look like clean-cut college kids, talking and laughing in the hallways between classes. In the focus-group sessions, they become very serious much of the time.

Future Leaders

I call the young people we shall meet future leaders. I mean by that, first of all, that they have been through a process that singles out the best in the country. So, by definition, graduates of leadership incubators have a lot of chances ahead. It is not just formal education that helps them along: some come from dynasties of diplomats and specialists in ministries. Internships are required for all of them, and the schools will help to place them. While there, they meet people and do the work they might well continue after they graduate. Some of the young people in the focus groups are already partially at work—consulting for private companies, for example. Some have jobs promised after they graduate: they will go right into the Ministry of Foreign Affairs as budding diplomats or other ministries as expert analysts.

Considering chapter 2, where the participants volunteered (we never asked them to render political judgments about their rulers and certainly wanted as much spontaneity as possible) what they think their leaders are like and where Russia is going, I had to ask myself why they were going into the leadership. As a quick summary, to be unpacked as we go on, I would say that these young people are devoted to the specializations that will become their professions. Their talk is not about power. It is about excellence of their preparation and the opportunity to be the best professionals. They will be involved in economic planning, searching for and analyzing geological finds, and researching languages and keeping Russian grammar alive before it is thoroughly butchered by television. They will be lawyers attached to ministries or private and public/private firms. They will be working with urban planners and municipal administrations. They will be doing chemistry and physics for private and public institutions, and they will go into the diplomatic service. At times, these participants may seem cynical, but they are not. They are skeptical. When we see in subsequent chapters how they talk about trusting people and trusting internet sources, skepticism is a very good intellectual tool. Still, they do want to make a contribution. They will be the best prepared to do so; they will be professional; they will perform as well as they can. If they make some difference and foster incremental change, that is what they realistically accept. They have no illusions; some sound like rancid idealists.

INTERNET OVERVIEW

Every generation is different, at least for a while, until they become their parents. In Russia, a huge fissure has appeared; the leaders-in-waiting are on one side, and current leaders are on the other. Internet use is growing fast in Russia, but access is unevenly distributed, as shown below. It is a different story for the focus groups in Moscow, where participants have easy access to computers of their own and in the university; they have mobile devices as well. Moscow and St. Petersburg, the two capitals, and other large cities look very different from the rest of the country.

Take the issue of broadband access: by the end of 2012, one-quarter of the households in Russia were wired. By 2016 that penetration is expected to rise to just over 30%. Internet use at home has drawn ahead of personal use at the workplace, but that, too, varies. Taking the Russian Federation as a whole, in the summer of 2013, 46% of the population 18 and over, comprising over 50 million people, used the internet daily and 57%, monthly.[8] By the winter of 2012/13, regional differences for daily users had been reduced quite substantially: lowest usage was in the Far East, a region that is farthest from Moscow and includes the Pacific Rim lands and Sakhalin. There, 30% of the population uses the internet daily. In the northwest region, the number is 51%; in the central region, 42%; Urals, 38%; Volga region, 34%, Siberia, 34%; the Caucasus, 33%. In Moscow and St. Petersburg 65% and 70%, respectively, are internet users.[9] It was not always this way; in the winter of 2003/4, the Far East of Russia had only 9% daily users and in the St. Petersburg–Moscow region, only 17% used the internet daily. The rate of growth of mobile devices is exploding and heavily skewed toward the young.[10]

WHAT IS OUR WORLD?

Where in the world do these future leaders stand? Where will they find mutual understanding in values and geopolitical affinity? In the sessions they did not hesitate to rank the important countries in the world, America among them. We chose some seven countries and passed out a form in which they were listed alongside a column with three options: "very interested in reading about them on the internet," "not at all or not much interested," and "sometimes yes, sometimes no."[11] Germany was in the pack: the EU powerhouse is tied to Russia through the energy business and Putin's own history, as a KGB agent stationed in Germany. France, the second largest anchor of the European Union, has had cultural ties with Russia's elites for centuries, and former president Nicolas Sarkozy and Vladimir Putin had a much publicized personal relationship. Russia's increasingly powerful neighbor, China, was also included: beyond the obvious factors of rapid economic development and nuclear capacity, a sign of serious political cooperation between the two nations came startlingly early when China's new leader Premier Xi Jinping made Moscow his first foreign visit. Japan is there as an Asian power, a disputant with

Russia in a low-key contest over ownership of the Kurile Islands. Japan, with its catastrophic earthquake and tsunami that destroyed the nuclear power plant at Fukushima, turned up on everyone's list of "very interested." For that reason Japan's place in the "score" relative to other countries is doubtlessly quite inflated. Descriptive words for Japan always begin with the disaster, but other words are few and emotionally detached. Ukraine, with its large Russian and Russian-speaking population, especially those compactly settled in what used to be the Russian Crimea, where the Russian Navy is berthed and the population is 60% Russian, is on the list a short time before the peninsula was forcibly detached from Ukraine and annexed by Russia. Russia's insertion into every Ukrainian electoral campaign and American interest in Ukraine as a buffer and potential ally add to the tension. Especially after Ukraine overthrew its leaders in the "Orange Revolution" in 2004 and began talks with the European Union. Vladimir Putin and his supporters watched their southern neighbor with caution, as a source of possible contagion. The overthrow of the pro-Russian Viktor Yanukovich a decade later was even more menacing for Putin. With the pro-Russian leader thrown out, the view from the Kremlin saw that NATO and the EU and, of course, voracious America, were after the West-leaning and more nationalist Western Ukraine. For President Putin a great danger to Russia was building up. Finally Turkey is in the group, because of its growing visibility and assertiveness as would-be—but unsettled and divided—leader among Muslim states, a history of conflicts with Imperial Russia, and also because many Russians vacation there and believe they know it well.

There is no question—and this is even more apparent in the discussions—that the United States is easily in first place, notwithstanding the temporarily skewed pattern for Japan. Nevertheless, its coming in first in the "interest" category tells us nothing about approval and empathy or disapproval and hostility: this is about perceived importance in the world. Taking the responses, we subtracted the "no or little interest" from "most interest" and ranked the countries as shown in figure 1.1.

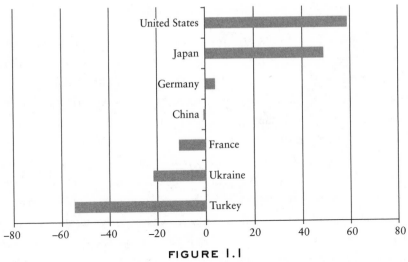

FIGURE 1.1

Interest in Individual Countries

Europe is psychologically and culturally much closer to Russia than is Asia, and neighboring Ukraine sinks under disapproval: it had its Orange Revolution and went into economic decline, political paralysis, and repression. The words focus-group participants used to describe Ukraine include "funny," "absurd," "senseless," "poverty of people," "mess," "violation of law," "autocracy," "falling apart," "collapse," and "totalitarianism," with only an occasional positive feature breaking through.[12] (See Appendix B for all the three-word descriptions.)

What is amazing is how *little of compelling interest there is in any country but the United States*. Note well: however much or however little attention is paid to Russia by the United States, the very fact of it will be hugely magnified in Russia. The two countries have a wildly asymmetrical interest in each other: these elite Russians consume all they can about the United States and mistakenly imagine that America's interest in and coverage of Russia is similarly strong. For these future leaders, as figure 1.1 shows, the United States is the world, and except for their powerful attachment to Russia, very little else matters. The bars of figure 1.1 depict a lonely outside world for Russia; it and the United States inhabit a rather barren field.

America Is Our World

At the time of the focus-group discussions, it appeared to many of the participants that American foreign policy consisted of bombing third-world regimes and fomenting revolution. Vladimir Putin argued that "outside forces," clearly the United States, had made revolutions possible in Ukraine, Georgia, and Kyrgyzstan. Most participants believe American money or military or intelligence intervention tried to foment regime change in Iraq, Egypt, and Libya. Bombing Serbia remains a live and nasty issue; they do not see it as having been about the Serbian massacre of Kosovars, but an attack on a fellow Eastern Orthodox neighbor that had had ties to Russia for generations. Libya was a different case. As these participants put it, the United Nations mandated only a no-fly zone over Libya, not an add-on of regime change. But the mandate was exceeded over Russia's strenuous objections, and the planes went on to effect the end of the Qaddafi regime. They consider externally designed regime change in sovereign entities a major threat to the Russian Federation, full-stop. As we shall see, bombing, regardless of which country or alliance is proclaimed to be in charge, is attributed solely to the United States and figures in the negative judgments of these young leaders.

Of those who ranked America most interesting, only 17 judged America uniquely as positive and influential. Another 6, though placing America in the middling interesting category, used words to denote that it has a "soft power" capability. *Unalloyed positive views, then, came from just 23 out of 108, or a fifth of these future leaders.*

What is America Like and Liking America

This first focus group that we meet has been talking about the internet and so the moderator asks about how they use the internet to find news about the seven countries. Katya is specializing in municipal administration and has come to Moscow from a distant city. She says that she has not yet decided to vote. The United States interests her very much; on a day when she has free time, she typically includes the National Geographic website among the four she regularly goes to. The words she uses to characterize America are a mix of positive and negative: Obama (she provides no clue about liking or disliking Obama), Progress, Aggression. But speak of America, and she is someone whose fear is palpable. America, she ventures, "generally, it's a big theme for me. I don't know why....Sometimes I don't like their positions." She is afraid of America, because she is afraid of destruction, her own destruction at the hands of the Americans. "I don't want war; I'm very worried about these questions." Katya wonders how far America will go. She says that when they bombed Serbia, they might have kept going on to bomb Russia, a possibility she takes seriously. She wonders just how far they would go to put the Russian army on alert: "I'm always interested in the conditions that will put our army on the defensive." Katya goes even further: "Generally we wouldn't have to watch out [for attack], if it weren't for the U.S.A."

Since the next two participants are in Katya's group, and we shall later meet others, it is a good time to describe a focus group, the feeling, the look of it. Mainly they wear "universal" college apparel: jeans, shirt, and sweater or jacket. During these two hours, no one furtively glances down to the new text message. Here, in the group, the agenda is serious and absorbs their attention. Much of the good feeling in the group of strangers is due to the moderator's ability to establish instant rapport and still retain an unobtrusive authority; she also keeps the overenthusiastic from dominating the two-hour discussion. I thought it notable that during these long sessions, the participants rarely interrupted each other or showed any condescension or impatience with a fellow participant. They disagree, as we will see, without the slightest hint of hostility.

Back at Katya's focus group, Anatoly and Dmitry—at the same round table—have a similar evaluation of the United States. Ilya's field is economics; he is from Moscow and well connected. When he had to put down his first and second most important source of news, he said internet first, as almost everybody does, and then, notably, "insider information." He does not intend to vote—another future leader who evidently considers the legislature useless. Ilya, in this conversation, calls Americans "aggressors, huge aggressors...." He associates "finances," "science," and "airstrikes" with America. It is perfectly logical, he thinks; it is a reciprocal relationship: "to support finances, they have to kill someone." He is referring here to weapons production as an engine of the economy. He is aware of the "military-industrial" nexus in the United States and he links the armaments industry to the health of America's economy and job creation.

Dmitry is a native Muscovite. When asked, on the pre-questionnaire before the session, about the top two sources from which he draws his news and information, he puts the internet first, but his second choice is low-tech: books. Dmitry says the internet distracts him from what he wants to do. I don't want it "to interfere with my doing something. What I read is a higher priority and fundamental. In my view the internet does not take away so much time as interfere with something else...." When Katya and Ilya go on about American aggression, he joins them, saying: "This is a country that attacks everybody who doesn't believe in democracy." A few minutes later, he will qualify what he means by "democracy." He adds that he means not just any system calling itself democratic, but only those who follow "American democracy." Dmitry goes on, "But Russia one way or another does not believe in American democracy....I don't know, whether America believes in democracy in general, but I doubt it. I suspect that sooner or later they will be attacking, and if they attack us, then it will raise the question about the existence of human civilization." These are the young elites of Russia, ready to step into the real policy process in the bureaucracies that run the country. They fear an American military attack on them in their lifetime. They are earnest; it is not empty hyperbole. In their one-word associations with the United States, in the "most interested" column, we see "aggression," "nuclear war," "military might," "expansionist," "arrogant," "hostile." I do not mean to imply that these are the only words; they are not. But they are severe. These attributes were offered during a period of American military involvement in Iraq, Afghanistan, Pakistan, Syria, and Libya. But when these rising elites with whom the United States may one day be negotiating relate American actions to nuclear war and threat to the people of Russia, they are thinking of an America that continues the Cold War and may likely end their lives.

Artyom is also sitting at this table; he studies economics. He wants to take the discussion a different way, or rather he wants to theorize, try to interject a deeper philosophical inquiry. He is a thoughtful person who speaks when he wants to say something he has carefully formulated. When, in the next chapter, he speaks about Russian Federation leaders, he is passionate and voluble. He is still thinking about whether he will vote. Artyom joins in to ponder the nature of democracy itself and human frailties. "It is interesting in general, from the point of view of how long such an arrangement of society can last. When societies are founded, they are based on values and freedoms, but in practice these founding principles can't be fully realized. First of all, everything has its costs and benefits, and secondly neither democracy nor socialism can exist in an ideal form. They are extreme poles, in which they mutually balance each other to some degree. But in its pure form democracy is an abstraction."

Fedya is in another group; his specialization is chemistry, and he comes from Moscow. He intends to vote and is interested in two countries: one is Japan and the other is the United States. Like many others, bombing Libya angered him and the double standard does, too. He says, "If we invaded Libya, the Americans would drop bombs on us right away." We will encounter this bitterness and sense of unfairness in specific cases. Russia, Fedya believes, is unjustly blamed by an international press that should know better, and this miscarriage of justice is probably the result of a conspiratorial convergence of Western media. This point of view was common in the Soviet Union during the long years of the Cold War. These young people learned of it second hand, but, more importantly, when they themselves articulate their experience with it—and they offer examples—it is apparent that it has made a powerful mental impact that colors their experiences. The Cold War, as a specific or technical term, has been over since the Soviet Union fell apart in 1991 or earlier, in 1989, when the Berlin Wall came down. Memory of the mutual fear of those days—of what exactly it was—is fading fast in the United States. In Russia memory is still alive, because the leaders stress the continuing threat from the United States, which still actively pursues it, they say. Cold War habits can be useful: Beyond the Urals Mountains, in 2013, a meteor split apart with enormous force and the sound of a giant bomb, heavy meteorites boomed as they hit the ground all over the area. One middle-aged teacher immediately called for Cold War defensive measures to protect her pupils: they all crouched under their desks. The meaning of the Cold War is not merely archival for Russia.

No matter how much some focus-group participants criticize America, there is universal agreement among *all participants in all groups* that America is the leading country in the world. America is still at the center of their attention. As they often say, it would be foolish or "idiotic" to ignore it. These elites have studied international politics and economics, law, and geography, among other disciplines. Many will be working in responsible positions with international ramifications. Paying close attention to and understanding America's place in the world is important to each of them personally. Whether on political or economic dimensions, or for assessing military intentions, they all have reasons to be au courant and consult a formidable array of international sources regularly.

In the very first group we met, the one with Katya, Dmitry, and Ilya, we hear from another participant with a worldview where America is at the center: Olga, from Moscow, is specializing in economics. She describes America with the words "democracy," "freedom of speech," and "modernism." There is no ambivalence here. Clearly, she has an unalloyed positive view of the United States and patiently points out to others at the table, that no matter what they like or dislike about America, "I simply think that it is one of those countries that occupy a very important place in the world and which influences both us and everyone.... you can't get away from it. We must simply be informed about what goes on there." Anya, in a different group, says, "It seems to me that it would be simply naïve and infantile not to watch what goes on in the States."

Not keeping up with American policy moves is just plain absurd. Not only is America's power abundantly clear; it is knowledge about America that these elites consider essential for success in their future positions. As several said, it "defines the world structure." Besides, says Rauf in Fedya's group, America is a competitor, and you should always watch what "the competition is up to." This geography student from one of the non-Russian ethnic zones (an internal Russian republic), does not visit internet sites on some kind of schedule; he has no set route, but reads "things that come up" from search engines. That is the way Rauf is: he is open to the unexpected, to unfamiliar arguments, to broadening his own worldview. Rauf believes America is a close friend and "we have trade relations. We trade a lot with them." In fact, there is rather little trade going on between Russia and the United States. It is ludicrously small when placed beside US–China trade. If the focus-group participants feel little affinity toward China, they are certainly aware of its growing military power. Alexander has grown up in a highly developed former Soviet republic and studies now in Moscow and clearly feels a strong tie to Russia, where he might remain after university. He will definitely vote in the parliamentary elections. He raises the threat of nuclear war hanging over both countries: "China is a power that has a very definite weight in the international arena, as does the United States and maybe still other countries. Second, we have the power to bomb each other. We will have to know what's going on there." Participants know about the dramatic rise of a powerful China, but, as the graph shows, they have very little real interest in the country. In a later chapter, when we look at where they might work in the future, they talk occasionally about employment in China, where, it appears, good jobs are available.

So many of these future leaders see America as the "competitor." Aleksei's corrective is: "We don't trade anymore." But for Andrei, studying to be a financial analyst, "objectively [the United States] is not the world leader now, the leading country ... unconsciously we're competing, and that's why it's especially interesting to read [about them]." Rud is in another group; we have not met him before. He is preparing to be a lawyer and in his spare time organizes environmental events. His position is defensively prudent: knowing about America is essential, because you have to know the "face of the enemy." Attitudes toward America are divided and contradictory because that is exactly the picture future leaders of Russia have in their heads. They carry with them images of hope and affinity, as well as weakness and alienation. Rauf, when asked if America is friend or enemy, says, "of course, friend," and Aleksei adds "of course."

Russia—the homeland—is the core of culture and attachment. Alla, a student of applied policy, is in another group. She says: "I can't single out one particular country that would excite me a lot. Probably I'm still more interested in Russian issues than in what happens 'behind the mountain.'" Dmitry says: "I like Russia. I would of course travel with pleasure, but I want to live in Russia." Foreign study can be professionally helpful back in Russia especially as an added value to a resume. A Master's degree or certificate from an American program would be economically useful at home.

Why Does America Diminish us?

The Russia–America connection is the most important in the world. Focus-group participants speak with such assurance, that they thoroughly believe that it is the same for the United States as well—that a symmetry of interest must exist. Yelena, a law student, believes America "is a progressive country, and we have very special mutual relations with this country." This talk about America in the focus groups runs from alarm to admiration for constantly innovating technology and education. There is nothing quite like Airat's confession. "You know that I consider myself a patriot of our country, Russia, but still, when I hear United States of America, right away I feel grow inside me an association with the homeland of democracy. And from this history of its existence as a state—it's not such a long history under the operating constitution—I feel I have some special relationship to this country...."

That intense searchlight fixed on America mistakenly expects equal light in return. That is why these young Russians are so irritated and disappointed when Western media at times get the facts wrong and when it is unwarranted, blame Russia. They believe these mistakes happen on purpose and prove that, for America, the Cold War is very much alive. Earlier, Fedya complained of the "double standard" the

West applies to Russia. Darya's specialization is physics, and she has a busy life on the internet. She believes that unreliable information about Russia appears on the net "by design." Sergei, her group-mate, also studying physics, is particularly interested in U.S. foreign policy on the Web. He continues the thought, "it's political intent…it's like a method basically of pursuing war—resources, territory."

THE GEORGIAN–SOUTH OSSETIAN–RUSSIAN CONFLICT OF 2008

In seven of the twelve focus groups, participants brought up the Russian–Georgian conflict over a region of Georgia. A very brief account of the conflict: with Russian military assets placed in its internal region of North Ossetia, which is just over the border from South Ossetia, one of several breakaway regions in the Republic of Georgia, Mikheil Saakashvili, president of Georgia, ordered an invasion of South Ossetia. No one could expect that the south would go up against the colossus of the north, but perhaps the Georgian government expected that surprise aggression might trigger help from Western allies. The Russian military roared into South Ossetia and kept going. They announced their mission was to stop the damage done to Ossetians and Russian peacekeepers stationed there. The Russian response was massively disproportionate; the president of Georgia retreated and South Ossetia became nominally independent or autonomous under Russia's overwhelming influence.

While observers and historians always battle the "fog of war," this case was especially murky. Official Russian news told of an unprovoked invasion by Saakashvili. Coverage elsewhere showed less certainty. Some in the focus group heard Western coverage blaming Russia for initiating hostilities—yet another example of that double standard by which Russia is always blamed. For the participants who dislike America and believe in American governmental power over the media, this misreporting of the conflict rankled. Here is Sergei, studying physics while also working as a commercial crystallographer. When the war broke out he was at a resort in Sochi on the Black

Sea. He says, "All Europe thought it was Russia that attacked and all Russia thought it was Georgia that attacked. Even now, it's not understood who attacked whom. In the summer I argued with five different foreigners about this. They were all certain that Russia attacked." He was right next to the conflict, "and it seemed to me that Georgia started it." He rejects what he sees as pro-Georgian Western coverage and calls it the result of intentional American policy. It makes no difference if the "news" comes from the "private" or public sector—the leash is in the hands of the government. "If you believe that the governments of countries don't pay them off...." The moderator adds that news outlets are supported by advertising, but Sergei does not believe a word of it. In practice, no matter what the source, "there have been lots of precedents when foreign media knowingly gave untruthful information." The moderator wants to clarify: "so you think [deliberate misinformation in the news] happens only because the government pays them?" Rauf, who is also at this table, says "yes," and Sergei strongly agrees, "Yes, of course."

The moderator throws out a question, "Which is better? Several sources of information, even if diametrically opposed in their content of events, or one?" Sergei answers without hesitation: "several and you need your own head." Sergei observes that the rush to judgment always goes against Russia: his method is devouring contending explanations and arguing with their proponents; and, finally, weighing all of them by himself. Rauf echoes Sergei: "You need to keep your own head on your shoulders." Roman, a mathematics student from a different group, has this same calm assurance that with multiple sources, a good education, and individual analysis, even this strangely covered event (clarity about who invaded whom came late in the West) can be deciphered: "...it's necessary to look at the problem objectively from different sides...we watch objectively. We can read about or watch the conflict in South Ossetia, then we can watch how the West evaluates the news and how Russians evaluate, and choose one's own point of view." Roman has come to Moscow from a former Soviet Republic. He does some tutoring in mathematics in his free time; his second most important source of news is CNN; his shorthand description of the

United States is "news" and "power." He is interested in every country. When he says he uses the comparative method and then evaluates for himself, he has many sources in mind. Participants regard the World Wide Web as just that: a world to investigate, and they are not hampered by finding information in other languages. Roman also offers this comment, "I say that any information can be biased."

Kostya will be a mathematician. He is not into blogging; he does not visit blogs or have his own. He goes often to Euronews, "which I think gives a rather unbiased opinion to all questions, and plus, there are all kinds of imports, CNN and BBC. If there is a situation, like the war with Georgia, I simply watch all sources, because everywhere they said different things: on CNN, they said one thing; on BBC, and about the same on Euronews...and on our channels, something else." He is open to a variety of conflicting opinions, but that makes the news so much more complex. He either lives with the dissonance, or comes to his own reasoned conclusion. That is what Roman does, too: "You have to look at the problem objectively from different sides...[about] the conflict in South Ossetia...we can watch how the West evaluates the news and how Russians evaluate it and you can choose which is your own point of view."

These well-educated young people practically all believe that the story of the Georgian–Russian war was misrepresented in the United States because of a continuing anti-Russian sentiment, deep, they think, in the political leadership of America. In fact, they are partly right. Georgia's leader initially was a "poster boy" for what appeared to be the beginning of a Western-oriented democratic leadership supported by the West. He grew into an impulsive dictator stifling diversity of viewpoints, but he does speak English well and looks good. He could have walked right off an American college campus. Small as Georgia is, and embarrassing an American ally as President Mikheil Saakashvili became, his country is a southern buffer next to Russia. The woefully mismatched war between Georgia and Russia was bound to end the way it did: in hopeless defeat for Georgia and the loss of two separatist regions. But because the Western press by and large could not figure out who did what and how it all started, Russia became

the initiator (incorrectly) and, in any case, even *The New York Times*
justified blaming the wrong party by focusing on Russia's having been
ready for provocation and prepared in its response with disproportionate force.[13] Georgia deployed a sophisticated, rapid-response public
relations campaign; Russia had none, enclosed in itself and the harsh
words of its enraged leader.

The war was hard to sort out. It began early in August; the
Western media were at a loss to say which country started hostilities. CNN at first reported the confrontation by simply passing on
the Georgian president's self-serving version in an exclusive interview with CNN.[14] *The New York Times* focused its first coverage
on Georgia and South Ossetia. Russia was not even mentioned until
the last paragraph which located South Ossetia "on Russia's southern border," and ended with "Georgia has accused Russia, which
maintains a peacekeeping force in the region, of aiding rebel fighters
there and in Abkhazia, another separatist region of Georgia." This
was puzzling and largely uninformative coverage: in the words of
the *Times*' ombudsman, called there the Standards Editor, "...it's
clear we don't have any idea which side started the fighting."[15] In
the late edition on August 8, Craig Whitney noted that the paper's
report "makes clear we still can't really say who the aggressor was."
On August 9, Michael Schwirtz, Anne Barnard, and C. J. Chivers
wrote from the region, beginning the article with "Russia conducted
airstrikes on Georgian targets on Friday evening, escalating the conflict in a separatist area of Georgia..." and focused almost entirely
on Russian military incursions into Georgia; one sentence attributed
to the Russian Ministry of Defense noted that the Russians arrived
"to help Russian peacekeepers there, in response to overnight shell-
ing by Georgian forces, state television in Russia reported...."
Whitney regarded the focus as warranted: "There is no suggestion in
the report above that the *Times* has taken sides and decided that the
Russians attacked without provocation. But it's also clear that the
Russian actions serve Russian foreign policy interests, in Georgia
and beyond." I take issue with Whitney. Broadcasting a statement
made by a military official on Russian government television hardly

counts as advancing the diversity of viewpoints and the market of ideas so important to journalism. After a lengthy piece the next day, Whitney noted: "There are obviously problems understanding who did what to whom and why, and this is not infrequently the case in reporting on conflicts of this kind." Nearly four months later, the independent non-Russian military observers who had seen all of the war, wrote their report. It "called into question the longstanding Georgian assertion that it was acting defensively against separatists and Russian aggression. Instead...Georgia's inexperienced military attacked the isolated separatist capital Tskhinvali on Aug. 7 with indiscriminate artillery fire, exposing civilians, Russian peacekeepers and unarmed monitors to harm."[16] Apparently cluster bombs were also used against civilians, according to Human Rights Watch.

Apparently, the start of this short, but costly, war was not as "foggy" as most news organizations claim. Details began emerging quite soon, but did not become widespread until much later—partly because of apathy in the media audiences; partly because the favorite turned out to have been aggressively off the leash, but also because Europeans especially were calling for Georgia to join NATO, and the impulsive aggression it launched ran counter to NATO's way of operating. In September 2008, the German investigative journalism magazine, *Der Spiegel*, published a detailed study of the war: who started it and why? What were Georgians up to? And were Russians prepared for and provoking a skirmish leading to massive invasion of the southern neighbor or themselves caught partly unprepared? The article quotes Republican presidential candidate John McCain declaring "Today, we are all Georgians," and "public intellectual" Robert Kagan, likening Russia to the Nazis. But, the investigative piece goes on to say that within five weeks after the end of the short war, "the winds have shifted in America." Early on during the hostilities, officers at NATO headquarters in Brussels "believed that the Georgian attack was a calculated offensive against South Ossetian positions to create the facts on the ground....Even more clearly NATO officials believed, looking back, that by no means could these [earlier] skirmishes be seen as justification for Georgian war preparations."[17]

These matters are too complex and too fraught with massive consequences for former presidential candidates and respected lawmakers
with apparent military expertise to engage in instant compassion and
retaliatory plans. If John McCain was a Georgian, without knowing
all the facts, he did the same with the annexation of the Crimea in
2014. With barely a thought about the consequences of his unlimited
emotional commitment, he declared, "We are all Ukrainians," before
calling for new moves to condemn Russia at the United Nations, sanctions against Russian officials, and the installation of U.S. missiles in
the nearby Czech Republic as a show of American regional strength.[18]
McCain was quick to call in the missiles; apparently being a "fellow-
Ukrainian" (Ukrainians are also Russian-speaking and culturally
Russian on the eastern side). His acceleration to dangerous solutions,
with no room whatever in between for the workings of diplomacy, followed the same pattern as his reaction to Georgia, years earlier.

————

Think again about the strategy the focus-group participants used.
They, too, did not know what happened earlier in Ossetia. They do not
trust Russian media, though they always want to know the Russian
version. Then on the internet they find fairly large numbers of other
sources outside Russia. They find the BBC, Euronews, and individual
mixes of the press from perhaps three to five more countries and talk to
people near the area. This is an enormous commitment, and it is what
these focus-group participants do for practically every international
story. They know that the story on their domestic channels cannot be
trusted, and to seek the truth, they compare: probably the single most
important verb in their minds. It takes a great deal of time and effort,
and that is time taken away from studies, but also from rock stations
and games and friends. But they trust no other way.

THE NEO-NAZI ERUPTION IN MOSCOW

Fedya, whose group includes Darya and Sergei, remembers the
incredibly off-base American coverage of a deadly serious event in

Russia. On December 11, 2010, two incidents occurred in Russia on the same day. One was much less newsworthy—most media professionals in America would probably classify it as "human interest" and put it at the back of the news, if anywhere. In the Far East of Russia a few thousand people gathered peacefully to register their dissatisfaction with the president's decree reducing the number of Russia's time zones to nine. On the same day, something unheard-of took place in the very center of Moscow. Violent racist organizations streamed into Manezh Square to inflict vicious beatings on anyone who did not look Slavic.

All demonstrations or parades must have advance permission from the municipal security department of the city of Moscow. Demonstrations are restricted to particular hours and areas, which definitely are not in the very heart of Moscow with the Kremlin just feet away. But here, at the end of 2010, with no permission, a riot of fascists, "ultras," neo-Nazis, and violent soccer fans—all young, Russian, angry males, most in black leather, some wearing black balaclavas—erupted and swung clubs and used their knives to rid Moscow of ethnic minorities, "chanting Russia for Russians only." They beat people who did not "look Russian"; ambulances came to carry away the wounded. The rioters gave the Nazi salute and waved banners with a symbol mimicking the Swastika. The few police present stood by and watched. Eventually, riot troops arrived late. Barreling down into the subway station at the end, the rioters terrorized people on the escalators, throwing them against the sides (if they were lucky), and then the angry mob took over the platform and the trains. The initial spark had been the murder a few days before of one of the fans' leaders by a non-Slavic brawler outside a bar in Moscow. Then after the soccer game on the 11th, hardened and frenzied, skinheads, fascists, and neo-Nazis exploded in a mass of violence. They were not only soccer fans with a culture of violence, but, more importantly, they were joined by organized fascists—"professionals" who worked to increase the disagreements into hatred and to expand what might have been limited pushing and shoving into a politically pointed and deadly inter-ethnic riot.[19]

Fedya was watching the news: "I saw the video on CNN news. There, the anchor says with a serious expression, 'in Russia, thousands of people came out against the change to winter time'...Here, if you please, is a world channel." I watched it too. CNN's anchor—her face serene throughout the short piece—doggedly talked about quaint opposition to a time-zone change, while *at the same time, behind the anchor*, there was footage of the violence in Moscow, the clash of black-leather jackets and clubs, blood, hatred. For the future leaders it bespoke the lack of importance America attached to Russia. The Moscow riot was serious. That it could happen there, that the ethnic hatred had gone so far and was at the boiling point, certainly deserved serious attention.

That riot on December 11, 2010 was very different from the next year's gathering of peaceful and relatively privileged Muscovites protesting election fraud. That was a milestone in civic outpouring on behalf of democratic rights to contest power. They impressed Vladimir Putin and Dmitry Medvedev enough that promises were made for some easing of centralization of choice at the gubernatorial level (later revoked), and for removal of some obstacles to formation and registration of political parties, and therefore, ostensibly, allowing for more potential competition.

FAVORITE NEWS SOURCES

Focus-group participants use both Western and domestic sources. Andrei prefers to use Google instead of Russian search engines, because, he says, "Google searches better than Russian search engines." He says he "*never* uses Ria-Novosti [the official wire service for feature stories], because it is extremely politicized and loyal to what takes place in the country." In the view of the Kremlin, the service was not, perhaps, political enough, and at the end of 2013, the president abolished it, putting in as head a much more hard-line chief to renovate the organization. Kirill, in Fedya's group, says foreign sources actually tell more about Russia than do domestic ones: "say, when there were problems in Chechnya in the '90s of the last century, in Russia they provided very little information about it.... The Germans wrote more about this problem; they studied it and supplied more information than Russia did." Many participants regularly use foreign sites, such as Euronews, Deutsche Welle, Agence France Presse, BBC, *The Economist*, and *The Guardian*. The moderator asks: "What do these sites and blogs you just named have in common for you, personally?" Vitaly, who is from another former Soviet republic, one that is to the west and highly developed, says simply, "authority." Then the moderator asks, "How does Europe differ from Russia?" Vitaly responds, "First, it's the thought process, yes, [a different mentality], second, we haven't got to that level of openness and development." Again and again, in so many ways, even these future leaders who doubtlessly will work in some way with the West, answer the question in terms of Russia's isolation: they do not (or do not yet) belong in the European world.

A Country and Three Words of Association

When asked to provide words to describe each country off the top of the head, the responses the students give are curious and vivid and often unexpected. Appendix B gives them all. Ukraine is identified, for example, mainly by *salo*—a slab of salt pork lard. For France, it is wine, snobbery, perfume, fashion, and some other quaint epithets that have nothing to do with power. We can take a look at them and see the gamut of their "gut" reaction to the most and least interesting countries to read about on the internet.[20]

America is the country to watch, but, as mentioned earlier, often from fear of what they see as an unrestrained foreign policy relying on bombing. Different aspects of America may coexist: the ones that advance innovation, science, and democracy, and others that threaten them with unilateral use of military force in the world. The participants do not draw a distinction between America-led, NATO-led, OSCE-led, EU-led, UN-led, or France-led; for them if it is Western, it is America-led. Some say, in discussion, that they now feel personally at risk. After the United States' bombing of Serbia, Iraq, and Libya, Russia could be next. American military actions were on the minds of most of the focus-group participants. A second quite common objection to America is related to its financial mayhem: they use words including "scandal" and "financial crisis."

President Vladimir Putin chastises the United States for a wide range of what he considers threats and attempts to dismember Russia. The wave of revolutions that spread from Serbia to Georgia and Ukraine and across North Africa on to the Middle East were all, in Putin's view, a direct result of America's policy of interference and the money and hardware to implement them. The crowds that turned out in Moscow in 2011 and 2012 were there, he believed, because of foreign involvement. The nonstate organizations (Russian and international) were creatures of American policy. The independent Russian election observation committee, *Golos* (Voice/Vote), was handsomely supported by USAID. As we shall see later, after violence exploded in what was supposed to be a peaceful "middle-class" citizens' demonstration, a surge of anti-foreign, anti-American restrictions came out of the Kremlin.

The line between "democracy assistance" and "interference" in a sovereign state can be thin to invisible. It is important to be clear: Putin's anti-American vitriol comes atop Russia's already disillusioned and negative view of America. Russia's future leaders are even more critical of their own leaders.

TWENTY-FIVE YEARS LATER: REWRITING THE HISTORY OF CHERNOBYL

Though it has been over twenty-five years since Chernobyl blew up in the worst nuclear catastrophe in history, the event has become, once more, a live topic of discussion. Julia relates a remarkable "truth" she was taught in her university class. She did not mention any dissenters to this story: "Not long ago, in the university, in environmental law, they talked that there was a cloud above—it formed over Chernobyl, and began to move around the planet. A great many Western politicians did not want it to get to Europe. They forced the cloud to be shot down over the territory of Belarus and Ukraine. Why did they [Belarus and Ukraine] suffer more? Because the cloud was shot, but it didn't land in Western Europe." Therefore, it follows that the West saved itself, while destroying much of the farmland and the second largest city in Belarus. The moderator could barely hide her surprise about this tale, and I found it altogether a fantasy. That the airspace of a sovereign country could repeatedly be breached and continuous bombing take place strains reason. Besides, Vladimir Putin did let most of the real dramatic story out many years later.

When the Chernobyl nuclear plant exploded in 1986, it released a heavily radioactive plume. "Particle sizes within the plume were the most dangerous range for inhaled aerosols."[21] The scope of the consequences is still uncertain.[22] When Julia refers to "shooting the cloud" to make rain, she means cloud-seeding, which has been widely in use since 1945. Pellets of silver iodide are delivered by planes to induce rain. It has been used to stimulate rainfall in South Africa and by the United States military during the period of March 1967 to July 1972 to extend the monsoon season over North Vietnam's Ho Chi Minh Trail, so that columns of fighters would be mired in mud. It has been used to increase snowfall at resorts. At least twenty-four countries on all continents engage in cloud-seeding.[23]

The radioactive cloud formed from the Chernobyl explosion produced "radioactive trails on the ground in both westerly and northerly directions." A large part of the plume was headed east to Moscow and would eventually cover the capital and several large Russian cities on the way, doing indescribable damage. Soviet leaders decided to force rain to fall and the cloud to disperse over relatively unpopulated Belarus, though it would hit the second largest city, Gomel, and contaminate farmland. The Soviet military determined to send their most powerful bomber to seed the cloud, but first they painted the military plane to look like one of the civilian air fleet. Pilot Aleksei Grushin, who already had experience flying the "Cyclone" TU 16 (named Badger by the U.S. military), led the mission. The Cyclone could attain a speed up to 615 miles per hour and reach a height of 7.5 miles. Grushin said, years later, that they took out the nuclear weapons and put in special cartridges filled with silver iodide. One cartridge, recalled Grushin, could make in the cloud a "hole" with a radius of almost a mile. No one explained to Grushin the dangers of the mission; the crew, including the commander, was refused pistols and parachutes. This mission had no back-up safety measures. The cloud rained down mainly on large parts of Belarus. It was a heavy black, radioactive rain. Moscow and the large cities east were spared, and for his bravery, Major Grushin was honored by Vladimir Putin in 2006—but for what? The mission was not named.[24]

Vitaly Rybchinsky, secretary of the editorial board of the historical study "Military Air Force and Chernobyl" and himself chief engineer of the service for radiation, chemical, and biological defense of the Military Air Force, maintains that by causing the rain to fall on Belarus, Grushin's Cyclone saved not only Moscow; "He defended the entire country!"[25] Disseminated a quarter of a century later by those who ought to know better, the rewritten history with the West as villain aroused no doubt in Julia and her classmates.

THE DEEPEST FAULT OF THE WEST

Trust between individuals is the glue that holds society together. Without it, there can be no society at all; according to the ancient Greeks, a man whose life is outside the city is a monster. Here I want to bring up the very thoughtful comments of two participants. They regard the assistance of the West, when the Soviet Union was dissolved, as the source—symbolic and real—of the worst of Russian life, because it destroyed trust among people. Misha is in the very first group we encountered. He considers the West morally responsible for the export of what developed in Russia into unchecked capitalism and the creation of conditions in which it is folly and dangerous to trust others. In Misha's words: "There are stereotypes about people's behavior and [they] form some kinds of images of life, which, for example, are dictated by the West. These images of life are based on a strong belief that people are often driven by their own personal advancement and are moved by all kinds of profit motives. Therefore I would not trust all of them [people in general]...well, the majority...."

Artyom, the thoughtful economics student, continues: "I think that it is possible for people in whatever countries, to trust appropriately—to a greater or lesser extent—but not here, at least not now. Because we have a system built for the satisfaction of the personal interests of concrete people."

The moderator asks, "And do we know these people?"

Artyom replies, "Yes, I think so...."

Through their eyes, the West has been successful, not in exporting democracy, but a way of life and values of constant deceiving and fraudulent competition, scrambling for riches on the backs of others. The contribution of the West to today's Russia, which, in the participants' words, may not be forever and is different from other countries, is rampant corruption and monopolies of state property and natural resources by a small ring of vicious cronies. Though the participants understand that society is built on mutual trust, they are not inclined to begin with trust, because trust is a risk: it involves self-disclosure in return for the same from one you hope you can trust. Olga says, "I agree with the guys that a person by his nature—I think that the majority of people are not altruists. And one shouldn't hope that everything will be done to help you.... Therefore I think that their position in life is correct: It's more likely that a person [should] not trust from the first meeting, [for if you do] then there's a huge likelihood that you'll simply be made a fool of. And that is the product not only maybe of human nature, but the times in which we live."

———

Blaming the West for the unrestrained corruption and the environment of deadly competition may be in large part a rationalization for Russia's swirling corruption and protection rackets creating a stratum of thieves on a huge scale—tycoons or oligarchs. The decades of the Soviet Union certainly made trust untenable and dangerous. Many in the focus groups, aware of the current state of affairs, nonetheless regard it as a byproduct of the Western belief in and spread of a market capitalism that has been rapacious and has plundered the goods of the country. This state of affairs prevents the strengthening of ties of trust—at least for now and at least here.

CHAPTER TWO

RUSSIAN LEADERS

On the Internet, It's Unimportant How Important Someone Is

In an environment of many news sources—foreign and domestic—and the deeply ingrained habit of comparing them, no single individual is regarded as untouchable in authority and wisdom—not by these focus-group participants. There has been a leveling. Focus-group participants regard themselves as co-equals with their leaders. They have strength of character and knowledge. What they were not taught formally, they have at their fingertips on search engines. With this expanded sense of capability comes an expanded sense of self. Their lives in their world have enhanced their self-worth. Pavel Lebedev, a Russian analyst, put it well: "It turned out that historically, precisely the strength of the internet-user [lies in being] more educated, he is better educated and he has more income. He has what is termed an inner locus of control: these people do not need to be taken care of by the state; they, themselves, take responsibility for what they do; they are more critical in relations with reality. Therefore, there are themes that cause outrage."[1] For example, the massive insult to individual autonomy of bald and crudely self-confident vote fraud sparked mass protests in 2011 and 2012, as we shall see in chapters 5, 6, and 7.

Many of the future leaders on the threshold of entering decision-making bureaucracies have been simmering internally, if not publically. They are not docile, not unthinking megaphones for the ruling leaders, but very often, they display a very surprising anger and bitterness. Yet they are deeply attached to their homeland.

ALEKSEI NAVALNY ON THE WEB

Aleksei Navalny has become the public face of online activist movements. He is a skillful internet user. As his activism and daring public challenges to the Putin government quickly expand, Navalny moves into new areas and even embraces new ideologies. Some of the focus-group participants follow him on his escalating internet investigations. He has been at it since his twenties and was not quite forty in 2013, when he ran for mayor of Moscow (while his court case was postponed).

The postponement was conditional on his staying put. When he went to protest the 2014 verdict for the second Bolotnaya protestors, he left his permitted radius and was put under house arrest and, most damaging, forbidden to use the internet and telephone for two weeks—a crippling, but limited punishment, while others were still pending. As he rose to greater and greater prominence in Moscow, he reached out for new ways to challenge the stability of the regime, including running against the powerful mayor of Moscow. He did not win, but he defeated decisively every one of the old, familiar parties and proved he was without question the leader of the opposition. There are many sides to Navalny. He appears to have changed his ideological direction more than once. Should we see these moves as different facets of a supple, larger-than-life challenger of the frozen system? Or are his changes in ideology steps in a journey of evolving values? Or are they various masks fixed to a man with a central core that has been fairly consistent? Before the large Moscow demonstrations, Navalny had been building up first one anticorruption blog—, then more and then organizations to expand their reach. Still, even among the well-informed focus-group participants, Navalny is not a household name: followers of his websites knew a whole host of details; others, practically nothing at all—and this is in Moscow. His site has something followers especially respect: steadfastness in pursuing important issues, even when they no longer command headlines.

He gave up all revenue-producing activity to do investigative reporting full-time. He puts up on his website not only what he has found out and with what methods, but, and this is the very impressive part:

he puts up facsimiles of all the corroborating documents and other evidence for his stories. He has gone after corruption in banking and the secret service. Mainly, he is after corruption in state purchases. His team follows every instance they can across the face of Russia. One story was about the government of Chechnya, where the president ordered online four Mercedes-Benz cars; the cost of the contract with the German company was estimated to be $727,482. The team found similar state orders in the volatile Dagestan Republic in the Caucasus and a new state order for a "light automobile for the regional court of Yaroslavl," north-northwest of Moscow. As the team makes clear, there is no limitation or oversight by the government in these cases of likely corruption—four luxury cars for a regional bureaucrat looks pretty suspicious. What the Navalny group did was to lodge formal complaints in the judicial system, especially about purchases by the state, since they are at present often absurdly luxurious. In watching out for state purchases, Navalny also exposed a bank and two factories engaged in gross money laundering, and even the secret service.

In one of the focus groups hardly anyone followed Navalny's anti-corruption blogs. One Navalny reader explains to the rest of the group: he blogs, his team of young lawyers help to gather evidence, and, most important, full documentation and reproduction of all business agreements he has uncovered. A chorus of voices is heard at once: Anna, Peter, Dmitry all say "yes [I want to go there]"; Nariman says, "I honestly never once heard of him, but I shall go today." Ilya says that Navalny's activities are merely the government's strategy to divert people from looking around them to see the vast inequalities in Russia: "There are different versions," he says, about "what kind of person, he is, but one of the versions is that the Kremlin created [him] in order to lower such social tension in the internet and in society."

Many in the groups speak about being drawn to Navalny's blogs and following them. Quite a few had never heard of them. Rita is an economist. She comes from a medium-sized city, not far from Moscow. She visits and contributes to blogs. She also has her own blog, about her personal life. She is registered in three social networking sites. Rita is tuned in to the blogosphere. On the current politics side, she does not know if she will vote; she does not know who the British Prime Minister is or the second largest party in the Duma. She compares then-president Dmitry Medvedev's blog with Navalny's. She says about Medvedev, who was tasked with ending corruption: "Not once in a hundred years would he write with such impact as Navalny." Lucia, who will be a lawyer, finds time to spend in three social networking sites. She definitely will vote, yet appreciates Navalny, especially for his exposés of politicians. Lucia says his blog and his behavior are what leaders should be doing [but are not]:

> Yes, everything he does is verified, documented. He has all the documents, all the data, all the numbers....He's not unsubstantiated, as opposed to many of the politicians who say "Oh we're such great guys; we do everything." He says, yes, he exposes politicians, but he always brings out the data and he always has all the documents.

She is impressed with Navalny's work on the internet and how he expands it with lawyer-interns and has even given up his job to devote more time to investigative work. She believes Navalny is so influential that he could and should become president. She thinks he has the makings of greatness. "I think that he has enormous popularity; if he brought out just this [most recent exposé] before elections and provided [material for] the next elections."

We will see more of Navalny in this book as his public defiance accelerates. Even in 2014, while under house arrest, he was getting out blog posts and messages through his allies (a violation of his court-ordered probation). He wrote the messages and essays by hand, and his wife and allies disseminated them whenever possible in social networks.

Focus-group participant Boris is thoroughly realistic when he explains Russian elections. He says before the vote, "We have a problem here in Russia: there is no party to vote for except United Russia....that is, they are all one and the same party." Boris will have a position in international economic relations and, in spite of his hard-hitting realism about the Russian political party environment, says he will definitely vote in the elections, another seeming contradiction. Stas, who is not a Muscovite, will work in international affairs. He definitely will vote, even though he says it's about the four parties in the Duma, it's "as though everything comes from one source."

It is amazing that 18% of the future leaders were certain they would not vote in the parliamentary elections of 2011. Another 30% could not say they would definitely vote; they said they had not decided. *Almost half of the future leaders of Russia were essentially dismissive of their civic duty and exercise of their rights.* It is not surprising when explained by one of the young elites we met before: Rauf, the geographer from a region distant from Moscow, asks Sergei, a physics student, if he is going to vote and Sergei replies, "No. It's absolutely useless."

We met Sergei in the previous chapter, when he explained that the United States was engaged in a communications war with Russia: that is, a concerted and organized attempt to reap the spoils of war without war. At the same time, he pragmatically thought of the United States as a place to look for work. Here, when turning inward and looking at domestic politics, he represents the critical and bitter dominant sentiment in the focus groups when he says: "That's how it always is. He [Dmitry Medvedev] elected himself, whatever we did. It's all the same, they elected him and they elect whomever."

Look at the inconsistencies, the dissonance, with which many of these young elites live. Lucia cheers on Navalny for exposing the crooked thieves who operate in broad daylight and yet she plans to vote for the regime responsible for the deception. Since the candidates may hardly differ from Navalny's targets, in terms of their lack of accountability and their powerful patrons, will she simply be adding to Navalny's docket? Boris says that there is only one party in Russia and yet he will vote, with the full realization that it is meaningless. In part, the intention to vote is a matter of civic duty for those who may serve the state at home or abroad. I would go further, to relate this apparently contradictory behavior to the preceding chapter—to the attachment that the focus-group participants have to Russia and not to any other country. The civic ritual of voting is an emblem of that attachment. And at a psychologically deeper level, she and Boris and many of the other participants who register their intention to vote live with psychological dissonance. Human beings do. We are able to compartmentalize contradictions rather than face them to achieve consistency. We do it all the time; we eat candy bars while bombarded by the crusade against obesity; we smoke, knowing the consequences, but we separate those consequences from the moment. Consistency of values, emotions, behaviors, and knowledge is impossible for human beings, and it may be both personally and politically healthy that it is. Zealotry might be the opposite. A great many of the focus-group participants wrote "No" or "Don't Know" to the question of whether to vote. For them their powerlessness and ineffectual Duma sessions could not be tolerated. Each had his individual threshold.[2]

THE RUSSIAN SYSTEM

When we talk about trust in the next chapter, there are two principal components that bear on the operation of a political system: (1) the expectation that the system will implement its own rules; and (2) the risk a citizen takes in disclosing personal information. In the current Russian system, where bribes and corruption are ubiquitous, neither of those components of trust can be said to be operative. Corruption happens from the lowest level (motorists driving lawfully might be stopped by traffic police who demand a bribe or threaten jail) to the highest level (the oligarch's theft and money-laundering). The culture of expectation that elected representatives will both represent voters and also be accountable to them is missing.

When Boris Yeltsin faced crippling gridlock in the legislature, and the threat of rebellion in parliament to cancel his plan of destroying the economic power of the Communist Party, he issued a call for a referendum on a new constitution. In the new constitution the powers of the legislature were hacked away, while the presidency amassed enormous power in what turned out to be a very unbalanced system.

Yeltsin's successor as president, Vladimir Putin, used all of those powers and went far beyond them. After two terms without possibility of an immediate third term, Putin became prime minister and Dmitry Medvedev, Putin's choice, became president. Had the division of power on paper been real, Medvedev could have had the great power Putin did, but for four years he exercised very little of it. He *looked* good—a Western-oriented fellow with more cultured speech than his tough-talking predecessor and an interest in tennis, badminton, and Silicon Valley. I do not mean to demean what Medvedev did succeed in doing, such as working with his Human Rights Council to address some important issues and make incremental improvements. His paper powers, though, were so much bigger, and he invoked very few of them, while Vladimir Putin, in the lesser position of prime minister, made the decisions. In 2011, Medvedev chose not to run for president again and instead headed the largest pro-government party to become prime minister. The next year, Putin returned to the presidency, which now had six-year terms. Again, Putin was a visibly powerful figure, activating the powers of the office—and beyond: to global admiration for the Winter Olympics in 2014 and then to the West's surprise, shock, and disorganization at the lightning absorption of the Crimea. Putin's second term was to be a confounding one for Russians and foreigners alike.

At home, Putin's appointments to his presidential administration were powerful, experienced, and loyal; Medvedev's ministerial appointments were, on balance, much younger, more regionally diverse, and several had good backgrounds in modern communications technology. Which group would have the last say? I heard no one, even Russians pleased with the new presence of younger people with technological skills, surmise that in cases of disagreement, the president's administration would defer to Medvedev's appointees. Power remains centralized, personalized, and unaccountable. The reader will hear participants in the focus group speak of "the government," by which they mean the Duma; they speak also of "the Kremlin" and "the power," by which they mean the actual holders of power: Vladimir Putin and his administration, which includes a good number of former secret police officials with whom he served and whom he especially trusts.

At the next level down are governors of the many Russian economic regions (many including some of the compactly settled non-Russian ethnic groups). Under Yeltsin, governors were elected; under Putin, the process was changed to appointment by the president. After the large peaceful demonstrations of 2011–12, new concessions were granted, including a partial return to direct election of governors—but less than a year later, changes started coming down from the president, canceling the vote.

We return to the question of expectations and taking on the vulnerability inherent in risk: at the level of the citizen, there is little to nurture the growth of true citizenship. The future leaders who will speak throughout this book analyze the roles of leaders, both economic and political (understood as public policy, not partisan politics) with their eyes wide open and the determination to put their professional excellence and dedication to the service of improvement in the areas of their education. For the most part, they are not firebrands, but they also do not appear to be self-serving leeches enriching themselves on the backs of ordinary citizens.

Moscow is not Russia

The new phenomena of mass gatherings after the deeply flawed parliamentary vote of 2011 were amazing. Even under the Soviets, there had been protest demonstrations for years. Sometimes the leaders had received permission and a spot to stand and sometimes they were "unsanctioned," without proper permission and with punishment to follow. Pushkin Square was the place for muzzled writers to meet. From 1960 on through the 1980s, intermittently, protestors defied the rules and occupied the square. They read their own poetry; they were not present in large numbers. They moved past literary protest into political opposition. They were thrashed, dragged away, and came back.

Early in 1991, breakaway Lithuanian Television was stormed, and Lithuanians who tried to fight the unequal fight were killed. The story was repeated in Latvia. In March 1991, Moscow faced a demonstration unique in its history: about 100,000 ordinary people said "enough" and went to demonstrate their refusal to sit quietly, without any civil rights, and with only the barest means of subsistence. It was an outpouring of protesters, who had no permission to gather and were willing to challenge the system. They were unarmed, of course; most had no way out of the angry crowd in this heavily protected sector of Moscow, just steps from the Kremlin. They came to demand that Gorbachev and Communist rule end immediately. The streets and squares were lined with security troops, who looked on and then went back to barracks. Nothing like it had ever been seen in the history of the Soviet Union.

After the Soviet Union fell, protests continued. In 2006, 2007, 2008, and 2009, and later, there were demonstrations in Moscow for gay rights. The first demonstration for gay rights was sanctioned and set upon by a counter-demonstration. It happened again the next year while the police watched. Turnout was fairly small but these protests were truly dangerous for the participants, who would get no protection from gay-haters.

As the numbers waned in 2012 and the hopes for genuine self-government became less grandiose, it was only too clear, as has happened time and again in Russia, that Moscow was a world unto itself. The exclusion of the rest of Russia from this encapsulated land of Moscow is worrisome as the capital shows a singular lack of compassion and identification with the rest of Russia, where very many people eke out a living in substandard housing and with debilitating medical conditions, especially the very young and old. In one of my earlier books, a self-confident, college-educated, young woman from Moscow—Lena, age 24—candidly described what it was like to be a Muscovite in vast Russia. She was annoyed by the constant menu of disasters on the news, such as the deadly floods in the south.

Of course, because it turned out they were not ready for winter. They weren't even ready for floods from melting snow. It's like that all the time...Yes, it's them—it's them. I, for example, absolutely do not feel anything in common, nor with the people who live in our South, where the Kuban overflowed....

I am I. I live in Moscow. I consider that Moscow is a state within a state. It has nothing in common with the rest of Russia. That's why when I say "we" I have in mind Muscovites. When foreigners ask, say, what is

your opinion there or what is your average wage, or do you have something or other, I answer them, without a second's hesitation, I answer:
"well that isn't true because I don't have an understanding either about
what they think, or about what they say, not about Yekaterinburg, or
about Sakhalin. What they get, how they live, I haven't the faintest
idea."[3]

Is it not a bit late for Aleksei Navalny to acknowledge "that the opposition [his followers] had failed to extend its reach outside the capital"?[4]
And when Michael Schwirtz provided analysis in an article in *The
New York Times*, was it not a phenomenon of very long-standing,
instead of a recent strategic mistake, that: "This was one of the biggest
miscalculations by leaders of the protest movement. Energized by early
success, they made little attempt to project their message beyond central Moscow and a few other large cities."[5] Nor should it be assumed
either by Navalny or Schwirtz that the message from Moscow will be
eagerly assimilated by the rest of the country, for which the capital has
stood for opulence, selfishness, and inequality.

Moscow can be an inward-looking centralized capital for which the
rest of the country is almost invisible. Failure to include minorities is
common, of course, but it is also a recipe for instability and division.
Inclusiveness is hard-won and requires distribution of both symbolic
and real resources for all. Ukraine is much less homogeneous than
Russia—not in numbers of ethnic groups or breadth of geographical
variation—but in the deep cultural, economic, political, and linguistic
division that runs like a huge trench up and down the entire country. During the Soviet era, differences were defanged by orders from
the Kremlin. So, in 1954 when Party leader Nikita Khrushchev simply
gave the choice strategic, historic, and much loved Russian Crimea to
Ukraine, the impact was muffled—all were bounded by Soviet power.

When the Soviet Union dissolved, so did the cage into which all the
different peoples were packed. In Ukraine the western part was mainly
Roman Catholic, Ukrainian-speaking, and Western-oriented, and
included a Muslim Tatar minority. In the east, people were Russian
Orthodox, mainly Russian-speaking, and the area was the center of

industry, mining, and railroading. Crimea was granted special autonomy and rights for the Russian navy berthed there.

Ethnically divided countries are not a rarity. But they have to be handled carefully and that means efforts at inclusion. In 2014, after street fighting in Maidan, Ukraine's central square, and over seventy deaths, Russian-leaning elected President Yanukovich was overthrown and an acting West-oriented president elected by parliament.

The actions of new Ukraine in Kiev and other western cities were incendiary for the Russian-speaking east. Kiev passed—and rescinded—a law removing Russian as a second official language. The previous president, Viktor Yushchenko, gave posthumously to Stepan Bandera—a famous and controversial partisan leader—the highest honor in the country—Hero of Ukraine. Rather than patriot and fighter for Ukrainian independence—as he was seen in west Ukraine—in the east, he was burned in effigy. Polish, Jewish, and Russian groups see Bandera as a front for the Nazis, fighting alongside and ordering horrifically large massacres. Tens of thousands of Jews perished in actions instigated or ordered by him, and large numbers of Poles and Russians were killed. Bandera went to live in Germany after the war until 1959, when the KGB found him and assassinated him. In 2014, political parties competing in Kiev included Svoboda (Freedom), whose leader Oleh Tyahnybok refers to the "Muscovite-Jewish Mafias."[6] Parties and their leaders were getting ready for the elections, and Svoboda was a minority party at the time.

Vladimir Putin's disregard of Ukraine's sovereignty, conviction of the importance of the fascist faction, and appropriation of the Crimea, gave Russian state-controlled television a platform of unusual effectiveness. The pictures and concentration on the fascist element in Ukraine were powerful themes, though they were by no means the whole story. As the demonstrations in Kiev grew in size and violence, Russian television focused on what it showed as the brutality that kills whole peoples in the name of nationalism. Stepan Bandera was shown in footage from wartime together with horrific, unforgettable scenes of masses of limp bodies, nude or in rags pushed over into trenches. An enormous heap of dead leaves shoveled into the earth.

President Putin had other motives for the recapture of the Crimea, and although they were not nearly as emotionally evocative, they had been consistent and powerful drivers of his views of the West and his policies. We have seen Vladimir Putin's aversion to possible "contagion" from the string of revolutions sweeping along North Africa, Georgia, the Middle East, and it is especially Ukraine, a huge country strategically situated, that was viewed with apprehension in the Kremlin. We know Vladimir Putin's powerful conviction that these upheavals all around him were conceived and financed by the United States to destroy and dismember Russia. Regime change, he believed, remained a central motive of American foreign interventions, and the new and violent Ukrainian disorders were the product of the American puppetmaster. In scale and seriousness, it had gone too far and was too dangerous for Russia.

When Vladimir Putin addressed both houses of parliament in March 2014, his triumphalist emotional speech was delivered with strength and fluency. Justifying the annexation of Crimea, he said that all the minorities and Russians there could now be free of Ukrainian fascism. "Banderitsy" will never be allowed in the new Crimea.

That Putin speech signaled a new turn, provoked by the successful excision of Crimea: after the fall of the Soviet Union, Russians were scattered all over the former republics and were now a diaspora in a dozen states (the Baltic countries are never formally included—their pre-war independence and solid ties to the West make them an exception). The president of Russia was addressing a new thread of policy for the future: with passion, he delivered a super-patriotic, effectively emotional speech, saying that Russia is a power on the world stage again. How much greater a counterpart to American hegemony would be a Russia to which the dispersed Russians had returned? It would be a return to greatness, with Russians together. The rash of American-generated revolutions brought increasing world power into its orbit. Russia was announcing something less detailed than a blueprint, but also something more. Victory in Crimea (against a decidedly unequal foe), returned to Russia its historical centrality. It pinched off a piece of land laden with Russia's past from the time of Catherine the Great and foiled America's plan to take apart Russia, to relegate it to a triviality.

I was in Moscow those days talking to well-known editors, journalists, owners of media properties, freelance investigative writers, and others representing a spectrum of values and views. Big questions were in the air, and the biggest was: was the plan for Crimea a spontaneous and impulsive move? Or, was it planned and carried out with thought-out precision? During the lead-up to the taking of the Crimea, there were signs that supported the thought-out policy plan. Three news sources of integrity and real journalism were dealt punishing blows, from which survival was unlikely. *Rain*, where diversity of views and superb journalism abound, started as streaming video on the internet. It moved to a subscription-based satellite channel. The Kremlin came down hard on its unfettered ways and, a short time before the Crimean move, cable operators, on whom *Rain* depended for its audience and financing, started to stop carrying *Rain* in their bundled packages of television programs. By March, few operators were left in the stable and finances were desperate. New investment was badly needed, but at least at that point, could not be identified. A fine internet channel, Lenta.ru (Tape.ru) came under official criticism and owing to Kremlin displeasure, the wealthy board members withdrew financing. There were massive reductions in personnel and most of the staff announced they would resign if Lenta was mortally wounded. *Ekho Moskvy*, that well known and experienced internet radio and blog combination, was warned to pull in its horns. As we know, Aleksei Venediktov, who, incredibly, succeeded in keeping this program alive for years, had a successful plan: he was not a foe of the leadership. His programs did have differences of views, but the tone was kept mild. His winning compromise was to convince the Kremlin that among the diverse guests, he would invite a very large number of government bureaucrats, who could explain and advocate policy. This compromise held. Before the Crimean campaign *Ekho* came in for criticism and after Venediktov went to argue his case in private, was allowed to continue. Some say the program seems watered down. The Kremlin's strategy in moving in on these mavericks whose disappearance or diminishment would leave only state news and views was economic and administrative: *Ekho's* fine-tuned policy was not going to be enough. The chairman of the board was replaced by a person whose line was tougher. Economic pressure could effect control and even disappearance, and these three cases were especially dear to liberals and, indeed, anyone who wanted to know more about what policies and directions were trending in the Russian Federation.

THE VIEW FROM VLADIMIR PUTIN

IMPULSE OR PLAN?

What did Vladimir Putin tell about how he took the decision? In that patriotic speech, full of the emotion of restoring Russia to world great-ness, he said he began to think about it as part of his political agenda when he observed in newspapers and on television ethnic conflicts, such as the ones in Yugoslavia. His own action in the Crimea was righting an historical wrong. By the beginning of 2000, in his first presidential term, he gave "a command to activate work on the final definition of the Russian–Ukrainian border...So we finished work on this ques-tion and at that time there were good relations with Ukraine...and mutual friendly visits and the issue was suspended....But others had different goals. They were preparing a coup d'etat, planning to grab power....The chief implementation of the coup were nationalists, really neo-Nazi russophobes and anti-Semites. They are the ones who to a great extent still define life in Ukraine."[7] The judgment of the law was simple: Nikita Khrushchev violated the Soviet constitution in the initial giveaway, and he, Vladimir Putin, was putting it right twenty years later.

At the end of the speech, the president turned to Russia and the West. "Some Western politicians sow fear from the perspective of tightening internal problems [in Russia]. I'd like to know what they have in mind. The actions of some 'fifth column, different type of nationalist traitors' or are they expecting the worsening of social-economic conditions of Russia and provoking the dissatisfaction of people?" Of American political leaders, he said, they are sure that they are permitted to decide the fate of the world, that only they are right. And that they ignore international organizations completely. Two countries—and only two—were thanked by name: China and India.The speech, given in the magnificent great hall of the Kremlin palace, was received with tears of joy, and that night fireworks burst over Moscow and the Crimea.

NO MORE AUTHORITIES

One hundred percent of the focus-group participants use the internet daily. Today's political leaders in Russia now apprehend that their replacements, the future leaders, are suddenly wholly inaccessible in that very strange virtual world of the internet, where different forms of "speech" are used: where linear thought may be replaced by nearly simultaneous reference to five open screens and sites; where it can be uncertain what kind of person is in virtual "close" contact; and where the entire world can be accessed. The country's leaders have not been living in the world of the internet; future Russian leaders have been living nowhere else. Julia specializes in international politics and comes from an ethnic republic inside Russia, but at some distance from Moscow. She gets her news mainly from the internet but is also a great newspaper reader and microblogger on Twitter. She rather astutely sees how few are the options for anyone from any previous generation. She observes how partitioned off young people are now: "Basically the entire young generation is on the internet…they are 90%. They don't watch TV; if they read newspapers, then they regard them as prejudiced. And it is necessary for a new approach to the new generation. The old generation also needs a new approach and are allies of the current government. They need to think of some new approach, and to do something for their self-advertising to attract a bigger public from the new generation." At the same time, this growth of intellect and self-confidence is threatening to the old order. On the nationwide Russia Channel, a program called "National Interest" was shown live as the huge protest demonstration was taking place in Moscow, in December 2011. Maxim Kononenko, a provocative and experienced internet personality, has his own show on NTV, a national television channel owned by giant Gazprom, the natural gas producer, in which the state owns the controlling interest. He was among the half-dozen discussants on the television show and was unsparing in his description of those like the future leaders in the focus groups, who, he said, place themselves "deaf, behind a wall," a "wall of hatred." According to him, they revel in their protected state on the internet.[8] Vanya, a student of physics, intends to vote. He has learned about Moscow and power: "In Moscow, if necessary, say, they will crush the opposition in Moscow or something like that. [Putin will] do it on the internet, because all the opposition lives on the internet."

When the Moscow protests began to shrink, Kononenko wrote in his blog: "What can be done by the opposition? And what bones should the power throw to calm popular dissatisfaction?" Besides, he writes, vulgar and pornographic acts [such as desecration of churches] and demonstrations only "result in support for Putin abroad."[9] This comment, referencing the 2012 incident surrounding the band Pussy Riot, was a faulty prediction as sympathy and free speech arguments overwhelmingly supported the rock band treated so harshly by Putin.

Vanya is angry and puzzled at the fawning attention official media paid to something treated as a breakthrough—the president starting a blog. Vanya says, "The Medvedev blog is generally idiotic. The president of the country should not be involved in such things...cavorting around with iPads...I don't understand this cult of fame, of personality. So what, that a lot of people were watching you, let's say. I don't understand why I ought to." He speaks to the fall of the pundits, the fracturing of the famous of the pre-internet world. Among these future leaders, it is the end of the mentality that authority confers wisdom and a status immediately seen as worthy of its position. Vanya has no interest in Medvedev on the internet, and when Yanna, sitting nearby, says that Vanya could ask questions of the president, Vanya replies with asperity: "Why is he better than, let's say, the same person from Germany?" Yanna cuts that off: "Crudely speaking, he decides more and that's it."

In the preceding chapter, the participants said they got more news about Chechnya from foreign than from domestic sources. The advent of the internet parallels the upending of the automatic linkage of high political position and depth of knowledge. Moving around the internet, from the BBC to Euronews to *The Economist* to Russian news aggregators to any number of sources, personal and public, appears to have reduced the impact of an individual in a leadership position, claiming authority only *because* of that position. In parallel fashion, living in the internet world, where what matters is the message, the result is emphasis on *content*.

CONTENT: THE ESSENTIAL TEST

These future leaders lack a reflex of bowing to authority. It is proof, tangible evidence, convincing information that they seek, and they will do whatever is necessary to get it. It is likely that Dmitry Medvedev did not understand the bitterness and contempt with which many of these future leaders greeted his blog. The more powerful Putin has his own way of appealing benevolently through what the participants call "playing." He kissed a puppy's nose; held a bear cub; helped tag a Siberian tiger and was called a hero for saving the TV crew that surrounded him. He shot the tiger crashing through the taiga—with a tranquilizer rifle prepared and handed to him by an off-screen expert. He showed himself a plane jumper and a scuba diver finding an ancient amphora. Most of these stunts were staged, as Putin later admitted.

High position has no particular impact, even if these future leaders intend to keep an eye on what people in power are publicly planning for them. Life online and the participants' likely path into leadership merge to give them a strong sense of their own worth. Every day that sense of self expands, as the online world reveals more and more of the unknown from all varieties of sources, domestic and foreign. They are not arrogant but have a keen sense of their abilities and expectations. It is a further source of real power that they are themselves set for entry into the leadership because of where they have been educated, what connections they have made, and what they know: not only because they were born in Moscow—many were not—not only because they are from wealthy families—some are, many are not. There is financial assistance at all the universities. The largest school, Moscow State University, has over 40,000 students, 85% of whom pay nothing; the other two universities offer stipends. When focus-group participants see platitudes instead of political platforms, when they see the tremendous inequities in the country, and when the current leaders have the temerity to enter their world as rank amateurs, these young people find it especially galling. They say harsh things about their leaders in this chapter; they expect little enlightenment from those higher up, and yet they know their skills are needed and they do wish to serve in a capacity to make incremental change. They know the limitations too well to have the hubris to think of the great things they will do in high office. But they are better educated than their predecessors, far more worldly, and dedicated to the application of their own learning, of which they are proud and which they want to put to use as best as they can. While their comments on the state of things in their country may appear cynical, a reading of all they say and a look at their attention, candor, and energy around the table, dispels the notion of cynicism. It is skepticism that is required in that system. They will work hard and well; change, if it comes, will come from the inside. They accept that.

Life on the internet is a life of digital texts: whether in video, alphabetic characters, equations, models, or any other form. Contentless messages are thinner than empty balloons. It is content that creates the threshold of attention. Bureaucratic hot air fails to engage the user and is not amenable to cognitive processing and storage in memory. These young people are used to multiple, horizontal sources of attention. They look at several screens at once, and therefore, even if their multitasking does not yield as much as it could if only one task were on the agenda, nonetheless, they are absorbing content at great rates.[10]

Russian social networks differ from American ones. Russian networks have personal messaging and virtual friend interaction but also very large numbers of blogs (and communities) on a wide variety of topics—from politics to hobbies to personal issues and others. Social networks in America generally do not mix in a large population of blogs.

Bloggers, such as Aleksei Navalny, write on these multipurpose social networking sites; his is mostly on *Live Journal* [ZhZh]. Some activists may post four or five times a day. Though in the United States the blog may have ceded position to Twitter, both are used in Russia. For communicating a lot of often complicated content, blogs are favored.

When Kostya (Konstantin), a student of economics who is not from Moscow and doesn't intend to vote, started talking in his focus group about the president's blog, he said that he rarely, if ever, sees the blog: "Of course not. I haven't been there for a long time. What is there to read about?" Kirill says: "A person can be famous [or not]; it's just that he has something to say. I think if somebody has those ideas, he ought to have something to say to you. If he has nothing to say to you...." They expect leaders, of all people, to be passing on content to them; they expect to see discussion—as they do in school and on the internet. There is nothing to give them confidence in the superior policy-making skills of the Duma. Some important economic policy proposals are drafted by experts from the Higher Economic School, but the groups as a whole do not hear concrete statements of proposed policies, plans, and programs in election campaigns, and they do not see any party in the Duma that is worth much. Without hesitation, all of the focus-group participants say the Medvedev blog is a public relations move, period. Unanimously, these new leaders recognize that the motive for projecting the president onto the internet was "PR." Public relations—just by itself—is a sarcastically pejorative term.

Many in the focus groups are incensed that Medvedev could so thoughtlessly make a decision to become one of them: to come late to a whole world that had been formed and that requires navigation with special skills and, more importantly, a whole different way of looking at life. It does not matter to them whether Medvedev or his staff writes answers.

ALL IS PUBLIC RELATIONS

Public relations is associated (among Russians who remember) with the shocking first political advertising on television. Boris Yeltsin used it to support the critical referendum on the legislature and his continued stewardship of Russia in 1993. Access was granted to no other party or point of view. A brilliantly conceived series of television spots was contributed by an extremely good American professional.[11] The genesis of this powerful innovation occurred quite by accident: the son of a liberal Russian playwright met Ben Goddard in California. Goddard and his partner ran an advertising agency in Malibu. The Russian urged his colleagues back home to hire the Californian. The Goddard/Claussen First Tuesday ad agency had worked on Robert F. Kennedy's campaign and others more conservative. U.S. political advertising (especially issue advertising) was revolutionized with their "Harry and Louise" campaign against the health care plan during President Clinton's first term. Goddard was intrigued by the idea of the Moscow showdown and agreed. In Moscow, Ben Goddard sketched out the campaign on a napkin at Moscow's fanciest hotel. The ads would be based on the view that voters vote for their self-interest and the "key to winning is aligning your position with the needs of the electorate, so that they see your position as in *their* self-interest."[12] Each spot was short and addressed different elements of the population. They all started in black-and-white, with an ominous voiceover and pictures of Soviet leaders grimacing in anger, with violence, the deadly Civil War, and placards brandished like weapons—symbols of the old life. It showed the statue of feared KGB chief Dzerzhinsky being hauled back up on the tall pedestal from which it had been pulled down by angry citizens when the Soviet Union was dissolved. Immediately after this grim staccato beginning, the ad changed to brilliant sun-drenched color. Young people could have their music; mothers could show their babies an optimistic future on a grassy field. Then came the pitch for the government's preferred votes on the referendum. The message was that there was a choice between the black-and-white images of frightening repression or the color-saturated future, and that four answers to the referendum would lead to the latter. That is when the public first became conscious of this new and mysterious form of persuasion—they were old hands at the heavy-handed Soviet style of propaganda and could easily take it apart. Actually, public relations efforts on a large scale came earlier, with democracy assistance from America: for example, to help Russians understand the voucher system by which they would have a piece of paper representing their apartment or "piece" of their factory and then could sell it, if they wished.[13] Russian advertising agencies make use of sophisticated equipment and analysts using the latest metering devices to gauge positive and negative sentiment and mine "big data." For this reason, public relations and the subset of political advertising are often called the "black art" or "black PR." The most outré embodiment of the hyperbole was the best-selling novel *Generation P*, or in its English title, *Homo Zapiens*, by Victor Pelevin.[14] The summary on the inside cover refers to an advertising copywriter who is so successful that he no longer knows "Who is the boss—man or his television set? When advertisers talk about 'twisting reality,' do they mean it quite literally?"

Public relations has become so pervasive, and the media so cluttered, and the population still so concerned about the "black art," that the focus-group participants are keenly aware of it on the internet. They examine messages, including the ones from leaders and presumably neutral parties, as public relations products. Almost nothing is taken at face value. Offline current leaders employ teams of specialists to advance their strategies; future leaders see public relations motives behind almost everything. Public relations can be a profession for persuasion, yes, but also can serve to clarify and broaden understanding. Public relations has such a negative reputation in Russia that it is dismissed as (in one of their favorite terms) fake. It has acquired the place of ideology and propaganda, left over from Soviet times, but now with new technologies and expertise. If advertising eviscerates content, then it has no effect on the brain, on memory, and is simply brushed off. In this sea of despised advertising, the skepticism that we have often noted as a vital instrument of navigation and information processing looms ever larger.

The form of social networks has also contributed to skepticism. The participants approach virtual individuals sometimes with trust, often with overcautious examination. This process is the subject of later chapters. Here, I want to call attention to the migration of the habits of social networks as applied to the communications of offline leaders. On social networks, personalities and histories can be made up. That, too—that uncertainty about who is really who—accelerates the decline of trust in titles and positions. Ordinary people as well as public figures are analyzed the same way. Sonya, who is studying economics and will be working in marketing, begins the following exchange; Nika, who is also an economics student, from outside Moscow, and intends to vote, is next; and Camilla follows.

> SONYA: I wanted to say that I don't feel any difference in my level of trust of public and nonpublic figures. A fairly private figure can form an image, different from his real one, and so can a public figure. And correspondingly, trust depends on information. If information appears personal and not biased then I'm more inclined to trust it than the real image. If underneath this information [something else] appears, then it's for some purpose, then there is less trust.
>
> NIKA: I agree.
>
> CAMILLA: I also agree. Exactly, it depends on information.

Claims of authority are of little use to the participants; public relations, advertising, and insistent selling are self-defeating as they recall the Soviet era and the chaos of contemporary competition. But it is content that is, finally, the measure of the message.

A New Blog Appears

Right after the election of 2008, the Putin-Medvedev campaign to "modernize" Russia began in earnest. It would be Medvedev's portfolio until Putin returned to the presidency. One of Medvedev's first moves was to learn from Silicon Valley to see how it was done.[15] His hosts gave him an iPad. He was visibly delighted, and came back determined to set up industrial parks in Russia, to leapfrog the present right into the thoroughly wireless world of communication and commerce. Russia, as of the fall of 2011, had about 5 million blog posts and 30 million monthly readers.[16] Most are personal, but there are also ones dedicated to games, music, communities, politics, and more. Medvedev's blog is one of them.

Medvedev's videoblog debuted in 2009. He sits on a stool in a small hall, shirt open, no tie, no notes, and addresses a different policy issue in each of the frequently updated blogs. Usually he speaks to a small group of activists from the ruling party, United Russia. On November 21, 2011, the videoblog was dedicated to housing. The presidential power to devise and implement substantial and desperately needed policies for a population without a safety net, suffering ill health, poor public education, and substandard housing had gone basically untouched, except in the larger cities, as it had been under Putin.[17] Investments in the welfare safety net are far back in the queue behind building up the state's natural resource revenues and the defense sector. The Winter Olympics in 2014 in the southern city of Sochi took another big bite out of the economy. The country is shrinking because of infant mortality, low life expectancy for males, low birth rate, and unhealthy levels of damaging particulates in the air, but that is mostly happening outside redesigned and apparently rich Moscow.[18]

Vladimir Putin's promises during the 2012 presidential campaign to increase the income of pensioners, doctors, teachers, the military, veterans, and others are badly needed. However, to implement them, adding up these promises and the improvements in military hardware and personnel, and the development of Siberia, does depend on a price of oil that must remain high. And there are many more who need help and an infrastructure that needs repair or replacement.

Medvedev's point in his videoblog on housing problems was simple: companies themselves should stimulate the housing market and help their workers find adequate homes. In his November 8th videoblog, in the same format, he took on the problem of alcoholism in children. He noted that each region (the South, Siberia, etc.) had different problems. The fact of these different needs enabled the federal power to defer to the regions, as Medvedev disingenuously said. He had solid praise for the Soviet system: "in Soviet times" selling alcohol was strictly forbidden; the prohibition was implemented and potential sellers were frightened off. Now, he said, without promising federal funding or any kind of tangible help, it was up to the regions. One of the party activists present suggested that regions develop "hotlines" for prevention and assistance. Of the 131 comments, there was one from a region well outside Moscow. It said "What hot lines?...Today there are already organs that are supposed to monitor such problems and not only those. [And they are corrupt.] The very same [corrupt] police. Let's now create 'hot lines' for the sale of poor-quality food, even though there is Rospotrebnadzor [acronym of Russian Food Supply Monitoring Agency]. How can the problem be solved with some line or other, if we can't solve the problem with our [established] oversight organs? And D. A. Medvedev said correctly: in Soviet times there were no such problems with alcohol and cigarettes for children and adolescents. Problems like the ones we have now did not exist."

A change-of-pace curiosity was his videoblog of November 11, 2011: here he was, in a pale blue tracksuit, holding a badminton racquet and addressing the viewer directly. He talked about how the sport was popular in foreign countries and that the first man in space, Yury Gagarin, had been an avid player. Then Medvedev said it should be introduced into schools and universities, because it contributes to physical fitness, hand-eye coordination, and making quick decisions. At the conclusion of his talk, the video showed a rather anemic display of Medvedev playing badminton.

Dmitry Medvedev's blog is not laden with heavy-handed propaganda; it is as smoothly and quietly vapid as his normal speech, even though he did raise issues of great moment—and tentative, ruble-free solutions. To the educated elite he is addressing, it is a misstep. The 108 know that they are living in a world separate from the ruling power and are therefore unreachable.

SOCIAL TENSION

Curiously, it is precisely the debut of such a high official's blog that sets off an often bitter consciousness of the senselessness of Russia's path over the last twenty years. It is typical of all of the focus groups that so many of them take part in the discussion and that for so many, the issues are taken so seriously. Misha tries to see a possible positive function in Medvedev's blog. Misha, in the previous chapter, talked about the "stereotypes" of human behavior the West exported to Russia—maximizing personal interests by ruthless competition for wealth. Here, Misha is trying to see what function Medvedev's blog is supposed to serve. He thinks it is meant to contribute to lessening acute social tension in Russia, a tension many of these future leaders bring up often. They regard the level of social tension as possibly building to a cataclysmic outcome: rebellion. Medvedev and the leadership think of sterile solutions, with apparently little idea of the seriousness of the tension and the looming threat. This is Misha's explanation of the much-heralded Medvedev debut in the blogosphere. His comments are followed by those of Ilya, whom we know as an outspoken critic of America, calling it Russia's foe, hostile, and "aggressor," and then the words of Artyom.

> MISHA: It is an attempt to create activity. I don't know…on the part of the government, whatever, or organs of power of the state, to be more transparent, more open. But that is somehow only an imaginary attempt. Just so [the critics] get off their backs. I don't know, I have a certain position about the government. We have a ruling top and beneath it is a pyramid of these ants, well, bureaucrats, the state administration. And then there are the people. So I think that the life of the country is the life exclusively of that top, which seems to subsume the entire state administration in order for the top to live well.
>
> MODERATOR: Misha, you say many interesting things. I don't want anything to be lost here. Did you say that this is an effort to make the activity of the rulers more transparent?
>
> MISHA: Yes, in order not to have such social riots, shock waves about what is happening there. We know nothing. In order for those who are beneath, that is, the people, or somehow to throw something into the mob—to shut them up.
>
> MODERATOR: But after that you said that the attempt failed?
>
> MISHA: The attempt failed on the level—well, if you look at it from our point of view, because it [the attempt] doesn't reflect anything. It is

simply a piece of meat thrown to a pack of dogs, which the dogs rip apart and won't bite and won't yap.

DENIS: The situation hasn't changed in principle.

ILYA: Do you know why it hasn't?...Because our incomes from the budget grew. Our holes could be plugged by that same budget, and then the people began to understand that systemic holes were happening—mistakes in the state's policies. They have to be plugged with something.

MODERATOR: Which people started to understand it? Ilya?

ILYA: It the intelligentsia rioted almost the entire time in the span of the twenty-first century.

MODERATOR: And what do you mean? Give an example of rioting.

ILYA: I mean that minds were rebelling.

ARTYOM: In Russia...

ILYA: The youth is extremely dissatisfied with the pronouncements of highly placed people...about what has taken place. The crisis simply exposed all these....All the illnesses of society and all the mistakes that were made both before Vladimir Vladimirovich [Putin] became president and after he became prime minister. Therefore...simply as the economy began to crumble, immediately, in 2008, the people began to express their dissatisfaction massively.

Future leaders of Russia say they are inner rebels, cognizant of how ineffectual are the government's self-serving attempts to reach people, especially the inhabitants of the internet world. In the focus groups, they recognize the mass outburst of fury in 2010 for what it was: they take it more seriously than the government did. Official blogs as safety valve or diversion is, the participant Katya says, just "a drop in the sea." She is the one who considered that America might bomb Russia in the future. Here, she is fed up with her own country's leadership.

MISHA: The government simply has no direct access to such people [young people living in the internet world]; there are no chances to enter directly into their discussions, to introduce or bring them answers, explanations. "Here, we, too can start blogging," implying "Write to us; maybe we'll answer."

MODERATOR: Let off steam.

DENIS: Yes.

MISHA: No, disorder.

DENIS: Yes....It's not a matter of effectiveness, but of the principle...that people are going to comment in blogs and thereby remove social tension, as if the effectiveness of this had been predicted [as certain].

DMITRY: But, note, December 2010 [when riots broke out in the center of Moscow] happened in the era of blogs....That is, if before that, nothing at least as visible existed. Now supposedly everything has to go according to the plan of those who wish people to express their opinions and dissatisfaction in blogs; instead, people started to go out on the streets.

KATYA: For me, I don't think that it can be used to lower social tension. I think that in Moscow, in Petersburg, in any large cities. And so in Russia. So, I think that in general it's like a drop in the sea.

ARTYOM: With me, it switches to the negative side. Because I understand very well that it's still another invented way, although there are already enough of them, to try to catch up....Yes, it's like a little of bureaucracy, a little of some political technologists [public relations consultants] mired in mud. They are just a bit late, but just the same they are making up for lost time. Here is the internet....But it is simply another method of manipulation. Fine, another one, good. But for me, it's a more negative signal, because what other nonsense will they come up with?

The frequency of references to social tension and the seriousness of the issue for the focus-group participants is everywhere, in all the groups. To put the question of social tension in a larger, national context, it is revealing to consult the Russian Academy of Sciences' long study analyzing twenty post-Soviet years. Its direct language of warning based on the studies is extremely rare for such a body. This authoritative study is shocking to the authors themselves. "Social tension" is so serious all across the country that the eminent scholars conclude only bold and very large-scale changes must be made by the national leadership—immediately. The problems have gone beyond the local and regional, and have reached, as they say, a "macro level" that requires major responses. The research findings suggest that the tension between the top rulers and the rest of the country needs to be addressed in a manner different from the first twenty years of independence. A crucial change has taken place: instead of anger at "the system," it is now specifically the rulers who are being held responsible for the severe difficulties experienced by so many.

There is a powerful sense of unfairness in social relations in Russia, the research finds, but now it has reached "the delegitimization of the rulers in the eyes of a significant part of our fellow citizens, happening in the last years. And, judging by certain other specifics of the dynamic of social-psychological conditions of Russians and the role of social-psychological factors in the protests; one can hardly relate calmly to the development of this tendency."[19] Low income and a fear of crime figure in this overall judgment, but perhaps the most startling change is the most unexpected in terms of the stereotype of the Russian nation, a stereotype held by its leaders, as well as by outsiders. The change is this: Russians now, according to twenty years of surveys, "do not believe very much that *one must endure a little longer and life will work out*" (emphasis in the original). Whereas in the past, dissatisfaction was related primarily to what Americans call "pocketbook issues," that is no longer the case. With pervasive and frightening crime and corruption running rampant, a sense of personal helplessness, and a strong sense of unfairness, has come a significant change in society.

Social tension, smoldering so far under the surface of society, can suddenly pour out into the streets and not at all in decent and institutionalized forms of meetings and demonstrations (it is not important whether sanctioned or not), but in forms which Moscow and a host of other cities confronted in December 2010 and before. In any case the basis for such manifestations has already formed in society and it is connected precisely to the social-psychological condition of the population and not with some kind of personal material interests, which can play a role of detonator, but do not appear to be the deep reason for such manifestations.... never in the entire period of observation, even in the mid-1990s, was there such potential for aggression as now (emphasis in the original).

Most likely, the analysts believe, it would be manifest first of all in interethnic conflicts and secondarily against the newly rich. The greatest hatred and propensity for aggression, the study concludes, is in fact, in Moscow.[20]

Inequality in Russia has stayed high all through the post-Soviet period, even increasing since 2000. To put it in stark detail, the top 10% is estimated to get "30% of the total monetary income in the economy." The gap comes mainly from the difference "between incomes of this top 10% and all other incomes."[21] Russian official statistics use an official subsistence level covering a minimal subsistence basket to preserve health, enable normal functioning of the body, and for the "preservation of health and required for the satisfaction of the main social and cultural necessities." A specialist on the topic at the Organization for Economic Cooperation and Development notes that "it is widely believed, however, that the official subsistence level is enough for survival only and does not meet current requirements for sustaining health."[22] Particularly vulnerable to sinking into poverty and/or failing to get out of it are: "large families; single parents and more broadly, families with children; rural households; households with heads who are unemployed or were owed wage arrears." As we might expect, "Economic growth almost halves the chance of getting into poverty. At the same time, the chance of escaping poverty is also lower during a period of economic growth, thus putting those still in poverty during the economic upturn at a high risk of prolonged poverty....Economic growth tends to lower the probabilities of entering poverty, but families that enter or remain in poverty during periods of strong economic growth have a lower chance of escaping poverty. These households often face multiple barriers to participation and require extra support and attention."[23] Revenue from energy industries has made a difference to large cities. They have been the chief beneficiaries. Leaving their boundaries, however, even in the "bedroom suburban communities," the scene can worsen dramatically in terms of standards of living.

In this state of tension it should have been recognized long ago that there will be no quick or cheap fix. The future leaders in the focus groups think they ought to keep abreast of policies the leaders are launching, and for that reason occasionally dip into the Medvedev blog and watch First Channel's television news. On December 10, 2011, when the program *National Interest* aired, as demonstrations were going on outside, a range of viewpoints on the mass demonstrations was presented: from liberal democrats to dizzyingly vituperative anti-American conspiracy theorists. The editor of the newspaper *Izvestia*, though scarcely in favor of the purpose and action of the demonstration, said, however, that something should have been done a long time ago to help the poor and hungry and that the inequities in society should have been addressed. Though it might not have been his explicit intention, by linking the demonstration to the underlying social tension, by implication, he condemned the two-decade inaction of Russia's rulers.

CLOSER TO THE PEOPLE

In every focus group, at least one of the participants would label Medvedev's blog as "going to the people" or "closer to the people." They are referring to a specific and tragic period in nineteenth-century Russia. "Going to the People" was a famous, doomed time in nineteenth-century Russia, a time of altruism and idealism of the young. In 1861 Tsar Alexander II freed the serfs, a mass of millions. Between these former, but still destitute, slaves and the urban European culture of Western Russia, there was a dangerously wide chasm. In the cities, the young and educated idealists had visions of the peasantry as pure, shepherding their flocks in a green Arcady that Poussin could have depicted. Thousands of young people, many of them students, went out to rural Russia to teach and treat (the young doctors among them) the masses, and to impart the wisdom of elevating culture to them. They found instead people who were "as coarse and rude as the lives they led." A young woman confessed her fear and disillusionment: "I was lonely, weak, and helpless in that peasant sea...[U]ntil that point, I had never seen the true ugliness of peasant life at first hand."[24] Looking into the abyss, the mission of these noble souls willing to serve and to sacrifice by "going to the people" ended. They went home, disillusioned with the tsar's regime and the 85% of Russia the rural inhabitants constituted.

"Going to the People," that nineteenth-century sweep of idealism and altruism, ended in tragedy. Some of it was personal, as the young woman who was frightened, dazed, and disgusted recounted when she got back to "civilized" Russia. The young people—students, young professionals, the best and brightest—came back disillusioned with the strategy, and different and opposed reactions emerged. Two modes— neither monolithic—of thinking and action were moving in quite different directions in Russia. One wing believed the problem in Russia to be much greater than the disparity between newly freed serfs and the rest of the population. The problem was the whole Russian hierarchy of power and institutions: only terror could shake the system to its foundations, and the radiating shocks would create something new through mass revolution. This wing turned radical and terrorist, although there were numerous splits within it. The most serious—for whom revolution was both vocation and "religion"—adopted terrorism as a way of life and total dedication. Tsar Alexander II was assassinated, as were other high officials. Predictably, repressive measures followed.

The most famous revolutionary was Sergei Nechaev, whose *Catechism of a Revolutionary* was to be used in the mid-1960s by the Black Panthers in the United States and the Red Brigades in Italy. The latter believed and took to heart what Nechaev had written a century before: "The revolutionary is a dedicated man; he must not be driven by his personal impulses but must be directed by the common interests of the revolution. For him the only thing that is moral is that which contributes to the triumph of the revolution. All that obstructs this is immoral and criminal."[25] I do not mean to attribute the terrorist movement in Russia in the late 1800s only to the disillusionment of the returned, failed idealists. Revolution was in the air in many places in Europe. But the profound impact of "Going to the People" had a lasting meaning for Russia and is raised by the focus-group participants to refer to the chasm between the political leadership and the dwellers of the internet. However, the participants do not link the gap and Dmitri Medvedev's feeble attempt to bridge it with the inevitability of violence, as had happened a century ago in a very different Russia.

Rather different groups of the returning, defeated idealists in the 1800s went in another direction. Before the serfs were free, Russian populist philosophers pressed for their freedom, and the Slavophiles, as they were called, saw in Russian rural life and especially in the self-organization of the serfs a uniquely Russian way of organizing life. They, too, "went to the people"; they lived among them and tried to educate them, and suffered both suspicion and attacks. They came back, defeated in their immediate goals, but inspired by what they ardently sought: a unique path for Russia. Russia should keep faith with its traditions, and in its own traditions lay the basis for a different kind of society. They should reject the cold, calculating, purely rational Western values and how the West transformed human beings into disassociated individuals: numbers in account books of the market. When they lived among the peasants, when they studied traditions, they found virtues and self-governing institutions that were uniquely Russian. This group of educated city folk combined the populist respect for older ways, proven by time, and the central role of the Russian Church. The peasants by tradition came together into a collectivity of self-organization for the common good. Unspoiled by expanding urban life, the Russian way offered the chance for continued community and humane relatedness. This group of urban idealists parted with many Russians, who, at the time, looked to the West for models of "modern" societies. Populism and elevation of the "purely Russian" can and did also spawn, among other directions, extreme movements of exclusion, intolerance, and barbarous nationalism.

To this day, Russia is torn between its historical traditions, many of which are no longer natural or accessible after over seventy years of Soviet repression, and what it must give up to join the West as

Westerners. In his long and comprehensive "Address to the Nation" in December 2012, Vladimir Putin made it very clear that Russians support democracy, but that it will never be imposed upon Russia from outside. Rather, it will develop in accordance with the unique traditions and structures of Russia and will follow a Russian road. It, and other ideas we shall discuss later, appear to point to a brewing national idea reaching back beyond the Soviet period to the nineteenth century.

TWENTY-FIRST CENTURY "GOING TO THE PEOPLE" AGAIN

In every focus group, when talking about why Medvedev might want to start a blog, the young future leaders almost instantly said: "to be closer to the people," a cliché that at once expressed futility and the distance between leaders and the population, especially the country's young who had already decamped to the internet world. A highly placed official in Moscow told me in 2011, that he was conscious of growing inequality in Russian society and worried that such conditions over time were leading to a generalized anger among people. It is, he said, the main reason the Russian government, unlike that of China, with its Great Firewall, has generally chosen to regard the internet as a source of diversion—a safety valve for this buildup of resentment. There are, increasingly, serious moves to narrow that latitude, but no impenetrable wall has been built. In chapter 7, we will look at the legal environment of Runet.

All of this effort to be "closer to the people," to become known and "vivid," as one focus-group participant said, to present both authority and knowledge, while appearing approachable, human, congenial; all of it is crowded into the mission of the uninspiring blogs of leaders. As in the nineteenth century, the top senses the gap yawning underneath. They are particularly concerned about the coming "replacement" generation of inaccessible younger citizens.

In the large protest demonstrations in Moscow—so many people for the first time joined together. Many came to experience a public event: some were apolitical, and many represented a variety of

different and incompatible political leanings; many saw politics for the
first time; and some brought their children to enjoy an oddly beauti-
ful December day's clear weather. It was a Moscow event. Very soon
came the opportunity to "go to the people" again and reach out to the
regions, to vast Russia beyond Moscow. On July 9, 2012, in the south
of Russia—in Krymsk, a small city near Krasnodar—in the quiet
nighttime, when the city was asleep, a gigantic wall of crashing water
flooded the city instantly. There was no advance alert, though there
could have been and should have been warnings from the managers
of the system, who knew hours earlier what was going to happen. The
town was destroyed. At least 171 people were killed and many others
left dazed and homeless. Volunteers came from Moscow to help. These
were not the "volunteers" of Soviet times, performing enforced and
required public activity. Volunteers came on their own. To the locals,
as a Western newspaper reported, they were "a bewildering array of
strangers.... There were sunburned, tattooed volunteers who traveled
from Moscow; the supermodel Natalia Vodianova, others came with
opposition leaders, and about 150 volunteers came from pro-Kremlin
youth movements and stayed in tents in the center of town."²⁶ They
all pitched in. But they did not understand that Krymsk and the area
around it is a crime-ridden region that, since the time of the later Soviet
leaders, had been virtually turned over to the Cossacks to govern and
police. Cossack country was going to be difficult terrain for the young
volunteers. Cossacks had served the tsars—and at times rebelled—by
guarding the frontiers of the empire. For this, they were given special
privileges, such as land and self-government. Living out on the edges
of the vast empire, they were fearsomely brave or cruel. They were
extraordinary horsemen and devotedly hierarchical and formal about
traditions. They were mainly Slavs, divided into settlements, each of
which was distinctive in its traditions and features. They were also
ruthless in the Krymsk region, driving out a non-Slavic, Turkic local
population of long-standing residence. Rule of the flooded zone was
given to the Cossacks of the Kuban River in the south. "Rule" is not
too expansive a word; they had been told by the municipal authority that "what the police cannot do, you can do." These hardened

warriors with handlebar mustaches met the volunteers with suspicion, irritation, and anger at their "intrusions." Though at first heralded in the Western press as a new age of internet-organized voluntarism in Russia, the facts on the ground were not so warm. Some of the volunteers on the scene blogged about the situation as still another failure of the Kremlin. Colonel Ivan Bezugly organized a thousand rescue workers in 90 minutes, saying that "Cossacks, not just the Taman division, but the entire Kuban Cossack army, began to gather on their territory clothing, food, blankets, pillows and everything that is needed."[27]

The scene was not what the volunteers had thought; they were not hailed as young hands joining the gnarled ones of victims. Instead, the city administration ordered the volunteers to move their camps from downtown to the outskirts. The Cossacks announced that the volunteers were moving to better areas and amenities and emptying the center for citizens' recreation. Volunteers told a different story to the press on- and offline. Ecologist Suren Gazaryan "told the [Voice of Russia radio] daily that the city administration doesn't want volunteers to snoop around and report on the restoration process....Besides, when the bulk of the hard work is over, it's time to ride the publicity wave—and authorities don't want to share their spotlight."[28] Volunteering to help the less fortunate while also preaching opposition is an old strategy for building grassroots support.

It was not the way to expand the Moscow demonstrations and what they stood for to the country-at-large. It was naïve grandstanding and politically juvenile, even though some real help was given at real cost. The Cossacks had had enough, and they never cared about rules other than their own. By July 18, four male volunteers were sentenced to fifteen days in custody for "hooliganism" (the same charge—disturbing the peace—was used for the Pussy Riot punk band stunt in the Cathedral of Christ the Savior in Moscow). Here in Krymsk the hooliganism charge was made after the young men "interrupted a public meeting to argue that the government was hiding the true death toll. A police spokesman told the Interfax news service that the men introduced themselves as volunteer rescue workers. They 'behaved aggressively and provoked a conflict with the Cossacks who were maintaining order,' the spokesman said."[29] And, in the final act of this well-meaning debacle, Moscow stepped in, creating new regulations to control nongovernmental organization of volunteer activities.

"Going to the People," the nineteenth-century phenomenon, crushed the hopes and illusions of educated city youth sacrificing everything to go help the newly freed, poor, and uneducated serfs. They shared no common language, sentiment, or behavioral norm with the former serfs, and they faced dreadful material conditions. The bringers of enlightenment returned defeated. The volunteers of 2012 went to help a town near the Caucasus destroyed by a 20-foot wave of water and sludge from a dam. The victims could have been warned in this poor region, but they were not. They suffered and died. The volunteers did not all think alike; they had a range of views. They did not recognize that when Cossacks rule, there is no recourse and that they are notably distrustful of outsiders, for the warrior horsemen take the "us" and "other" as guidance and will expel by force or, especially in older times, kill intruders. The volunteers made the huge mistake of not understanding how to work with unfettered rulers or that they should not, as some did, jump up to propagandize anti-government issues in the middle of organized meetings of profound loyalists. Did "going to the people," then, help to expand the base for the Moscow demonstrations—something the organizers badly needed to do? Or did it create a nasty backlash and isolate them still further? These young people found themselves in the latter situation. But had they not come as superior Muscovites riding roughshod over local customs, they might have accomplished more. Yes, the flood victims were angry with a government they believed had failed to warn them of the coming disaster. But complaints about the Kremlin did not translate into friendship with loyalists.

CHAPTER 3

SHOULD I TAKE
A CHANCE ON TRUST?

WE SHOULD TRUST—EVERYBODY

In the focus groups some participants—a minority, but still, some—believe wholeheartedly that, of course, they trust people; of course, they trust everybody. *Because, how can we live in society without trusting others?*

In each group the moderator asked: Do you think most or all people should be trusted? Some of the participants talk like a textbook: societies are founded on trust and that is how they develop. But these are abstractions that will soon come down to earth for them in a very different and contrary form. Mostly, the future leaders—who are, after all, going to be in positions where they have to be trusted—hear the question with their emotions. They imagine, vividly, life without trust and speak fearfully of the consequences: their horror that people all around them do not trust them. Others are even more inclined to trust everybody: some take it so seriously, that it is painful for them to think of massed human beings who do not trust each other. Lucia is studying law and is worried about what will hold society together. Law is based on mutual trust—that contracts will be performed by both parties, for example. She says that "without trust there would be no interactions among people, no friendship, love, mutual understanding." For some, thinking about a community without mutual trust is painful and only trust can relieve the anxiety and grant peace. And trust benefits the one who trusts. Many of the participants who are inclined to trust in general, do so because it is simply easier to live that way. Yakov thinks it gives a person peace. Pasha says, "I trust because it's easier to live and easier to relate to life when you trust all people generally." Seva thinks about a world in which no one trusts him; "imagine that each person with whom you communicate, beforehand perceives you as undeserving of trust. It is monstrous, without doubt.... " Tanya, a geographer, has come a long way to Moscow from an ethnic region where forms of respect are still used and old ways of hospitality endure. She says it actually physically hurts her not to trust; "you just can't live always in a state of stress, always thinking how you will be betrayed." Another participant says she is frightened to be alone and not to trust. Some are afraid even to think of living in the midst of a society where trust is absent—it results in isolation, constant reinforcement of personal insecurity, and terror. They cannot live in a state of psychological tension amid lying, grasping, predatory people.

This picture of society is one in which there *must be trust*, because the consequences of constant conflict among all—the Hobbesian nightmare—are too scary to promote a livable, creative life, and civilization itself. A different kind of society might be one in which all trust each other.[1] There are people who have this personality trait, say psychologists. Some theories say trust is an individual personality trait. This psychological approach maintains that individuals may vary in their personalities and that this variation affects their willingness to trust. They believe that trust given will be returned by others. A trusting personality may trust others even before any information about that other is received. Trusting people as a first response or inclination rests on a belief that other people—people in general, all people—are inherently good. Some, such as Kirill, see human nature as good. When asked if he means that human nature is "a priori good?" he answers, "it seems so to me." This is also what future lawyer Alla says. She does accept as true "the presumption of good conscience. All people physical and legal have good conscience and do not try to deceive." Roman says he is ready to trust. Camilla, Nika, Olessia, and Lena in a different group all agree that all people can be trusted. Camilla cannot imagine that there are people who don't agree. Each of these participants (who are a minority) believes in generalized trust; each begins with a strong affirmation of readiness to trust all, and they come from all three universities.

It sounds so natural, so simple, so reflexive to trust, when we hear these young people speak. It shames us; most of us are cautious, fearful, don armor for safety and are very, very careful about taking chances based on the idea that "all people are good," as these future leaders believe. Trusting may be a personality trait—some have it; some don't. But far more frequently, we think of trust in behavioral and cognitive terms. This gets more complicated and more enigmatic and leaves us with a big job: How shall I determine whom to trust, if I do not instinctively think everyone is good and everyone can be trusted? Even among the participants who think they trust everyone and that everyone is, by nature, good, as discussion progresses to specific instances of conferring or denying trust, this sunny view begins to disappear. The argument fades away, and they, too, join in the discussion of criteria of trust, suggesting that criteria are necessary because there are those who are not trustworthy. The trust-all default position falls away, and they all look at real situations and real choices. Sooner or later, as Marina put it, one encounters fact: people are "egoists who wish to receive benefits" from her trust. But the participants who are ready to trust and think it monstrous if no one trusts, insist still that their default position is trust—a trust that has to be broken repeatedly, before it is abandoned. Yet, as we shall see, all of them know, the ground below is thin. Dmitry says, "people bring in aggression."

Should I Take the Risk?

One of the Russian participants says that if there were perfect trust, we would need no judges and no courts. Trust among individuals in society has long been thought to be the glue in the foundation of democracy. Trusting can eliminate the overhang of regulatory and penal institutions; transactions are carried out in so many trivial and large ways without the need for enforcement. Social trust is "widely believed to be a key factor in promoting healthy societies by reducing transaction costs, which are eliminated when the parties involved in a transaction no longer need to pay a third party for enforcement of an agreement."[2]

Robert Putnam and colleagues have shown that repeated, cooperative, freely initiated group activities—it can be sports groups or choruses or cooking enthusiasts spontaneously acting in concert—can result in familiarity and eventually trust.[3] A web of them can underlie more generalized trust. In enumerating the dimensions of trust—from personal mutual support to a theory of the foundation of democratic society, we tend to neglect the other, not so sunny side of trust. Trust thrives only when the parties take on risk. Trust will not take root without opening oneself up to another. There is a very substantial cost to deep and true friendship: self-disclosure makes one vulnerable. You have given up the defensive cloak of secrecy for the sake of a trusting relationship with another. It is a risk to open oneself up in the hope of mutual self-disclosure and the hope that deeply private parts of one's life will be protected by the discretion of the other and will not, as the participants consistently say, be "betrayed" by that other.

We know others are free to choose among behaviors, some of which will violate trust. Therefore, it follows that it is most important that the risk of exploitation of vulnerable "me" by "others" should be avoided. Miss Havisham, in *Great Expectations*, deserted at the altar, sits alone in her great room, staring at the decaying, once-pristine wedding cake of decades ago crumbling in a cobwebby room. She has resolutely locked up her trust for fear of a second betrayal. When conversation around the table focuses on a normative understanding of trust and society, everyone is serious, and contributions are to the point, but volunteered at a slow tempo. When talk around the table comes to a consensus that perfect trust is not at all real for them, no matter what the textbooks say about the foundation of the polity, the whole group becomes lively, talkative, sarcastic, or funny at times, and eager to put forward their points. They address each other across and around the table to get their ideas across and to meet what bounces back. In fact, they are so engaged, that at one point, when the moderator had to leave her place for a few minutes to go fix some equipment, the group did not notice, wrapped up, as they were, in the energy and fountain of talk around the table.

OFFLINE TRUST

To be trusted, one has to appear trustworthy in the offline world. Most important are three criteria:[4]

- Reputation: the record of past deeds available to the person evaluating the other individual's trustworthiness
- Performance: actions, current conduct
- Appearance: how the other looks, self-presentation

Intriguingly these same criteria will appear again, as the participants search their repertoires for criteria by which to judge giving or accepting trust on the internet. If we start on that ladder from offline to online trust, then we see that the three criteria above are the most valuable. As the participants move up the ladder into the online world, they keep coming back, in different contexts, to what they have learned offline. In an imagined world of certainty and complete information, trust would be unnecessary. We—none of us—live there. Accepting our own vulnerability in a world of uncertainty of how others will behave is how we have always and will always live. The risk is often well rewarded: "Based on cross-national data, economists suggest that a *15 percentage point increase* in the proportion of people who perceive that others in their country are trustworthy raises per capita output growth by 1 percent for every year thereafter" (emphasis in the original).[5]

THE MARKET AND TRUST: THE RUSSIAN VARIANT

In the previous chapter, we heard from participants who despise Russia's flawed market economy and resent the culture of exploitation it has ushered in. Many of these future leaders see the effects all around them both in institutions and in individuals, and understand that competition involves incentives to curb disclosure or, at best, to make sure it is asymmetrical. Artyom agrees and gives the reason: "because 95% of the population as a rule does not follow any ethical or moral principles." The moderator asks, "of any country?" and he says immediately, "no, not any. In this country 95%." Nastya adds that she agrees and that "it depends a lot on the mentality. If you speak concretely about Russia, then, here almost everyone thinks first of all about himself and that very powerfully interferes with trust in people." Striving at all costs to get ahead, to win the economic and political prize, to be "successful," even when it is defined as cheating and wounding others, is understood as the most predictable behavior by participants in the groups. The obstacles to trust are enormous, for true goals are hidden; this is not the territory of disclosure, and that includes trust in people, institutions, and the country as a whole.

Liubov announces, "It's complicated to trust someone because each follows his own goals and it's not clear whether they correspond to yours." Andrei goes further, "People as a rule do the opposite of acting right." For Nariman, "the majority of people are liars; they're all egoists and follow their own personal values." In another group, Georgy says he lives in a "world of lies." Peter agrees and is willing to locate the sources as he sees them: "There are times when a great many people lie." Who, exactly? "Power lies to the people; they steal; they get a bonus for power; many are tied to power and have an incentive to lie." Alexander says, "I think everyone lies and that there doesn't exist a person who doesn't have an imperative not to lie....I didn't say that a person is required to lie constantly. I said that always, there is no person who never lies."

It is a grim picture of the imbalance between disclosure and expectations of the benefits of trust. It is the self-disclosure—that you cannot keep hidden if you really want friends—that poses the risk. How to reduce the costs and retain the benefits of trust will be the main question for the Russian focus-group participants. They may not be able to find a balance between self-disclosure, on one hand, and expectation of true trust, on the other, without menacing threat. That uncertainty and its possible harmful consequences—writ large across the country—would be unfortunate for the prospects of a safer system of values and spontaneous public activity.

CRITERIA OF TRUST

APPEARANCE

Which clues signal trust? Appearance, we know, is one. Daniil does not trust whole categories of people: he would trust a Norwegian more than a citizen of Congo, and he would not trust the Chinese. In other words, white and European would be more trustworthy; they resemble him more. That makes it easier to infer traits and goals, he thinks. Diana, a physics student from Moscow, who is tied to the internet for news, in blogs and in social networks, says that "Slavic looks" are necessary to trust a person one does not know. When the moderator asks who agrees, many hands go up. Arseny studies economics, is not from Moscow, and does not intend to vote. He talks about certain ethnic groups in terms of bad feelings that he has had about them since childhood. He wants to talk about a difficult subject, which he says is "close to racism." Arseny is wearing a thick blue sweater vest and blue shirt, and has boyish features and close-cropped brown hair. He says he is going to talk about what others might consider ethnic prejudice, and he just says it outright, without falsely apologetic words. He speaks fast, as most of them do, and offers his experiences just as rapid-fire as the rest. He is telling what happened in his childhood and how it affected him. When Arseny first started thinking about the question, he says, "I will not trust, most of all, people of Caucasian ethnic groups.... People from the [former Soviet] Union republics. I cannot define the nationality of a person. I cannot say who he is: Georgian, Armenian, or Ossetian. But in general, they are Caucasian—Immediately I would not trust this person." Sasha, Alla, and Kostya all say that ethnicity is a major factor in trust. Lucia mentions fairness and is immediately contradicted by Arseny, who utters these words: "There is no fairness at all. What fairness is there in this world?" When the moderator asks, "No, Arseny?" he responds: "Don't start up demagoguery about fairness. There is none!" Again the moderator asks, "Exactly so? Nowhere?" and Arseny responds, "Exactly. There is no fairness in the world." In an unfair world, in a society in which the cards are stacked against you, defensiveness sounds like the better part of trust. Arseny reduces information and emotions about himself, while seeking what trust he can from others. The moderator asks Arseny about the roots of his distrust: "What you said about Caucasians, do you have the impression that these are people who are just completely 'other' for you?" He ponders his past and analyzes it this way: "I don't know. It's hard for me to judge. It just turned out that my childhood was spent in a region where there are a lot of people of Caucasian ethnicities...but we have one nice, little area. Therefore my negative bias began with childhood, because of the excessive arrogance...well, I think, from excessive arrogance and power, a feeling of omnipotence they some-how exhibited when there were a lot of them. That's why I can't say that they're like me and can be my pals. On the other hand I had good friends whom I really trust. But these are individuals I know from there." And Camilla, Nika, Olesia, and Lena, in their group, after hav-ing initially said that everybody should be trusted, turn now to ethnic group as an important criterion in determining trustworthiness.

The criterion of appearance as a signal expands beyond ethnicity; it is also about clothes and cleanliness. Mainly, it is someone like oneself whom one trusts: "tidiness," "isn't dirty, doesn't smell." Never trust anyone over 30 used to be the rallying cry in the 1960s in the United States. Age is still the enemy. Maxim says anyone over 35 should not be trusted; mainly because they cannot possibly "understand" what is so important to the younger group. The further from oneself, the less one trusts. Women participants tend to trust women more. Anya says: "If I go up to someone on the street to ask directions, I usually choose a middle-aged woman. I know that probably she lives around here. If she has a shopping carry-all, then she's middle class." In this one observa-tion Anya has summed up what many other participants say: for the sake of safety, women can be trusted more than men. For both safety and ease of communication, a local person is best. And the visibly poor are not to be trusted.

Participants can "read" a person if he mirrors them. Trust involves looking like you. Sofia says, "We are inclined to trust a person if from the first time we communicate, we see in him qualities close to our own."[6] Dmitry says that he would trust a "businessman. My personal opinion is that you are more likely to trust a businessman than a gypsy." Zhenya says, "an expensive suit tells a lot." Camilla says that it is important that a person's "clothes style is similar to your own. Somehow, unconsciously or automatically, clothes indicate something; they show he has similar thinking: a logic, and makes it easier to find a common language." Boris judges by the person's family background and education. Stas listens to the way a person speaks, his assurance, his self-possession, and ability to support the arguments he puts forward.

THREE KEYS TO SAFETY IN TRUST

Focus-group participants rely on the criterion of appearance, because, as Camilla says, "It shows he has similar thinking; a logic, and makes it easier to find a common language." Yaroslav finds appearance important and the commonalities it advertises important, mainly because it is a sign that "he won't betray you.... He has an opinion corresponding to the majority, and he won't turn out to be a fool; that's why you can trust him." Camilla draws the conclusion that "people want to fence themselves off; they want to find people who have the same thinking." Olessia raises the further notion of safety: "When you meet such a person, you feel better about him, and therefore it's harder for him to deceive you."

Depending so much on similarity to increase expectations of the benefits of trust and at the same time expecting none of these benefits from those of different ethnicities, the less educated, and people who do not look good furthers the enduring prejudice against the Roma. Yaroslav is not aware of his prejudice; it is so natural and approved by so many in his society. Yet these criteria, so starkly enunciated, stand in sharp contrast to what we have seen of these young people: we know they are widely read, cosmopolitan, open-minded—in short, these students represent the best of the best. It is surprising to see such insularity. But maybe not. This discussion is about trusting and betrayal. It has a very strong emotional impact, and betrayal could ruin a career. We are in new territory here, and it prompts a very defensive posture. While defensive rejection of the less fortunate is one element of withholding trust, there is another element in the defensiveness, which is equally pernicious. Yaroslav also finds that being in the majority confers trust. He means the majority, of course, that he is in, and it sounds as though he will not give due consideration to minority views.

Criteria are applied to prevent betrayal and deceit. These participants are wary and look to characteristics of social class and opinions that do not diverge from one's own fellow Slavs. It is a common strategy; one chooses friends, and therefore groups of friends are the least diverse of any of the other social environments. Studies in the United States find that when comparing diversity of viewpoints among friends, as compared to what is seen on television and other media, including the internet, it is consistently true that the least diversity is found among friends.[7] For the Russian participants, the motivation for choice may differ. Their primary focus is avoidance of risk and "betrayal." In the offline world they can see friends' appearances easily and directly, and they make judgments. Online, features of identity are much more difficult to determine with certainty.

Most participants say that gaining trust in the real world involves time—time to watch actions, time to assess behavior. Intuition, says Roman, is "built on experience from the very beginning. When for the first time you trust a person or don't trust a person, you already have some experience, some baggage of our own and when you meet a new person, our intuition is formed from personal experience." Tonia adds that "there is in the word 'trust' fifty–fifty: either you lose or you receive. But if you don't trust, no matter what, you won't receive anything." Tonia has a precise notion of what she means. She is like that throughout the session: everything about her is straight. She has long straight light brown hair. Her straight brown brows and her habit of looking directly at the person with whom she is speaking give her a somewhat stern face, but it is a face that looks unequivocally honest. What Tonia says, and what her fellow participants basically agree with, is that trusting people is a formidable game of roulette: reciprocated trust is merely random. Yet, you stay in the game because it is the game of life, and trust is so highly valued, that it is worth the risk at fifty–fifty. For many, the odds really are this random; they mirror the insecure and defensive vision of their own society. For many others, the odds are not even, but stacked against them. Their focus is, once again, on the exploitation of vulnerability that trust entails and the resulting fear of "betrayal." It is the risk element in trust that appears to dominate and not the benefits of trust. With material things, it is not so serious; their losses do not cut deeply into one's own core. Liza has said that there is not much damage from betrayal involving material things and money. They are trivial when compared to revelations about your behavior, your fears, and hopes. Ivan says, "If you trust everybody and everything; still, sooner or later, you'll make a mistake. You'll get burned or something and then you'll suffer." Tonia says, "You can suffer, but you can also receive." Time and experience add up to caution and trepidation. There is a layer of fear among the focus-group participants. There is no question that in this quandary, the risk of trusting is probably for them more critical than taking chances that the benefits of trust returned from friends enhances life and frees them from loneliness. It is a kind of mental negotiation each of the participants is engaged in, whether they recognize it or not. As in all negotiating behavior, increasing information about the other is a big advantage.[8] Participants apply heuristics to help sort out the ways the new person can be observed and evaluated. Similar appearance is the major factor conferring trust, and that includes, as brought up first, ethnic uniformity.

MATERIAL WELL-BEING: A REASSURING SIGNAL

Obvious signs of material ease also impress them, no matter how much they decry the race to riches in society. A few lone voices are counterculture in their judgments: one said he would prefer the gypsy look; another said he would welcome a friend with a beard, even a shaggy one—something the others did not think enhanced desirable appearance. One participant, among them all, bridled (sarcastically) at this show of conformity, and said, that as a matter of fact, he preferred the unkempt look, the untended beard, the ragged clothes. He was trying to make a point about walls erected to keep out threats.

Many see a pragmatic connection between giving up information about oneself and receiving material gain in return. Tonia says that since trusting is a risk, one might as well try it—if successful, a "bonus" awaits. Liza is sitting next to Tonia. Liza is voluble and so involved in what she is saying, that she is probably the most talkative of all. None of it is off the point or vacuous; she is serious. And this is a topic that engages her thoroughly. Though she is the same age as the others, her fuller face and hair, worn in a topknot on top of her head, give her a strangely matronly appearance. She has a bubbly (but very smart) personality. Liza wants to soften what she thinks Tonia means, by explaining that it may sound "pragmatic," but this is a "bonus" in quotation marks, not a literal one. It is the pleasure of a having a close friend. "Isn't that what you mean?...a 'bonus' that is not to be taken literally?" Tonia, straightforward as ever, means exactly what she says—reciprocal trust is unadorned profit: "A closer person who will also help you later." Yet fear is also used to determine personal safety, the likelihood of betrayal, and the loss of a range of assets from secrets to material goods. For so many, waiting it out, watching, observing, and withholding is the strategy of choice.

REPUTATION

Among criteria considered important to the process of trusting is the reputation of a new individual. What if a new person seeks admission to their circle of friends and rumors of something suspicious or unpleasant accompany the new person? When asked if reputation counts in their approach to trust, it is time that plays a crucial element. They say so often: Let us wait until we observe their actions with others; until then, let us become minimally connected, if at all. They ask themselves these questions:

- What might have influenced the creation of the reputation?
- If reputation is warranted, is there reason sufficient for offering a "second chance"?
- How do characteristics of reputation distort the truth or promote it?

Participants trust their own observations and interactions. Inna says that "reputation is like a broken telephone; it brings you absolutely distorted information, and when you communicate with a person one-on-one, you can even see in his eyes and really understand the eyes—they are the mirror of the soul and you will see; you will look at the person and you'll see him fully." Anatoly says that the reputation can come to you "from some person who misinterprets the information." Tanya asserts: "I will not believe talk in any case. I'd rather rely on my own experience." Though most participants really do wish to rely on their logic and experience and dismiss the effect of the reputation of a new person as likely to be distorted or untrue, knowledge of a new person's reputation, once heard, is adhesive, forever sticking in the mind. Dmitry says, "Unfortunately the majority, the absolute majority of people cannot eradicate the factor of reputation of a person in relating to him. If some rumor appeared, even if it wasn't totally direct, the listener will keep it on the level of the subconscious."

These young leaders reject rumor and gossip about reputation as insufficient. They know it is wrong and weak to rely on rumor; they do want to do the right thing and to uphold the values of their position and education. They say it is the conduct of the new person that counts, but observation of conduct is tempered by wariness and defensiveness. Earlier, Airat spoke of America as a historic achievement of democracy and that he had a special feeling for this country and its Constitution. Here, thinking about trusting someone new who is shadowed by negative talk, Airat does battle with himself. He is probably the most articulate person around the table. He is of two minds—the generous, rational human being and the superstitious, prejudiced weak man. He does not want "reputation to be borne as a brand, but there are boundaries. There is no smoke without fire....From the beginning I will keep in mind his reputation. But if he shows—really shows—that he is an honest and good person and has many positive criteria, then I will relate to him." Airat's caution is not generous, bold, or brave; he dislikes himself for going against his natural instinct of openness and acceptance, and yet, if he is to trust another person, that person must pass the tests of time and deeds. Why do these mentally and physically strong young people put weakness and fear ahead of public courage? Perhaps because the condition is so common and unremarkable. Lera, for example, responds to Airat's comments by saying: "If I hear of a bad reputation, I'm very careful around him. But I will also try to verify." Sergei says that in some situations you can verify something from the beginning. Then again, "you won't trust him with some personal things, secrets, which you talk about only with close friends." They monitor the level of dosage of disclosure they will impart, lest the stained reputation, even though investigated and found clear, still gets through the protective barrier of caution.

Though they are the smartest, the elite, they have surprisingly little confidence in their ability to deter betrayal or to be indifferent to it. The strong ought to be less careful, less mincing, and less timid in their actions. Why not take a chance? Is it that upward career mobility could be detoured by a friend's passing on what you had hoped would be kept in confidence? Who will take advantage of what kinds of personal information in this competitive world after university? It is sad to see these extraordinary young people, with their bright minds and dedicated hearts, reveal the hold that "betrayal" has on them because of what "other people" might think and—worse—decide.

THE JUDGMENT OF TIME

Usually after professions of freedom from bias, they may say, as does Tanya, "very often a person puts on a mask and his image is transformed." Sergei adds, "with good actors you can see very little." Boris says that "reputation is more important.... because as a rule reputation is put together over a longer period of time." The critical element of time surfaces in their judgments very frequently. It sounds reasonable; time reveals all. Yet the time of which they speak is illusory, the cliché does not fit. There is no "test of time." Soon they will disperse, and the "test" begins again and will do so again with new people at each stage and place of their careers. Time sounds like a logical ally in providing room for more information-gathering, but in reality it is another defensive posture to prevent exploitation of disclosure, the risky side of trust.

Do You Trust Anyone "Absolutely?"

Participants were asked if they have absolute trust in a person—anyone. Ivan says, of course, there are people he trusts absolutely, "but you can never tell anyone everything…because I don't know how it will be further turned and then what you've said is turned against you." Yana says that once you conceal it means you don't trust. Ivan does not want to disclose "[those things] you don't want to remember yourself." Liza says, "those shouldn't be talked about." Alla says that there are people she talks to about "various things…but not to whom she can say everything…all the mistakes [she's made]." Another side of disclosure is the permanency your shame can assume in your own mind. Confessing to a friend means your "mistakes" will never dissipate and cannot be sloughed off. They are now shared. Once what you would rather not remember about yourself enters another human consciousness, it can never again be repressed, or forgotten.

Disclosure and Political Repression

Trust is vital for mental stability, the participants say. Alexander says that "sometimes it's necessary to trust. You can't keep everything inside all the time." No matter how useful a relationship with any individual or institution can be, the groups never forget that it is set in a context, and that context is the country and times they live in. The society in which they live is fueled by personal advantage, and orderly, law-abiding interactions among people cannot be assumed and must constantly be verified. Masha says: "I think that it pays in our time, in such hard times, it pays for us really to be more careful.

That is, you can't open your soul to everyone and say everything, be sincere. Because sometimes people really use this information against you.... And at the same time, sincerity is really what we must preserve and which gives us peace and satisfaction...." It is exhausting to maintain a set of inauthentic selves, and it is psychologically unhealthy. Yet the times demand "pretending"; pretending was essential in Soviet life, and it is essential now, but when the tempo of life has quickened and uncertainties ballooned, the personality must splinter into more and more selves for success. After all, competition is everywhere, even for these young people who have a privileged future, there will be political and economic demands, as well as the pressure conferred by patronage to conform. Masha continues, "When you pretend, you are eternally trying to hide; you accumulate all this inside; you really play some role, and it's impossible to pretend and to play something your whole life."

Should they trust someone absolutely? Kostya says, "I can show you on one hand the people I trust deeply." Maxim says, "I don't think I can trust someone absolutely"; Dmitry adds, "That's a fatal end"; Georgy says placing trust in people is "deceiving." The best defense is to turn off trust. Alexander takes the totally defensive posture: "I think that it's much easier [not to have absolute trust]...when a person doesn't trust a person, then he won't be disappointed in the other one and it won't lead to extreme stress; if you don't trust there's no disappointment."

Absolute trust is absolute risk, and these future leaders are well aware of that, and speak of betrayal in this connection. Trust under current conditions only adds quite a lot of stress. Polina sees something like a state of war without war in which "betrayal" can strip you of your defensive shell. Inna repeats that trust can leave you "undefended." Lera says that when trust is betrayed, "Trust is lost and maybe even somehow your normal psychological condition is lost." Many refuse to risk revealing themselves because of the damage betrayal causes. Boris says that "it is almost 100% certain [one will be betrayed]...." Stas observes that "naturally the question of the amount of trust and the amount of betrayal that takes place....I can't say how much I'd put up with.... always these two categories are tied: what I trusted and how much they betrayed me."

Rauf, whom we met in chapter 1, initially answered in a second, without hesitation, that "Yes" he trusts all people. Later on, Rauf, noticing the narrower and narrower field of trust expressed in his group, concludes: "We all say the same thing about trust. Everybody says 'trust'; we talk 'trust, trust' and friends betray someone."

They know that trust is desirable, both for society and for themselves as individuals. It is the problem of the fulcrum they find difficult and that, ultimately, appears foremost. Is the tipping point of vulnerability far over on the side of damage resulting from risk or is it tipping the other way, with the benefits of trust outweighing the risk? These future leaders put the weight on the side of risk, vulnerability, and real damage to themselves. Part of the wariness and concerns they express about the dangerous side of trust comes from the context of the time and society in which they find themselves. There is nothing they can do about it; they express no interest in moving to other places. They want to stay in Russia, most of all, in Moscow.

ONLINE TRUST

Criteria for trust on the internet are like the ones in real life, but how they are expressed are different. The basic steps and criteria for online trust are born in offline trust. Even Skype does not make communication transparent. Participants are strongly divided about trusting individuals or "friends" in social networks. As we will see in the next chapter, social media are used very heavily in Russia, but among the group, the degree of trust and "friendship" varies significantly. Several say it is much harder to make a judgment about whether to trust online, precisely because clues found in the real world are largely missing. None of them is particularly reassured by Skype as a substitute for interacting with the person offline. Live interactive screens of individuals from social networks actually communicating in real time would, on the face of it, seem to be an adequate substitute for real-world interaction. Has Skype made the virtual, real? These participants do not think so. Lucia, the law student, has spoken up before for fairness and trust. She is also a user of serious and varied materials on the internet; she reads the best newspapers and watches television news online, as well as a good many sites. Mainly, she is drawn to sites about politics, economics, and society—the territory of a lawyer and a citizen. She is in three social networks but has left the Russian equivalent of "My Space." In her free time, she is not much on the computer, except for one site: VKontakte (In Contact), the most popular social network in Russia. We shall call it VK, as Russians do. She is there about three hours typically. So, Lucia has a good deal of experience and strongly believes "you will never know if you can trust, even if you're both live on Skype. He may be communicating with many people. You can't define the features of his character." There is no participant, even those who trust their virtual friends very much, who believes that Skype eliminates the distance between "friends," rendering the virtual as good as real. Many in various groups agree that, as Roman says, "When a person meets [you] in reality, it's so much deeper; you can precisely understand, can you trust a person or not."

COGNITIVE TOOLS

So, there must be cognitive tools at work for participants. Many of them argue, quite confidently, that it is their intuition at work. Olya looks for criteria to judge individuals. "I decided I will trust my intuition...and on the internet the same rule applies." We have seen the word "intuition" used several times in these focus groups and always with unquestioned confidence. Intuition for centuries has been understood as the power to see things in their wholeness and to apprehend that whole in an instant. The old connection of intuition with religion and mysticism has yielded more recently to a more scientifically based interest in intuition as a function of the brain. In our time, cognitive psychology and neuroscience, with new instruments of research, have revealed some pathways and connections in response to stimuli. As one study put it, "intuition is the ability to judge stimulus properties on the basis of information that is activated in memory, but not *consciously retrieved"* (emphasis added).[9] It is a form of understanding syndromes and puzzles with rapidity, taking in an entire set of individual variables and seeing them as a whole and presenting solutions for the whole. Such diverse areas as medicine, law, and management have developed a body of research to aid in decision making, and intuition has come back as a matter to be studied. Brain science technology has enlarged the field of intuitive understanding: intuition is composed of complex components. When the focus-group participants unsuccessfully push themselves to find the source of an attitude, they often fall back on "intuition."

In their early studies Tversky and Kahneman considered that what is termed intuition is the outcome of "pattern-matching honed through repeated training and practice."[10] Pattern-matching can occur only if the experience is already stored. We look to the capacity in memory that particular kinds of experience provide.[11] Intuition is emotionally charged and what the participants refer to could be colloquially defined as "gut feel." Matching the pattern of what is encountered in the real world with what has been stored is done speedily and produces an emotional gut decision in the person, who then calls it "intuition." Behind the sudden appearance of the "gut feel," the brain can be building the parts slowly and processing them unknown to us until the end point, when all of a sudden we are gripped by the wholeness of the emotion.

Conscious application of criteria for online friendship sounds a lot like what we hear in the offline world. Olya uses the same criteria on the internet as in real life. "His clothes are a symbol for me. What he chose...whether he's from a very good university; whether we have friends in common." Some of the participants say that it is easier, much easier to trust someone on the internet, because the danger of real betrayal or harm is far less than disclosing secrets and private thoughts to a real person in the same real circles of the university. Participants are split: some do trust their friends on the internet; some limit what they will say and are cautious. Some will not communicate with people they do not know as close friends or friends of close friends.

The "Passenger Effect"

The "passenger effect" makes it is much easier for the shy and socially unskilled to be open, frank, pour out their hearts to a total stranger whom they will never see again. This can involve self-disclosure on a grand scale. The passenger you sit next to on the plane or bus is a total stranger; you will never see him or her again—you may not ever exchange names. But nowhere else is there such freedom to pour your heart out, precisely because there is no second act. You part, unburdened, from the stranger.

Several of the focus-group participants have what they regard as close friends who function in just this way on the internet: as Olya says, she can "open up as you wouldn't if you met him." Because expressions of trust and self-disclosure take place there, the social network is seen to be much less dangerous than similar behavior would be in real life. Egor says that chances of harm from virtual friends on the internet is "much lower" than in real life. Lesha adds, "They can't get back at you." Once the potential danger declines, the ease of disclosing rises. Vanya cites the benefits of the "passenger effect." "You can talk to him about anything." The passenger effect is one of the most interesting phenomena of social networks. The "relative anonymity of Internet interactions greatly reduces the risks of such [self] disclosure, especially about intimate aspects of self." In this sharing there is a smaller chance of betrayal; the "friend" does not have access to your real-world social and professional circles. The second advantage of the passenger effect is the absence of "gating features." If you are shy, or have visible physical features you find embarrassing; if you are shy and lonely; if you stutter and feel socially unskilled and uncomfortable—all of these restraining gates disappear with your online friend.[12]

Liza says that on the internet, there is more trust. "You can say everything, because this person doesn't see you and doesn't know you, so you share information. He can't deceive you. He could talk all kinds of silliness." Liza, for all her enthusiasm, still applies the brakes: her default position is still watchful wariness; she does not communicate with people who are not her offline friends. Margarita says that "when you don't show your face, communication is more natural, sincere and you quickly draw together." In another group, Sam, who has the most mobile and engaged face in the group, says that "it's easier to trust when you don't see him live." Arseny answers sarcastically, "and he, you." When the moderator asked about putting absolutely full trust in people, Sam lights up, laughing at such an unlikely scenario. Alla and Rud find it satisfying to "idealize the image of the person you're talking to," and that's why it's easier to trust. And it's easier to idealize oneself, which is Alla's practice: "You want to give him some kind, good qualities and hope for corresponding ones."

Rud is tall, quite tall; his humor is infectious. At one point in the session, he had to make an important phone call. He went to the door of the small room and before opening it, said that it really was important, really. He was smiling and said the others could trust him. Throughout the whole session, Rud is one of the most thoughtful and expressive.

He had said in chapter 1 that it is essential to know about the United States, to "know the enemy." Here, he is talking about trust. As we shall see later, it is Rud who says that he loves to polemicize on the internet; that it is especially satisfying to talk with those who know more than you, so that your mind expands, and he would not hesitate to go to someone in the Stockholm School of Economics to have an online discussion.

Most of the participants are not so eager to have virtual friends and do not consider them friends. They have few illusions, and they think true virtual friendship is an illusion. So, they make rules for themselves: they apply limits to the subjects they share with the internet friend or are deliberately superficial, and mainly communicate about sports, games, and jokes. They do not expect virtual friendships to last long; they expect to run out of things to say to each other.

If the virtual friendship is converted to a real-life one, only then can it continue in real life, the only source of a more enduring connection. Otherwise, the participants make fun of virtual friendships. They are merely self-indulgent blather and a waste of time. Konstantin says they are also illogical; he is a mathematician who does not intend to vote. He wants to make sense of this process of making friends: "...you don't know and don't have: first, personal communication face to face and second, you simply don't know the history of the person's actions. You have nothing in common with him. It's strange to trust a person whom you know less than real life ones...." As a result of the anonymity, Sergei deliberately thinks up characters for those he meets online, any one at all he wants "to think up about myself and I won't even be ashamed about it. Because I know that the person I'm talking with is probably doing the same. It's just fun; it's interesting and amusing, but not more. Therefore, to trust a person in real life is much easier. I judge everything for myself."

Kristina, as her comments are shown here, might sound censorious or grumpily negative. She is just the opposite: in this extremely lively group, Kristina is among the brightest, and everything she says is in the spirit of the group's explorations of trust. She speaks with such good cheer and openness, that her trenchant, short questions about virtual friends are given and taken in good spirit. We have met this geography student with strawberry-blond hair before. She visits blogs, though she is not herself a blogger. She is in three social networks and gets all her information and news online. So, Kristina is no Luddite; she is keyed in to the same internet culture as her peers. When the topic of online friends comes up, Kristina says, "I'm not interested." But, says, Dmitry in the same group, conversation with internet friends doesn't obligate anyone to do anything. Kristina replies, "So why communicate if internet communication is needed to solve your problems?" Tonia turns to Kristina talking about her own need "for advice." Then Vanya describes his typical internet communication, "It's 3:00 in the morning, and our friends are sleeping." Liza retorts "and some nut is sitting there, right?" This makes Kristina question the logic still more: "Why is communication necessary? Don't you have enough communication in life?" The answer from Masha is "to think about known and unknown people." Kristina retorts, "The unknown remain unknown. That's why I ask.... Is it possible that in real life there's not a person you can communicate with?"

DISCLOSURE WITH VIRTUAL FRIENDS AND MENTAL RELIEF

There is a dimension to finding virtual friends on the internet that is disturbing psychologically. Is it a relationship? Is it truly trust if one is "using" the other to offload upsetting feelings and reduce mental tension, and there is no reciprocity? The participants are disturbed by the quality and imbalance of some virtual friendships. Rita has been listening to a participant who said that the passenger effect lets her release her problems. Is this friendship or a one-way street, with the weaker serving the stronger? Is this the mutuality of benefits or use mainly of one by the other? Rita says "to a certain degree this is trust—you simply say this hoping to lighten your soul...." Without an effort at least part of the time to dedicate conversation and concern solely to the other person and for the benefit of the other person, can one truly talk about real trust—a trust that enables the other end of the message to see into and help a "partner"? Rita goes on to say, "...I am not simply talking about lightening the soul, excuse me.... This [conversation with a close virtual friend] is an example of the effect of communication on the internet when you want to free yourself of everything negative or some bad emotions, simply to discharge, to analyze your bad emotions... this is use of a person and not trust.... Using a person for psychological improvement." In a word, the close "friendship" often born of the passenger effect is therapy—but perhaps not for both. When the moderator asks why many people communicate with people they do not know at all, Andrei answers, "loneliness"; other participants agree. In thinking about virtual friends helping the plight of the lonely, the American social scientist Sherry Turkle writes, "My own study of the networked life has left me thinking about intimacy—about being with people in person, hearing their voices and seeing their faces, trying to know their hearts. And it has left me thinking about solitude—the kind that refreshes and restores. Loneliness is failed solitude. To experience solitude you must be able to summon yourself by yourself; otherwise, you will only know how to be lonely."[13]

Turkle concludes that living in the world of virtual friends and backing away from real ones may not be therapy, but another layer of problems in forming the self. Findings of an experimental study from the United States suggest that the passenger effect really can have elements of therapy; it found that blogging reduced "social-emotional difficulties" in subjects. It enabled disappearance of the "gating"

characteristic of the internet, and thus removal of psychological deter-
rence. Though that experiment may have had optimistic results, it is
not an example of true internet communication. The subject blogged
to no recipient and therefore was not subject to any response from
readers.[14] The authors of the study acknowledge that "further examination of the effects of readers' comments on bloggers—including possible deteriorating effects of negative and hostile responses...should
be pursued."[15] With reduced time and space for a message has come
a change in norms of courteous communication. Such a change (several universities have initiated codes and impotent committees to limit
"incivility") surely points to a greater likelihood of encountering a
less than nurturing environment. If faster and more frequent personal
communication reduces the space for words, the first to go are those
"unnecessary" niceties that soften the tone of communication.

Therapy and "using" the other to unload emotional distress were
repeatedly brought up when the focus groups talked about friends in
social networks. Participants were divided on the issue, but few sought
these deep, confessional friendships of virtuality that remained only
online. If there were such friends, several participants expected them
to disappear as interests changed; it had happened in high school and
will happen again when they take their positions in the real world.

Distortions in User Personality

Ksenia finds she is morphing to suit her virtual friends and that internet
communication with a "friend" is actually uncomfortable for her. She
says with trepidation that she is turning into an "internet self." As she
put it: "Simply sitting [and writing] by myself, I'm doing it not the way
I would say it. That is, I think that there is some me on the internet, but
I'm not like that me; it's not the way I am." Ksenia has articulated a
serious byproduct of the world of virtual online friendships. Each message is the projection of the other person's interests and life. Think of
all of these converging on a single person. Ksenia finds herself getting
in the mood and talking the talk for each of the messages, for how else
could she respond and still stay the connected friend? And in each of the

interactions, it is a different Ksenia—one who fits the content of the conversation and its author. She is not bifurcated—she is more than bifurcated; she is practically disintegrating in the process and the wholeness of her self; her personhood is leaching away. Ksenia is not alone. Masha talks about her "splintered personality"—a different self for success in different internet contexts. It is not unnatural to have different personality features come to the fore in different contexts: parties, class, and job interviews each require different behavior. That is not what Ksenia and Masha have raised. In a young person, the development of the self is vital. The integrated self has a core, even though consciously adaptive behavior is learned for particular situations. Inside is the self. Ksenia and Masha, to the contrary, are worried that the inner compass, that center, the core is itself breaking down or failing to develop not because of external demands—the test, the interview, the party—but because their nascent inner core is forced to adopt so many different aspects that it is no longer whole and strong. They worry about the outcome and they worry about what is done to them, what, in other words, is out of their control. There is an essential difference between how these young people—and all of us—develop our inner core and how we adjust to varying external realities. These focus-group participants are concerned about the formation of that inner core, the compass, the integrated self. Turkle finds that "forming the self" is vital to subsequent development. It is the splintering of this inner self at a vulnerable age that Ksenia and Masha so eloquently deplore.

Perhaps social networking on the internet, bringing in millions of participants has no purpose at all. Dima says: "It's not about trust. But the thing is that internet communication can't lead to anything; it can't spark a flame as in real life." And that is a point so many of these participants make: Where can social media go? There is not likely to be a real-world mutual obligation issuing from online "friendship." They say that, eventually, they run out of themes; or over time interests diverge as do their activities in real life, and the "friend" becomes obsolete. Asking "where can it go?" does not prevent many from using it, but they have a rather narrow view of its relation to the thoughts they hold as most important.

No Echo-Chambers: The Thrill of Different Views

In choosing real friends in the real world and deciding whom to trust, participants strongly support the notion that a potential friend should be like themselves: ethnically similar, trim and neat, reasonably well off, educated at a good institution. On the internet the epitome of the person who will not budge from the narrow profile that does not differ from herself is Margarita: "All my friends on the internet think alike because I chose them.... Because people who don't involve themselves in my theme, in principle, I won't communicate with. Because what do I have to do with them? There's nothing in common." Some participants derive real satisfaction from finding those with whom they disagree. Anatoly says: "The internet is a rubbish dump. In a rubbish dump there's always something good.... There are authoritative people and leaders who have observations, blogs, etc. It is necessary to argue with knowledgeable people, independently of whether I share the point of view of the person and try to learn for myself something new. Because in any case a very small number of people look at a problem from all sides." Anatoly intends to continue to grow intellectually and professionally; he is not afraid to disagree and if the response surpasses his argument, he is pleased to have stretched his mind.

To enjoy this dimension of the internet one must take delight in arguing. Sasha says, "It's more interesting for me to communicate with someone who does not share your views, who has different views." Roman likes it when he finds on the internet "an interesting person you can talk to, with whom it's interesting to argue. They represent a different point of view. And I try to convince, or the opposite, retain." Dmitry, Vladimir, and Georgy in this group are all for argument. Peter says, "It's more interesting to argue when they hear your opinion too." Being "crushed" by the opposition is not true argument, as Roman elaborates: "A plus of the internet is that, unlike real life, where you can be interrupted and crushed.... on the internet that's not possible, you send your message, the person reads and sends you. The person listens to your opinion." Internet polemics provide the same rush of intellectual excitement, but preserve these participants from face-to-face degradation and humiliation.

Nariman says that "some people like to argue for the sake of arguing. They're not interesting. But when you argue with a knowledgeable person, you learn a lot that is new for you." The excitement of polemics or discussions in which disagreements arise is not defined by gender. Lena finds the "contraversion always more attractive." Camilla says she wants "new views" from the internet and has little patience encountering what she already knows. Or, you could be more ambitious and aim higher on the internet. Rud says, "If you do science and have a...question on, say, economics, and you find yourself, say, someone from the Stockholm School of Economics to talk to, and he has a deeply different position. In this case," says Rud, "you tell him your position....I think it could be an interesting field for discussion." He shows not a hint of hanging back, no fear in approaching the Stockholm School of Economics. Remarkable is that it is the *discussion, the polemic* that is important, and the excitement of learning takes away a feeling of an exposed self, a Rud that doesn't belong there.

The sport of polemics is irresistible. For Rita, it's much more than sport; it's the thrill of learning and pushing herself to take in and understand more and more. She says, "It's interesting for me to communicate with people of different positions, because I think that monotonous [talk] doesn't lead to any movement and development. Accordingly, if you communicate with people who have different views—and that doesn't mean that it will be an aggressive argument— it could be an interesting discussion. And it's always development."

Many Russian intellectuals find deeply ingrained cultural pleasure in polemicizing. In Soviet times, in the safety of one's home, around the kitchen table, one could find no greater meaning in life than in friendship and the upwardly spiraling arguments that would draw friends more and more deeply into fellowship at dizzying intellectual heights. If in the 1970s and 1980s, they emigrated to America, they found the joy of polemics to be noticeably absent. In tolerant America, it was puzzling why most rejected the notion that theoretically interesting disagreements had to be "solved." The commonly used American termination of an embryonic polemic, "let's agree to disagree" was truly baffling to people who would argue on until sunrise "to get to the truth."

Among the focus-group participants, opposing opinions are surprisingly well received and joined. Participants who are emotionally vulnerable to views unlike their own are many fewer than the more adventurous ones who seek the stimulus of engagement and the benefits of intellectual growth. One subject is termed taboo. After one participant says that she does not communicate about religion, the moderator says: "Are there any other taboo themes?" Anna says, "Religion—it's the best one." Seva agrees, "I think we will not discuss the comparative advantage of different religions."

Wary in Trusting Offline: Powerful and Confident Online

The pictures of the future leaders here are marred by the times and society in which they live. They know that trust is the basis of democracy. They also know that trust is made up of two parts: the benefit of pleasing expectations of friendship is the part they want. It cannot be obtained without the other side of trust: self-disclosure and opening up to someone to reveal the real "you." Without this simultaneous acceptance of desirable expectation and the risk of self-disclosure, there is no real trust. Self-disclosure is a risk, because you have recounted what is deep within about which you may be ashamed or proud, regretful or joyous. The participants focus most of all on the risk side of this intertwined process of trust. They worry most of all about "betrayal." They worry that what has been disclosed as secret will be released and touted about. In the skewed competition that lies ahead—skewed, because there are no adequately codified and efficiently and fairly implemented rules—"betrayal" can have life-long consequences affecting careers and one's person.

In company of each other, the participants describe the signs that strengthen the likelihood they will trust a person in real life. It is disturbing that, by far, the first one is ethnicity. Slavic is the first sign mentioned. They believe that friendship with a fellow Slav will come with a greater degree of certainty—a language in common and, possibly, religion and culture, too. But in doing so, they necessarily downgrade others; the traditional, unthinking, and total degradation of the Roma is not even questioned. Ethnicity as the first and most basic component of trust may affect their contributions to their professions; it may limit their range of colleagues and associates. The participants opt for conformity of external appearance. They believe they can "read" these factors and gain more knowledge and certainty and avoid "betrayal."

The future leaders are astonishingly different on the internet. They have less to fear about betrayal. They do not give up secrets; most do not look for enduring friendship. One student says that two years is about the course a virtual friendship runs before she gets bored; at that point they will have exhausted common issues and gone on to different lives.

More important and extremely impressive is the way most of them reject the "echo chamber," in which users choose only those sites and individuals who agree with them. Quite the contrary, the focus-group sessions were full of the excitement of discovery, as internet users described going to sites displaying opinions with which they did not agree; or finding entirely new ways of thinking about a profession; or seeking out experts and ways to enlarge their minds by moving into areas they did not know. They are adventurous and look forward to putting their education into practice. They are not cowed by the status of someone on the Web; they like polemics and all are attentive to civility. They will leave an uncivil site: as Robert said, "Why let them bring you down to their level?" These participants consider it useless to frequent only those sites with which they agree. Self-segregation is foolish, boring, and mind-numbing. They intend to explore new lands and new information. They use the word "development" often in this part of the discussion: they want to see their minds develop and here on the internet is the source.

Their tone is confident; their explorations excite them; they seek what they do not know and what contradicts what they do know. And they have the whole world of friends and contacts that the global internet offers. In these conversations they do sound like future leaders. Their online selves are, for the most part, continuously growing in knowledge; their offline selves are much more conscious of danger and exploitation. The context of the society in which they live gives shape to the habit of only warily disclosing. That is the key; this is the context in which they will seek their futures, even as their minds develop and grow. It pays to recall here why Masha feels her personality splintering: competition is everywhere. Even for these young people who have a privileged future, there will be political and economic demands, as well as the pressure conferred by patronage to conform. Masha says, "When you pretend, you are eternally trying to hide. You accumulate all this inside; you really play some role, and it's impossible to pretend and to play something your whole life." It is a serious incongruity, a dissonance that they will have to live with. Masha spoke of her "splintered" personality—a different self for success in different contexts. The gulf between offline and online stakes may likely result in a similar splintering as they advance through their expected careers.

CHAPTER FOUR

LIFE ON THE RUSSIAN INTERNET

Focus-group participants all use the internet daily, for hours. They spend a good deal of time doing their academic work and, in their free time, using the net for social networks and music. It is not so simple to navigate runet, the Russian internet. These young people have developed strategies to avoid attempts at persuasion by the government and commercial pressure. The net is full of shoals they want to avoid, and they have their own rules for evaluating what is truthful, real, and independently minded. In a country with strong government control and influence over non-internet mass media, getting solid and reliable information takes real work.

If we were to look at Russia as a whole, we would first have to settle on a definition of "user." Daily users are the serious ones, the ones analyzed here; users who drop in once or twice a month are not included here.[1] In 2007, Russia was inching along the bottom of a list of internet users in European countries, and remarkably, just four years later it was at the top of eighteen European countries in internet usage, even surpassing Germany.[2] Moscow and St. Petersburg are virtually saturated. And in the three universities, life without the internet is unimaginable. Some of the participants have their own blogs, do microblogging,[3] and read blogs. They can seek only views with which they agree; they can prefer to stay in a world in which their views are shared by others (the "echo chamber"), or relish striking out to experience the "high" of different views and the thrill of polemics (but not, they are quick to say, of unlettered or naïve debaters).

No Echo Chamber for Focus-Group Participants

The tendency of people on the internet (and those looking at cable television and print media, for that matter) to seek out just those views

that agree with theirs suggests that we ought to track "self-segregation" as some traditional platforms are toppled, while others prolifer-
ate. Mapping research seeks to see if there is self-segregation. So far, in
the American case, self-segregation is lowest on the internet and highest
among friendship groups.[4] Mapping researchers find that in the Russian
blogosphere, there is less "self-segregation" than in the American political blogosphere, which is more of an "echo chamber" of seeking agreement and avoiding views contradicting one's own. In the next chapter
we examine, among other things, how the focus-group participants
use clues and standards to navigate their way through the web to isolate false or biased information sites and maximize their capacity, not
only to understand more accurately, but also to experience contesting
points of view. We are buoyed that most of the future leaders are decidedly willing and often eager to seek and engage with different opinions
and convictions on the Web. They relish arguments and polemics; they
believe that their own thinking benefits from a variety of views, including those of well-known specialists, with whom they are not afraid to
disagree. For these future leaders, then, the Kremlin has a complicated
task if they wish to be persuasive or disrupt conversations and blogs on
the internet. All of these strategies have been tried but, for this group,
as we shall see, they are too simplistic and too easily identified.

WHY NOT MOBILE ONLY? DO BLOGS HAVE A PLACE IN RUSSIA?

Microblogging on mobile devices is the fastest growing social platform. The burst of microblogging has been built in part on lower costs
and enormously rapid penetration.

As mentioned earlier, Russian social networks differ from
American ones: the former contain blogs as well as personal social
network communication; they remain very important places for
political analysis, communication, political party platforms, investigative reporting, as well as social and personal linkages. The
blog is "long-form" (certainly compared to Twitter's 140 characters) and this longer form is essential for a more politically activist

commentary. It is required for complex actions such as the debates that determined an innovative internet election (see chapter 5) and helped to shape much of the online "opposition movement" and its supporters in 2012 and beyond.

WHERE DO RUSSIANS GO? FAVORITE SITES

An overview of the Russian scene shows us that as of the end of 2011, Yandex accounted for a "64% internet-search market share in Russia and it has been rated—and continues to be the most popular website in Russia."[5] Google has been trailing, though moving up; it has been making an all-out effort to be number one. In the category of social media, for runet users across the country, the most popular site is certainly *VKontakte* (VK, In Contact), a Facebook clone that dominates the field. Russian businessmen in 2006 were smart enough to see the possibilities at home before Facebook entered the Russian internet market. As of 2011, Facebook was number two, and although it has a commanding reach of the rest of the market in Europe, its penetration in Russia at the time was only 18.8%, the lowest in Europe.[6] For many in the focus groups, Facebook's advantage is that, in their words, it opens global doors more easily and thoroughly than does Yandex. Some of the most important political bloggers choose VK or Facebook (or both) to send out their calls for action. "As of January 2014, VK had at least 239 million accounts. VK is ranked 23 (as of November 25, 2013) in Alexa's global Top 500 sites [in the world] and is the second most visited website in Russia, after Yandex...As of January 2014 VK had an average of 55 million daily users."[7]

VK is a marvel and shows the prescience of Russia's young entrepreneurs when the internet was still new and Facebook far away.

LiveJournal (Russians refer to it by using the first letter of each word: ZhZh) is second to VK. ZhZh is generally considered to appeal to more educated and issue-oriented visitors, but it by no means excludes personal friendship communications, matchmaking sites, music, and games. Like other Russian social networking sites, it has blogs and communities. ZhZh blogs are heavy with big names in political discussions. This is where Aleksei Navalny has his blog, which has made it to the top 50 blogs on enormous ZhZh. We have seen focus-group participants describe Navalny's blog as something new, something special—a detailed investigative reporting format with all relevant documents reproduced. These blogs propelled Navalny into prominence and, as the next chapters show, set the stage for his dynamic and clamorous entry into public opposition activities and his run for mayor of Moscow.

The circumstances of his campaign are peculiar, to say the least. He sought one of the most important public offices while on temporary release after a trial in which he had been convicted of embezzlement and sentenced to five years in prison. The trial concerned a crime that he allegedly committed in 2009. The charges were dismissed and then reinstated in 2012. While waiting for the results of his appeal, he campaigned energetically against his more formidable opponent, the incumbent and Vladimir Putin's former chief of staff, Sergei Sobyanin. Against all odds, with blackout by government-controlled media, Navalny and his very modern and professional team made an extraordinary showing. He could not have won, of course, but he sailed past every familiar party and narrowly fell short of forcing a runoff against Putin's pick.

FACEBOOK VS. VK IN THE FOCUS GROUPS

In the focus groups, only 5 of the 108 use only Facebook and not VK; 9 participants log equal time for each. For the rest, it is a mix of unequal proportions (more for VK) or use of VK only. Participants who use both devote different amounts of time to each. Below are nine rows representing time spent by nine different users for whom Facebook and VK are competing. Each row represents information from a single participant's log, chosen from among users of both sites in all twelve groups. It is a record of VK vs. Facebook use in free time (no school requirements). It is not, strictly speaking, an iron-clad figure; eyes may stray to another window to see if there is a message there, but the participants seem to regard that momentary flicker as insignificant in their estimates of the time they spend on one or another site. The internet activity logs below show only the Facebook and VK comparisons. The fact is that these participants all show the same kind of behavior: they give some time to Facebook, but almost all spend much more time on VK. Time spent visiting the sites is starkly different. It shows a pattern of checking in on Facebook and "hanging out" on VK.

VK	FACEBOOK
17:00–12:10 a.m.	17:00–17:15
20:10–21:00	20:20–20:45
19:00–2:00 a.m.	20:00–20:10
16:00–18:00	16:34–16:40
19:02–1:00 a.m.	21:00–21:30
16:00–18:00	16:35–16:40
20:10–1:00 a.m.	21:20–1:00 a.m.
19:00–22:00	20:00–20:10
17:00–midnight	17:00–18:00

VK has already established itself deep in the culture of the young and the next generation. The future leaders are nearly all in at least one social network; only three out of the entire group are not. Of social networks, it is VK that leads. Although some might go to both sites, VK is the only site that has the most unshared users: of the group, just under half are exclusively on VK and quite content not to go elsewhere. The focus-group participants, if they have not already given up Classmates, a Myspace copy, talk about it as a weakening connection. Their interests have grown too far apart; what is there to talk about?[8]

Even so, the focus-group participants are so attached to the Web that, especially as Muscovites—the heaviest users—they declare their allegiance in the strongest terms. They take great pride in their unbelievably solid (and unique in the nation, they think) attachment to the internet. Dima says "without argument, for all of us, I mean Muscovites, at least, [the internet] is an extremely big part." The moderator, laughing, calls it Moscow snobbery, chauvinism, but Dima doesn't know what the word means. Nika says it's practically like nationalism. Dima thinks for a second and says, "So I'm a nationalist? Well maybe there's something in that....By Muscovite I had in mind not people born here, but all those who live and find themselves in this territory....The internet comes into our life very directly, with huge steps. Everything takes up more and more time. But I think it's necessary to try harder to limit all its powers." So, at the acme of praise and dependence the same user utters a warning—a warning that perhaps even such an educated and savvy young person cannot impose his rules on his own internet use. Oleg describes his nascent anxiety about losing control of his time: He was in VK. "I rejected [it] exactly a month ago...it's not that I resigned. I go there maybe once a week...I quit, well, I think that in part there were personal reasons....But in principle I understood that it is taking away a great deal of time. For me this is not substance; it was like a sickness." These notes of rebellion and rejection of the seductive are not typical, but they are heartfelt. Later in this chapter, when they think about how they will use the internet when they have left the university, the question of personal priorities becomes more acute, and some take a rather different look at their internet lives.

DOES A WEBSITE WITH A HIDDEN AGENDA GIVE OFF A WHIFF OF BIAS?

It is inarguable that the focus-group participants are extremely active users of the internet in university and in their free time after work has been completed. They take pride in their leading the country in internet use, but there is also an undercurrent—we saw it in chapter 3—that time is precious, even for the young. They must devise their own rules of navigation.

When asked: How great is the risk of receiving unreliable information on the internet? A great many, for example, Kristina, Vanya, and Liza say, "big risk," "very big." Margarita says, "huge, huge." When the question is posed as "how often do you encounter information trying to fool you?" Misha says "from everything," and Rita, Sam, Arseny, and Sergei all say "yes," and so do Veronica and Tanya: "of course." Sometimes incorrect information is the result of a rush to judgment; sometimes it is done deliberately. Every user of the internet everywhere finds a challenge in judging the reliability of a site—domestic or foreign. Russians have their own values and their own particular signals that steer them away from or toward sites. We know from chapter 2 and will see in the next chapter, how frustrated the Kremlin is in contemplating the moat that appears to separate internet users from access to the "normal" and traditional instruments of propaganda and public relations.

If the chance of bias, fraud, intent to persuade, and cheating is "huge," whatever can the user do? What tactics are in their heads? There are so many new entrants into the great sphere of the internet that these users have to make constant judgments. Attempts to persuade are often concealed. Sophisticated public opinion and marketing experts, including the ones who work on the staffs of political officials, are pushing their wares to potential users. Some are not so subtle; advertisements pop up with stubborn frequency on the Russian internet. The participants detest them.

Like a shot, Liza says "ads." Diana would immediately turn away from ads. Yakov hates the "huge number of ads on the side," and in his group Masha agrees. Yakov is especially irritated by the ads for prostitution, music, and "all kinds of different games that don't exist." He is irritated that links to other sites can be trickery: he relates that when he followed a link, he "got to a site of intimate relaxation."

How will they use the internet without getting their fingers singed? It is all a question of the hard work the user has to put in to separate the reliable and objective from the unreliable, with an agenda of persuasion. Most of them talk about the basic principle they use when making decisions about veracity, no matter where they hear or see it, and that is comparison. Rauf, in the same group, says "comparison, comparison, probably," and Veronica tells the group to "look at many sites." Konstantin and Mikael agree that comparisons are the way to judge the reliability of the site. Darya, like the rest, seeks comparison of sources to avoid being led astray. Well and good, but what if the sources disagree, has the compass of comparison proved useless? No one actually answers this—or can answer. In these situations, they say, with confidence, that their own educated minds must make the decision.

The work of comparison is work. These participants will be going through sources in Russian and also in English and other languages. They will be conducting the equivalent of a research project whenever they need to know how reliable the internet information is. When one multiplies a single comparison search by the many important pieces of information they must and want to know, it is a commitment of rather large proportions. They are prepared to take it on—almost every one of them is ready to compare when the slightest doubt is sensed. This test, and the considerable effort to conduct it, is undoubtedly related to the paucity of trustworthy information offline—or rather, the paucity of information in their country. The environment of information provision in Russia is poor; it is up to the user to go after the truth(s), and that they are not only willing but eager to do so is testament to their actual need for truth.

News sources are subject to the same test of trust as individual friendships: Darya says that reliability can be analyzed by "different factors, several sources. And if they are all different, then it's not clear which to choose, which is reliable." Well, then, says, Margarita, look for documentary sources: the "number of documentary materials, photographs." Reputation—a factor they use to form or avoid offline friendships—is important on the internet, as well. A good reputation signals absence of bias. Kristina would rely on the "reputation of the source." They are not willing to end their quest by brand selection only; it is not enough to have a good name. Olga's answer is the same as Kristina's, but Olga explains more: "branding": "for me the reputation of the site is significant; its resources which I can see before me and its comparison with other sources, too." Olga might first look to a brand she has come to trust when searching on the internet, but she will not stop there. Even when the "gold standard" has been reached, it is not enough; it, too, bears comparison with other sources. Roman, in another group says, "Yes, there's a brand. Reputation and appearance.... " Seva, Gulnara, and Rita in another group add another condition to determine the reliability of a site: taking responsibility and enabling accountability. Konstantin would turn away from information that's "unverified in other sources." A potential user's rule is that either the name of the writer providing information must be given or the source of the commentary provided.

POLITICIANS' SITES—DAMAGED GOODS

These focus-group participants regard sites of officials and sites related to politics with wariness. Darya would probably reject a site "if it's about public people." For Margarita, it is propaganda that sends her away. She says she will not use a site in which the reporter "biases his position, [by inserting] some of his own point of view [that] involves generally propaganda of something, and it does not present information." Zhenya rejects strong "propagandizing for some specific point." Tanya, whom we know well from the previous chapter, is sensitive and focused; she absorbs style: she says the "lexicon" (by which she means the dry bureaucratic abstractions) turns her right off. The news may have "governmental significance, but it was written in such a way that I lost interest. It was written in jargon." In view of this disconnect between politically motivated sites and user rejection, an official may well be communicating with no one at all; he may be writing to an empty chair if typical bureaucratic speech is used. Camilla says, "If you take, for example, governmental sites; there is the sensation that sometimes in some [of them] there is such a pseudopatriotic style." Though we know from chapter 1 that these students are patriotic, that they are attached to their country and value its culture, they despise trading on patriotism for cheap political gain and fakery.

Boris leaves a site when something "is announced by United Russia" (the party of the government). Seva says he is driven off, "and forget[s] about a search... if [it has some connection to] somewhere in the apparatus of [the government's party] United Russia." As we saw in chapter 2, the heavy-handed political leadership unknowingly drives a wedge between its agenda and future leaders. The focus-group participants have developed another standard, too, a deeper layer of principles and values. They share a strong common belief that fairness and reliability must involve at least two sides to a story. If diversity of viewpoint is absent, the site is doomed as a place of interest, much less of political persuasion. It is this essential, bedrock principle of the provision of differing points of view that renders the message objective. In life, there may often be many more than two sides to a story, but it is at least two contending ones that would attract these participants.

These future leaders have a whole host of tests to determine the veracity and integrity of a site in the world in which they live: the internet. First resort is the comparison of information and sites. When they come upon nothing but differences among the sources, they have the confidence to rely on their own education or to look to their network of people. Obvious public relations doom a political site, and if that site is associated with the ruling party and the leaders of the country, the site is discarded. These participants are inclined to deny trust to anything related to current politics and practitioners. If reasonably diverse views—of agreement and disagreement—were featured on a site, some of these irritable users might give it a try.

The attributes of a site—from frequency of updates, to design, to ads, to taste—are all noted and count in the evaluation. Users are conscious of the burden and conscious, too, of the resource they have that most other users don't: access to people who put the material on the Web and people who are in a better position with more experience and no need to deceive. And still, as Sam says about his time looking for information on the internet, "every day we are deceived."

THE TEST OF REAL LIFE

This search for signs of reliability harks back to the discussion in chapter 3 about reputation and trust. Stas is realistic when he says that the internet is too massive to be subject to his analytic powers. He says, "Globally, no way. More locally, yes, links to sources...there are some authoritative sources. To the source directly at the epicenter [of the event or problem] and legal normative documents." He brings up the tsunami and nuclear plant explosion at Fukushima. He understands this headline story is unfolding and that reporting is at any given time, only fleeting; the stories reflect the movement of time. While still "in process," all is contingent. Tonia wisely says that "maybe it [trust] depends on time." Tonya's sense of the role time plays in the bestowal of trust and the unwinding of acute and distant events is essentially the same strategy of holding back trust and waiting for the test of time.

Statesmen and political leaders must act and act honestly. Stas contrasts world coverage of Fukushima to Soviet news about Chernobyl. "They give there [in Japan] press conferences...when they know something.... When this situation happened to us in Chernobyl, people didn't know. Pilots were sent to put it out; spread sand on this unfortunate reactor and naturally they all died within a year." Boris reminds the group that "they [The Communist Party's Politburo] didn't plan to inform the population from the beginning. It became known only after 6 hours." There may be unreliable information because incrementally expanding reporting—learning more as the situation unfolds—does not get the whole story at once. But this, Chernobyl, was a matter of concealing known information.

TWO MAVERICKS AND A BULLY

ECHO OF MOSCOW [EKHO MOSKVY]

The participants seek objectivity; they are ready to hear conflicting sides. They know that it will never come on state-controlled national television news and information programs. But there is an original and interesting alternative in *Echo of Moscow*. Intellectuals, public figures, notables, and government people are all included in this long-running discussion program. The founder is a liberal, democratic intellectual named Aleksei Venediktov. He proclaims his individuality and defense of freedom of speech always, in every setting, often challenging the officials in charge of broadcast media. Venediktov recounts the story of being invited to a private meeting of the media industry in Sochi around the time of the Georgian War. At the meeting Venediktov was singularly called out and chastised in front of the entire group for *Ekho Moskvy*'s reporting on the Russian conflict with Georgia in South Ossetia. Putin considered it too favorable to the Georgians.[9]

Venediktov claims that freedom of speech exists [in Russia], but that the freedom of information has changed, giving rise to forms of self-censorship, which affects what can be discussed in the media—the zone of information has narrowed. "We have zones [in] which it is fatal, in every sense of the word, to dig.... Those zones are Chechnya, corruption, and corruption in Chechnya."[10]

Venediktov is an intellectual who looks the part. His unruly hair stands out as though electrified. He speaks directly and boldly in public conferences where the media powerful are present. His station was part of the holdings of NTV, the private television station that was taken down by Gazprom in 1995. Gazprom is an enormous natural gas company, and it is a vital source of energy for Europe, including Russia. This giant is a powerful political player in Moscow and a close ally of the Kremlin. Gazprom is trusted to keep a leash on the maverick radio station. When NTV started as a television station, its founder needed financing and took out a sizeable loan from Gazprom. The station was always lagging behind in its loan payments, but during the Yeltsin years, was allowed to postpone payment. When Vladimir Putin became president, Gazprom, always close to the government, called in the entire loan. NTV could not even hope to scrape together the large chunk of money it owed. NTV, always outspoken on air, then became harshly partisan and personal on air and attacked the political leadership. The station was a popular national television channel with an audience many times the size of *Ekho*, and that reach and vitriol [much of it based on fact] made it a target for elimination. *Ekho*, with Venediktov as its host, was allowed to survive; Gazprom put one of its people on the board of directors. Venediktov hosts the important discussion shows; other hosts the less potentially confrontational.

How does he do it? How does this maverick station escape the maw of broadcast conformity? Venediktov and *Ekho* keep on going because they compromise on inclusiveness and tone: the tone is never confrontational; the government supplies its policy makers as guests, to join the round table of journalists, specialists, and others. The show's survival is not guaranteed. What is the formula for its survival and why do so many of the participants respect it? Alla, the legal scholar, is critical of all news and information: "I think practically any information is embellished." But she goes on to draw an exception for *Ekho*: "There is, for example, a radio station, such as *Ekho Moskvy*, which has the right to abstract a little bit from the general colors and give an alternative opinion. But unfortunately his is probably one of the few mass media that is really permitted. But all the rest...." Sasha asks, "So, *Ekho* is honest?" Alla replies, "To a certain limit, yes." Rud strongly dissents, "There it's all party-line." But Alla, acknowledging that there is a good bit of official party representation, says about other guests, "There they really are allowed to speak criticism." Large numbers of guests from the teams of the president's and prime minister's policy officials are always invited; they make up the highest percentage of all guests over the show's lifetime. They get to say their piece to an audience with whom they rarely interact. That is the attraction for the Kremlin.

This high-wire act also has a finely managed safety net of several parts: the station is economically self-sufficient and not a drain on its owners' budget. *Ekho* has a loyal, if not very large, audience that is well-educated and mainly Muscovite. Venediktov is very careful to keep the tone of the show calm, low-key, and inoffensive. Specialists in barbed provocations act quite differently here; they engage in real conversation—these guests take it seriously, but it is not a platform for activism. Venediktov has been able to maintain the existence of *Ekho* not only by the calm tone of discussions on the program but also by compromises he has made with powerful officials.[11]

In the focus groups, everything is questioned; nothing gets a free pass. Misha isn't so easily persuaded: "And who said they don't lie?" He is skeptical about all he encounters. Grisha says, "And is there absolute truth?" Misha concludes, "Yes, but they are people always specially chosen...." These focus-group participants are realists, and the fact is that Vladimir Putin meets regularly with media heads: some he might criticize or ask for different material, but he stays closely in touch with the media and their leaders.

RAIN: THE STREAMING INTERNET ALTERNATIVE

In 2010 *Rain* became an important innovation and addition to the search for news and information in Russia. And again, the internet makes it possible. The channel started as an internet station streaming live video. It is privately owned, delivered live (with some programs archived for repeat showing) and most of its audience lives in Moscow. It delivers to a small public, it is true, and many of them are intellectuals; they are also among the most prominent opposition figures in Moscow. It is a bold and imaginative breakthrough; neither hosts nor guests mince words. They speak their mind in a way they cannot on *Echo*. There is real debate; there are real politics there; and there are cultural programs the intelligentsia find refreshing in an otherwise advertising-dominated, pandering media market. Free rein is not present, even in this, the boldest television: the Kremlin can and does signal its displeasure to the channel and quashes what goes too far. *TV Rain* made a shift in 2013 to become part of a bundled subscription by satellite.

Rain performed an enormous public service when it was the only channel to cover the 2011–12 demonstrations fully. And, as we shall see in chapters 5 and 6, without *TV Rain* it would not have been possible to institute an extraordinary feat of a real, democratic election on the internet. This process, too, will be detailed in the next chapter. *Rain* is unique; it is far more important than *Ekho* and far more central in enabling an unlikely internet-based alliance of the opposition to actually form a consensus about the most pressing issues, in which parties and ideologies do not rule.

Rain exists within a controlled political system, but its audience is small and rarely is considered to threaten the Kremlin. Exercising freedoms within a repressive society is just that: a cliff-hanger of avoidance, ingenuity, and rethinking old nostrums. It takes enormous commitment and courage. On the whole, repressive governments will give more flexibility to those outlets that have very small audiences that are mostly restricted to the well-educated; the intelligentsia, they believe, pose little risk in terms of national security. Their numbers are small; they are concentrated in the two biggest cities, and, I think, the government has a certain contempt for people who think and write but never wield anything more lethal than a pen. This is a familiar caricature that powerful, unchallenged leaders of non-democratic systems often harbor about intellectuals. The pen might be said to be "mightier than the sword," but teams of riot police and heavy armor impress the powerful.

First Channel

Ninety percent of Russians rely on television for news—far more than seek news on the internet.[12] *Vremya* (Time) was the official and first nationally televised news program in the Soviet Union. When a second national channel started operation, it, too, showed *Vremya*, and at the same time. There was no avoiding this mouthpiece of the state. During Soviet times there was a strict protocol regarding which subjects would follow in what sequence, with the top officials traveling or speaking or announcing policy at the top of the show, followed by the economy, sometimes brief coverage of foreign disasters and foreign injustice, and, finally, culture. This protocol was reinstated during Vladimir Putin's administration. Every segment is short. Context is absent. In Russia there are still only three over-the-air national news-gathering stations, one of which (NTV), the newest, began as a station with a different "take" on policies, and came under government control when Vladimir Putin became president.

Still, it is interesting to see now, in the internet age, how the most authoritative televised voice of the state, *Vremya*, has fared. If you examine the share for the top 10 news programs in the whole country of Russia for the week of January 13, 2014 *Channel 2, Rossia*, is first with a 21.2 share and *Vremya* a close second, with a 20.1 share. The rest of the top five are local and evening news, and First Channel captures three places. If the search is restricted to Moscow, then first is First Channel, Vremya (20.5 share) then three spots for NTV, and fifth for First Channel again (with 15.1 share). Share measures the program's audience as a percentage of all household television sets actually turned on. What is surprising is the figure for share for the top 100 programs for all of Russia, including all genres: news, entertainment, sports, serials, talk shows— everything. In the top five programs the same week, it is *Vremya*, that tops them all, with a share of 20.2 for one of the nights, and entertainment programs take their somewhat smaller share during the week.[13] The unique authority of *Vremya* has survived not only changes within the Communist Party, but the dissolution of the entire country, and still, in the Russian Federation, it holds that prime position.[14] This is hardly a stunning achievement considering that one has a choice of only two other channels giving the same news, but over the course of generations it has become a family "appointment" to watch the show. When the focus-group participants go home, they speak of the family watching *Vremya*, and they do too.

First Channel's continuing reputation of authority, as the voice of the rulers in the Soviet Union and later in the Russian Federation, is unique. Its serious anchors are formal and boring again, after a brief lively interlude during the administration of Boris Yeltsin, when real journalism was encouraged. First Channel catalogues Russia's achievements in terms of numbers of rubles, resources, and materials—in short, it broadcasts descriptions compressed into numbers. But viewers immediately forget these long lists of numbers which, according to the findings of cognitive science, are least likely to be retained.[15] Overall, the news is almost wholly without context and absolutely without diversity of viewpoint. First Channel is also another tool for Russian nationalism, exhibiting little attempt to present a genuine multinational environment and, on the contrary, reinforcing an aggressive Russian nationalism, as evinced by its coverage of the November 2010 riot in

Manezh Square.[16] In its presentation and the amount of information on offer, it resembles the Soviet news more than it does the news during the decade of Boris Yeltsin's presidency. For a good part of Yeltsin's administration, the Kremlin still controlled two of the three national news-gathering stations, but the third was privately owned. That third one, NTV, was owned mainly by a corrupt banker. But what was important was *what the viewer saw*. NTV was the beginning of real news, with several sides to stories, professional war coverage, and contextually based accounts of important and newsworthy items. It had the best crew of journalists, news direction, and guts.

It is surprising, given their dedication to the internet and impatience with official propaganda, that the focus-group participants actually talk about First Channel. They are far from national averages on so many dimensions. They have little in common with *Vremya* viewers who say they are satisfied with the broadcast. What is happening? Many state on the questionnaire that they watch it. They are aware that First Channel is the news source for the rest of the country, and, as Muscovites, they are inclined to believe that "others" in the provinces probably believe it, while, of course, "we" do not.

The participants refer to First Channel with bitterness. For example, Sasha is angry that the television channels, all three of them, toe the government line and often "lie or omit information." When Vitaly asks "Who knows the truth?" Sasha says that if you read the news about the same theme on French channels or a German one....Grisha interrupts, "And they don't lie?" Sasha mentions what a superior job German media did in covering Chernobyl and that Soviet leaders hid the facts from their own population. He also says that German coverage of Russia is to be preferred, because they present several sides of issues: "They say a whole lot more and...they speak about the bad; they don't speak only about the good in Russia." When asked by the moderator if omission is a lie, Sasha speaks her mind about her standards and values: "A half-truth is unethical." Leaving out information was the favored form of news presentation in Soviet times. There were very few outright lies; few total fabrications, but omission and innuendo were so widely practiced, that the slant of the "news" item was extreme.

Why then do the participants spend time on First Channel? They talk about their consumption of it and their low valuation of it. Both earlier and below, we see what they think of First Channel; their opinion is not flattering. It appears inexplicable that they should be First Channel viewers at all. Putting together the pieces of their discourse over the two hour sessions in the three universities, it seems, nonetheless, to be rational behavior. They must know what their own leaders have in mind as policy and what is being readied for the future. These participants can easily access policy documents, speeches, lectures, and internships in the ministries. But unlike these sources, the concentrated capsule displayed for public consumption on the television set is simple and final. There are no warring complexities. What goes out to the entire population simultaneously is a piece of evidence or knowledge the participants must know. They should know in what form Russia's population is told about a policy or event, and more importantly, how their leaders are framing it. Regardless of veracity and comprehensiveness, both of which are practically absent, First Channel displays the official direction and the authoritative voice of the state.

On the question of credibility, Daniil gives a biting description of First Channel, saying, "It's not worth trusting." When asked if they have personally encountered unreliable information, it is First Channel, flagship of government policy, that they cite as an example. Rita, Sam, and Arseny in one group all mention First Channel's unreliability. We heard them in chapter 3; they did not agree on much, especially Arseny, for whom boyhood conflicts with Caucasian groups became a defining element in his thinking.

An Audience of the Best and the Dissatisfied

The future leaders know that *Ekho* and *Rain* are exceptions in quality and integrity, and that the state can make ultimate decisions not only for the milder *Ekho*, but for the life of all three. They all have had experience with First Channel. On the internet when they find their way around sites of various untrustworthy kinds that signal or produce, by carelessness or design, what is incorrect or misleading, they say they are "deflated." It happens so often, that the moderator asked about them: How do they feel when it happens?

Pavel said that "you just don't believe this source and you understand it's propagandizing you," and he will ignore it in the future. For Margarita, "it's insulting even to stay there [on that site].... I was insulted when I read sites that want to force something on you; insulted because it means that [we are considered] users with immature brains....I understand that they are pressuring me. [I can delete it...] but there are people who take in this imposed information and that upsets me." When they do detect attempts at propaganda and "selling" the user a point of view or information, they find it absolutely unacceptable and expunge the site from their lists. Nariman, when he encounters such sales pitches says he is "sad." Alina says she rejects the so-called information; Sofia and Peter become irritated. Maxim says, "Aaakh, what's the difference; who cares?" Grigory has given up on all domestic mass media, because "it's simply that there's no need to expect objectivity from mass media." The failure of domestic, state-dictated mass media to engage, persuade, lay out the complexities of events and the contending views, infuriates these future leaders. Their dignity is insulted. They consider themselves different: well prepared, full of energy, and ready to put to the test in the real world what they have learned.

The focus-group participants bring up another grievance—it is the absence of news about Russia—and it exemplifies the constraints with which they must live. Rud is outraged by the absence of news; he does not even know that citizens in the next-door neighboring country (which is joined in a union with Russia) have taken up arms against their dictator. Rud talks about randomly surfing Euronews, and seeing large, violent demonstrations in a city. "They beat people with clubs....Naturally I turned to other channels to look—what is going on and what are they saying about it? They are people in the neighboring state, in the capital [Minsk, Belarus]. There is literally a rebellion. They're beating everyone, practically with water hoses and nobody, absolutely nobody, from our country was there. There is no information about it; no one knows."

In the larger sense, though, is it not logical that these future leaders in the focus groups might believe that for serious and comprehensive information, they can go only so far in the internet, especially about the deepest levels of issues about Russia, and that they seek people to provide truthful, usually insider, information? Inna wants to consider this strangulation of media: "Guys, let's look more deeply. Russia is big and how do our media work?...I think it is not a secret that we don't particularly have freedom of speech in the country and second, they are always soothing us—guys, everything's fine here. Medvedev does just the same: guys, everything's fine [he says]; Everything's fine here. This is done so that there would be no agitation, so that people would not rebel and these official pages [on the internet] they work the same way, and so does Medvedev's blog."

Sam says, "Every day we are deceived."

PEOPLE VS. THE MACHINE

The focus groups pick the internet as the first choice of news and information. Number Two is unexpected: people. As chapter 3 showed, these young people devise so many hoops for potential friends to leap through. It is baffling that these focus-group participants should say that after the internet, they would go to people for really important information and advice. Are these two different species of people we are talking about?

The moderator asks, "Are friends sources?" There is a chorus of "Yes, yes, of course." People, contacts, and family play a large role for these young leaders. This "pre-modern" source is vital for them in the electronic age. This search for help and information is almost entirely different from the kinds of relations with people we saw in chapter 3, and that is because the category of these people is significantly different. What we will see in the following pages is the elevation of people as a source, but they are special people and they are guaranteed not to harm one's career. This class of people also includes family, if sufficiently knowledgeable, and relevant specialists among students in one's own circle of friends.

In another group, the moderator asks, if the information is extremely important, where will you go? Sasha says immediately, "to that person" [the person who gave out the information]. For, as Sergei puts it, "You have to search the internet for all information, because that [person] will tell you that he probably got it also from the internet." Alla, we remember from chapter 1 as someone who is especially tied to Russia as the place she wants to know most about. She says that it is most important to have access to people who produce what goes on the internet. She says, "Often there are official sources and sites of the very organs necessary *if we have such access*." But access is not easily obtained, and one would have to "communicate with the people who create these articles for [official] sites." Mathematics student Konstantin's strategy is: "I simply look at the telephone, there's some 'superimportant' question. Last week there were two of them [questions]. At one time I called three people, so that some one of them was able to answer one question, and two other people [were able to answer completely] the other question." When the moderator asks if they can trust as absolutely precise what a live source tells them, Darya, Pavel, and Veronica all say, "of course," and [one goes to] "different people." What people? They must have friends whom they trust to be thoroughly knowledgeable. Then, too, if they use the internet as a guide to the source of some information, it is to the creators of information, even on official sites, to whom they would turn for more information—information that did not make it into the site or should be closely held. They consider this a logical and advisable route: it is not available to most people and few internet users in the general population would expect to have a line of communication to creators of these kinds of internet material. The participants have in mind the right kinds of friends—friends capable of responding authoritatively, and they are confident that they can successfully connect and receive. This matter-of-fact assurance of access and assumed welcome by the source is one feature of the path they are able to follow upon leaving these particular universities. No matter how they choose to begin their careers, they also have the network of faculty, many of whom are well-placed professionals in their fields. They have also had internships in institutions in which they will later work—the job already either partly started or settled after graduation. The conviction of having open to them whatever they need for success is not questioned. The points made by students in the conversation above are not pompous exaggerations; it is another aspect of who they are, because of where they are, among the elite.

They are interested in information that requires depth of analysis and expertise. Airat battles impulses of trust and suspicion, as we saw before, and is also an idealist about democracy. When it comes to professional matters, he is thoroughly disciplined about the internet and says: "A jurist always needs documents, concise, with dates, with numbers, so that all is official. These materials are stored in official sites, the presidential and the prime ministerial sites." Predictably, with her confidence even in virtual online people she has never seen, Liza says that people are the source of internet information, anyway, so why not go right to them? "No [it is not the internet one searches first]. First come people you know...students here form a very wide circle of communication...and all the people are working on different things.... You can [also] find among friends or relatives, rather competent people." Another participant says he relies on "insider information." Yet another obtains information "directly from competent people."

PEOPLE, CONTACTS, PATRONAGE, AND MOBILITY

Seeking people, absorbing their accounts of events and causes: what a curious and important phenomenon to encounter in today's future leaders, so tied to the digital world. Below, when we ask where they might find information relating to a person faced with a dilemma and asking on the internet for help, they constantly mention people as sources. The participants know the right people to go to; several would go to their parents, if they are on good terms. These parents would also be ones who are positioned to provide information on the complexities of a new Russia, in which their children are finding their way. Inherited status is an added part of their strength in the competitive world. Or the focus-group participants would turn to "other people" for important information.

Why does this happen? It seems an old-fashioned village approach to acquiring extremely important information. I believe that it is a result of a combination of tendencies, some of which we have seen in other contexts. If there is a personal factor, then trust becomes especially important. As we have seen, the search for a trusted person is governed a good deal by fear of the wrong choice. Relatives of the sort Liza believes can provide her with important information (not just headline material) must themselves have experience and status. Connections, internships, family ties—all add to the resources they will exploit in their careers. Life and work in Russia can be a zero-sum game without any rules, protections, or predictable punishments for infractions—in short, without a functioning regime of rules that applies fairly to all. And if it is the crony-laden market that dispenses rewards, how can one trust unconditionally? This does not sound like an environment suited to what these participants say they do. Listen to them talking about their enthusiasm for people; it does not sound like what they were saying before about trust. It is different, because *some people are different; they have different qualities to offer the participants; and they are trusted*. Who are they? There must be a good deal missing from the internet, to which everyone turns and on which they thrive. What makes the participants seek real people in real life for matters of great importance to them?

"MY LIFE DEPRESSES ME. SHOULD I LEAVE MOSCOW? I'VE LIVED HERE ALL MY LIFE. MAYBE SOME OTHER PART OF RUSSIA WOULD BE BETTER."

On a questionnaire given out during a session, the challenge was to think about where, among the five sources suggested and "other" (as a sixth), this statement might be found.[16]

The participants suggested first the social network LiveJournal (ZhZh), because there was just so much of everything there: blogs, chats, sites, communities, messages, and the political, the personal, the practical. As one of the participants says, it has everything. Misha says, " I chose ZhZh from this standpoint: I would look at [the person needing help], as I sit in the evening in front of the computer, and I'd think that I'm depressed in Moscow, so I go to sources, and I would take LiveJournal [ZhZh]." After LiveJournal, the number one source is people: the focus-group participants go to the "Other" line, where they write "people" and fill in specifics.

Parents and relatives are people who will never let you down, and they will always have your interests in mind. If they have the right knowledge and experience, they will be consulted as the most valuable of resources. The more the participants express closeness of emotional ties, the more decisively they turn away from the internet as a superior solution. Katya says she would "probably turn to people I know and look at places I've been to, but hardly the internet." Dima agrees wholeheartedly; he would talk only with his own friends, only with people, and then decide. That is why Masha says she would go to "both family and others close to her. I would probably discuss this theme mainly with them." Angelika was going to put down the social network VKontakte, but changed her mind. "It seems to me that friends, close friends, are still more important." Vitaly says in his group that "I think it's personal. I would want the personal experience of whoever is helpful: parents." Anatoly thought America "huge aggressors," in chapter 1, and, as an economist, linked the economic well-being of the United States to the armaments industry, hence to war. He appears to be rather well placed in Russia, with a network of people; as he says, he has relatives all over. "I have relatives in many regions of our country and if I have to decide this serious question, then it pays to turn to them." Thoughtful Artyom, who ponders democracy in practice and on paper put down "relatives," "because first of all [it is unimaginable] to make the decision to leave without conferring together and talking with close people." He obviously has been socialized in the importance of consultation, and perhaps his understanding and sympathy for democracy bears a relation to a family that practices it.

All the participants took the question seriously. In one group two of the participants could not imagine asking for help in leaving Moscow because it would not occur to them to leave Moscow. Dima compares Moscow with his own hometown and says he would not leave, "*Especially* since I'm not a Muscovite, and I like living here." Masha, sitting at the same table, says, "I'm from Moscow and I don't intend to leave." Artyom urges his group to think bigger; why be confined to the terms of the question? He asks why is the person asking about where in another part of Russia would there be a better future? He goes on, "This question confused me. Because why, if I went someplace, why go somewhere to a different part of Russia? If I went someplace, I would sooner go to Europe or Canada." Besides, the farther from Moscow one goes the worse it will be, he concludes. Here are more indications of the changes that would have to take place to draw Moscow closer to the rest of Russia. Having come to the top, they intend to stay there—and beyond. Artyom's aspirations have no boundaries, just like the internet.

Personal Influence, Patronage, and Mobility

In addition to study in an elite university, there are other resources the focus-group participants use; parents are often well-placed in Moscow and other cities. Many parents keep up with their contacts, and both can be helpful in moving up the ladder of success. Boris says that his father was a classmate of the minister of natural resources. The minister, says Boris, is not a party man. "It was through a different sort of patronage that he became minister. He is a protégé of the governor of a large city." Boris's father was also a university classmate of the governor of a major region: "I can say that according to what they said in university, this is a person who is used to lying—in the sense of those people who strive for power from the beginning [i.e., politicking]." Boris does not mean "lying," strictly speaking, but rather the kinds of "selling" and "promising" and maneuvering and forging alliances. It is politics, but quite personalized in Russia and opaque to the outside.

Stas had an opportunity to get to know the head of the Russian Communist Party: "It happened that I had the opportunity to communicate personally with him [Gennady Ziuganov] and I understood that this is a person who does not resemble how television portrays him; that is, he's not a fanatic. And this is not a person possessed by communist ideas. He's really a smart, talented, educated, and developed person with defined principles and ideas. He's a rather firm person, earning my respect." Stas comes from a smaller city outside Moscow, where, one might think, there may be less open-mindedness than in cosmopolitan Moscow. But that is far from the case; it is unexpected that like so many of the focus-group participants, Stas is very far from an ideologically rigid young person. Yaroslav in another group has his contacts, also high up on the ladder of success: "I communicated with Ilya Segalovsky on one occasion. He…co-founded Yandex [the browser]. It was a year ago. He said that Yandex was more Russified, that is, in Yandex there is a great deal of information about Russia. Google tries for both international and our Russian users." Yandex is far ahead; it is by a large margin the most successful browser in Russia.

Schoolmates, the ability to have one-on-one conversations with the head of the second largest political party—opportunities from family and school—are unmatched advantages. High-level officials come to talk to these students, and they mix with them and the students make personal connections. Boris gets insider information about Dmitry Medvedev's blog: "I have a friend who works, as it happens, for a famous journalist, who specifically related all this to me. All those communications, in his [Medvedev's] blog? These ten journalists do it."

MISHA: "You know this?"
BORIS: "[Yes, it applies to] all the discussions there."

In general the participants are not tense or uncertain about jobs in the future. In talking about changing lifestyles after graduation, Anya advises others in her group that you "have to imagine yourself where you intend to work in the future. If you intend to work somewhere in MID [the Ministry of Foreign Affairs] or in some organization or in the state structures...." She is almost nonchalant. These are most desirable choices, and she regards them as opportunities in the pool of likely jobs.

Masha intends to get an advanced degree and go into a construction company she has in mind. Sergei, as all the others, had internships in the summer, one of the advantages of an impressive alumni base from which to choose and get a leg up on future employment, as Sergei believes he has done. Oleg already has a business "I support my business [on the internet], [and use] several sites. So, on the weekends I can calmly devote [to the internet] 6 hours." Ilya has a job he's been doing on the side and has converted to real work: "My work is the same as my work studying; they didn't pay me money. Now I work practically the same and they pay me money for this."

FUTURE OBLIGATIONS AND LIKELY CHANGE

Most of what we have heard—with one or two dissenters nervously negative about the internet's eating up their lives—concerns the opportunities for learning and fun the internet gives them. But they are not always going to be in the special world of the university, possibly not always in Moscow, and all that time they spend on coursework will disappear. What will their internet future be like? We asked them to imagine themselves just months away, a short time into the future when they will have left school and will be working. Will online life go on just as now? Almost all of the participants say that, no; there will be changes in how they use the internet. They also say that the changes will not be total. The most serious change is the shift to use of sites they will need in their professions. Most expect to use foreign sites, for example, for "communication with other continents." Vitaly's main sites will be on "the law and constitutions." When the moderator asks what constitution, he answers "depends on where you work: if you work in Russia, then with the constitution of the Russian Federation." The participants who are working on international specializations—and there are several different types: economic organization, diplomacy, international organization, and others—see the internet as fundamentally essential to their work. Their work may deal with issues and peoples all over the world, so they want to keep what they have learned current and cutting-edge.

Strikingly absent in all this talk of the future is family. Perhaps it is especially likely that it is Rita who will bring it up first. In the previous chapter, she intensely defended the value of letting out your problems and worries on a virtual friend. She is sensitive to intimate ties and it is Rita who says that she might limit her time on the internet a little, but "what will concretely change your situation is how you have your own family. I think they [social networks] will be absolutely uninteresting." Mainly she will use them for writing something like "let's meet somewhere." Nastya agrees that "life" will change all of their patterns of use, and Katya goes on to explain that "I am sure it won't be interesting to follow too much what is going on with whom. I won't be up to it." Alla is keenly aware that after university there will be some transitional time, then "many will have a family and with pleasure will spend more time with family and children, than in communication with some old friends." Tanya in the previous chapter is also a sensitive person, who thinks it monstrous, horrible, to live in a world where no one trusts you, where there is no mutual trust at all. Now, thinking about the time when she has a position for which she has prepared, she will put her role as mother first and give that role an emphasis and commitment that exceeds the few others who mention it: "I think, in first place and most important is the family. Therefore, more time will go to family and to children....I think in general there is no time for the internet as such.... [when they grow up there will be more time, but] I don't know. In 15 years, maybe....It will be necessary to monitor what they say and also to know what's going on; what interests they have...in order to separate out [the bad and encourage] what will make them good." Tanya is saying that the most important time for a parent to be there, to communicate boundaries, to strengthen principles for the good [not merely the material] life, is not only when they are small and helpless. The most serious time for a parent to do what matters and to be there is during what she regards as the most vulnerable years in her culture: the years when peers can have a greater effect on young people, especially if parents are distracted and absent. Tanya is determined to take on maternal responsibilities for a very long time.

These women have raised a question and not a single male participant has offered solutions, including the notion of spouses sharing duties. Substantial resources have gone into the education of these particular students. All will be expected to do serious work in their specializations. In the past, the grandmother could function as a surrogate, while the mother worked. It is still seen, but for this young group the future is bound to be different: almost half have left their home cities, and with it, the rest of their families. All of the participants, if they are successful in their professions, will probably have to consider physical mobility together with professional mobility. And these are not Soviet institutions in which child care, vacations, social benefits (whatever their quality) were part of working in that institution. How available will grandmothers be to help Tanya's exacting and lengthy obligation to her children? Perhaps she will be able to afford superior child care, but this is not the European Union, where that kind of labor can be found in the flow of young people across countries. Some of the participants who come from privileged homes will be able to simply hire help, if they want to outsource bringing up their children. Most will not have that choice. Some women prefer to be housewives, but the participants are in training to be key professionals. They are thoroughly convinced that they have been given an extraordinary opportunity to be in these Moscow educational institutions. They intend to live up to expectations successfully. Expectations about family must seem problematic for the participants. Tanya describes the vigilant mother she wants to become. Who will help?

Overall, they agree, internet use will increase, and schoolwork will disappear. Most of the participants think their use of the internet will grow for professional reasons. They will have to know so much more to be competitive, to be in touch with so much new and updated professional material. When they speak about this new task, which far exceeds what they had to do at university, they are partly looking forward eagerly to an almost palpable growth of knowledge, and they are partly awed and sobered by the weight of their futures.

Attraction to online music will never stop; the games will likely continue too; and they will remain in touch with friends—as long as changing interests do not divide them as has happened in the past. On the other hand, the vast possibilities of the internet are their resources, endless in number and shoring up the first exhilarating steps into leadership.

CHAPTER FIVE

MEGADEMONSTRATIONS

While the focus groups were studying in their universities, two very different mass protests took place: one about the environment and one, a riot, really, expressing the growing support for ethnic cleansing in Russia. The focus-group participants reacted to both in the sessions. These are demonstrations that to some degree paved the way for the larger ones that followed. The environmental protest, in particular, led to a series of more and more massive demonstrations. Looking closely at the students' reactions to the demonstrations about Khimki Forest illuminates their positions on participation in demonstrations in general and expectations they are likely to have held when more demonstrations arose in an increasingly dramatic cluster before the regime's crackdown. Here we take a close look at two large Moscow demonstrations the focus-group participants have encountered and another one—a special demonstration with democracy at its heart. We will treat the last in Part II.

PART I

KHIMKI FOREST

These protests were a desperate fight by a very mixed group of people to save the one remaining forest on the perimeter of Moscow: Khimki Forest. Journalists, environmentalists, people living on the edge of the forest, and people from the center of Moscow were all involved. The protests, too, moved from the town at the edge of the forest itself to the middle of Moscow and Manezh Square. The protests went on for two years before hired thugs swinging clubs interrupted the previously peaceful gatherings. An ineffectual and lethargic police force turned a blind eye to the bloodshed and routed the young idealists. The protestors, led by a young, committed woman, finally had to give up; the highway that would cut through it had been approved.

Our focus-group sessions were going on while protest demonstrations were at their peak in Moscow's center and edges. These particular demonstrations to save Khimki Forest serve as an especially good indicator for us to understand the group's thoughts on the behavior of those involved, and their responses to the issues around which the protests galvanized. Do the focus-group participants bring up or act upon the well-publicized demonstrations going on around them? It is equally telling if we find that the participants do not bring up or relate to demonstrations in a personal way. Either way, we have 108 elite students to react—or not—to demonstrating as a form of effective political action.

The Protests and Their Consequences

Khimki Forest is a town on the edge of a forest originally surrounding Moscow. The forest has shrunk with deforestation and urban growth, but this remaining area stood as an obstacle to Vladimir Putin's plans to cut through it for a high-speed highway to St. Petersburg. Khimki Forest is Moscow's last undisturbed piece of nature. It is a unique ecosystem dense with masses of birch, venerable oak trees, and a wide variety of species of birds.

In the summer of 2010, because of protests from environmentalists, then-President Medvedev suspended construction of the highway. He announced that more experts should study the environmental impact of the deforestation. At the end of the year, the government reaffirmed its decision, but said that new trees would be planted in a different area to compensate for the loss. In July, the leader of the Save Khimki movement, a young woman named Yevgenia Chirikova, was attacked by a man who tried to ram her car, and a series of violent incidents were carried out against peaceful protestors. A journalist, Mikhail Beketov, started a newspaper with his own money to expose the violence and reveal the corruption of the mayor, for whom the devastating plans for Khimki would be profitable. Beketov was "warned" by unknown anonymous individuals when, in 2007, his car was set on fire and his dog killed. He wrote more investigative articles and accused the mayor of illegal activities. (He was indicted for slandering the mayor.) In 2008, he was found near his house in a coma—his skull had been cracked and his brain partially destroyed, and there were injuries to his legs and hands. One leg was amputated and he was left unable to speak. What seemed to have been desultory investigations into his torture were carried out with no success and suspended. Five years later he died of heart failure; he was 55.

Activists for "Save Khimki" were encamped, in the summer of 2010, in a clearing, where they lived in tents. On July 23, they were fiercely attacked by tattooed men wearing masks and Nazi symbols. Witnesses said the thugs looked like soccer fans from extremist right-wing groups, who were sometimes hired to put an end to interference with government plans, and sometimes came together to rid Russia of "troublemaker" dissenters. The soccer pitch was a useful organizing center. At Khimki, the head of a construction section for the road publicly admitted that the thugs had been hired by his company to provoke unrest and give the police a pretext to break up the camp. More journalists were severely hurt by these thugs and perhaps by others, too. The thugs wore black balaclavas and were dressed from head to toe in concealing black shirts and pants. Police arrested none of the masked bullies but did lock up journalists and environmental activists. Reacting to the impunity of Far Right violence, the anti-fascist left-wing attacked the Administrative Headquarters of Khimki some five days later. There were no injuries and not much damage to the building, but it served as a provocation to go after the activists more intensively—though none of them had been present during the anti-fascist raid. The neo-Nazis kept coming and violently attacked an activist in the presence of a member of the Russian Parliament who pressed for investigation and charges, but none was forthcoming. Other activists were beaten, kidnapped, and interrogated; thugs harassed a young girl, speeding toward her to run her over in their SUV, but then stopped just short—the fascist/nationalist groups appeared to hold sway.

In August 2010, a new stage was reached: the "famous" protesters held a peaceful rally in a nearby village. Riot police broke up the gathering and arrested the leaders of the left-center Yabloko Party and of the revolutionary extremist Left movement. Only two days later Chirikova was snatched by riot police in the middle of Moscow after her press conference. As the environmental activists and journalists were being beaten by neo-Nazi thugs, the opposite extremist movement, the "anti-fascists," called the "anti-fa," became increasingly active, and it was the action of the latter—the Far Left—on which the authorities cracked down. The sluggish police and judicial officials, who did not hesitate to crack down brutally on pro-environment activists and journalists, now went after the anti-fascist movement, who came to Khimki to rout the neo-Nazis.

On November 6, 2010, Oleg Kashin, one of the country's leading journalists and a star of the respected Moscow-based, national newspaper Kommersant, was beaten violently and left for dead. He sustained a concussion, broken shins, and a torn-off finger, and he had to be put in an induced coma. He did survive and became one of the leading figures in the internet-based movement of the opposition.

Rallies and Twitter-propagated flash mobs supporting the Khimki activists broke out in the middle of Moscow, and one, led by rocker Yury Shevchuk, brought some 3,000 people to the traditional home of dissent, Pushkin Square. U2 and Bono offered their support: when they were in Moscow for a concert, Bono pulled Shevchuk up on stage. All of the demonstrations and rallies in support of the environmentalist activists were unauthorized and put down violently by riot police. In the end, predictably, the ruling powers went ahead with the plan and promised again to plant new trees.

After all that heroism and sacrifice, Yevgenia Chirikova sought change from within, and she ran in municipal elections in Khimki. Her bid for mayor in October 2012 appeared reasonably fair and lawful.

She was decisively crushed by the ruling party, United Russia. She got about 17% of the vote, while her colorless, bureaucratic opponent pulled in 47.5%. Local management was deeply entrenched—Khimki was a fiefdom of the ruling party. It is one example of the grip United Russia exerts outside the very large cities.

Khimki in the Focus Groups

Without biasing the results, we wanted the focus groups to be able to talk about the Khimki demonstrations if they wished to do so. We wanted also to learn about the reputation of sites they may or may not frequent and presented a sheet of paper with choices they might consider. As we shall see below, we gave them a familiar trade-off news headline that could bring Khimki to mind, if they were so inclined. We gave them no prompts, and they were free to bring up Khimki, if they wished, at any time in the session. We presented three statements of (contrived) "news" and two requests for help, and we asked where these five would most likely be found; of what media source were they typical? We offered for each "news item" five sources and a line for filling in "other" (in each group the choices of sources were in a different order). Later we told the participants that these were not real news items, but had been devised for the focus groups. The first "news item" read: *Of course, our environment is very important. But we do have to sacrifice parts of it for projects that give people jobs. We have to put the welfare of our people ahead of everything else.* The possible sources of this were: "LiveJournal," "Channel 1 TV news," "A. Navalny's blog" in LiveJournal, "DPNI,"[1] "lenta.ru,"[2] and "Other source" (which they were asked to name).

The task was to identify the likely source and why it probably produced the information. But it was also a logical exercise during which to bring up Khimki, if it was on the mind of anyone in the group. Among the 108 participants, there were only 6 who referred in any way to Khimki. Ivan is concerned that the environment is so weighty an issue that the criteria should be more exacting and the evidence solid before any action is taken that might result in major alteration of an area.

He says, "If such a project, which is going to sacrifice ecology, exists, then we need to know a little about this project, right? It's necessary to analyze what's going on generally and what we are sacrificing when we cut down Khimki forest." In another group Andrei says the information probably comes from state-run Channel 1, which ignores environmental issues, "because ecology is not very important politically, [and therefore] not a big thing. Unattractive." Andrei's short comment on ecology is merely a comment on the government's "unattractive" position on ecology. Seva is equally detached saying only: "Yes, here it's now a basic theme—ecology." That is as far as he goes; he appears to show little to no personal involvement or emotion. Misha, who was so thoughtful in chapter 2 about rebellion inside his head and social tension in the population, says "I wanted to put down First Channel also, because [of] the formulation: 'we have to think above all else about the welfare of people.' But then I thought that somehow when they get into ecology and say that no, it's not what we [the government] are working for, then I thought it's more likely to be Navalny's blog, because it's completely likely for me that he would probably say that." Aleksei Navalny had not been associated with any environmental issues but Misha's brief comment, as one of the five who bring up Khimki, shows that he is thinking about the issue as contentious and possibly involving corruption. It shows that he feels some involvement in the question of the forest. On the other hand, absent from Misha's brief comment are the human tragedies and Right–Left warfare that defined the Khimki protests. Stas calls the statement "such a populist statement. At the same time, considering the trend, because ecology is also in principle a rather key element [especially in the West] which you can't disregard, then the government channel also should pay attention to it. Here, in the given proposal it's as though they disregard it. Therefore I put down at the beginning, First Channel, but then, thought. . . . " Stas doesn't finish his thought, and he does not seem to like any of the alternatives. He does relate the statement squarely to the government's responsibility for oversight of ecology, a topic in which the government has little interest and to which it merely mouths the usual platitude as a way of rationalizing its sacrifice. Stas has changed his viewpoint. Rather than taking a remote "scientific" look at costs and benefits, he challenges the government to stop riding roughshod over nature. Stas also warns that treatment of the environment can reduce Russia in the eyes of the West—he does not name America but, as we saw in chapter 1, it is the only power that matters.

There is only one person in the whole group who is concerned at the level of the human protestors and their sacrifices for protecting the environment. Olya says that "...recently I noticed a tendency that they [the government] are putting ecology in last place. I read a lot about the problems of Khimki forest: not long ago I ploughed through Chirikova's blog. I simply imagine that the position expressed here [in the statement in front of them] I would sooner relate it to the government's point of view." Yevgenia Chirikova has written many blogs and micro blogs. Olya is the only person of the 108 participants who has named Chirikova. In all of the sessions, not once is Chirikova's name mentioned. Rud is active in practically all the sessions; we know he studies law. It turns out that in his free time he organizes what he calls "environmental events." Here, where the environment is under siege, he utters not a word.

What are we to make of the little active interest in the Khimki demonstrations and, with the exception of Olya's response, so much emotional distance from it the few times it is mentioned? They are nearly all interested in the environment; some are studying environmental law. But in this case, they would not consider entering into spontaneous public activities and demonstrations. Were they to do so, their government or private sector jobs would be at risk. Faces can be identified in surveillance videos. The price of involvement for them, at the start of their careers, could be too high, and it might even be career-ending. The context is also important. Khimki was a very dangerous conflict: neo-Nazis and local authorities were going for maximum force and the law was absent. Of all of the participants not one mentions personally having considered becoming involved with the demonstration and certainly not as part of a crowd.

Others speak generally about the form of the trade-off used in the example. Dima translates the government's usual rationale, "good of the people," as simply an excuse for letting unregulated business take all it wants in the name of the development of the country at large and the trickle-down effect to households. Yegor turns the whole thing around and says that "you can't close your eyes to ecology, and here, if you observed, they never say that for ecology you can sacrifice a little." Like Dima, he is scornful of the government's formula "for the good of the people." It is a creaky rationale, and they can see through it as over-aged, oft-repeated, and unconvincing propaganda. Misha says he started to think that the statement came from First Channel, "because of how it's formulated—that we should think of the welfare of people before everything else. But then I thought they are strangling ecology, and they say, 'no, it's because we'll have work.' There [the leaders supposedly] care about everything and look after everything."

We shall return to the demonstrations to save Khimki Forest and the brutal tactics to suppress them, passively sanctioned by the Kremlin. We shall return to the events in order to ponder how, of 108 future leaders, only a handful mentioned them. These few were critical of the government's worn-out policy rationale: destroying one good for the "good of the people." Other than Olya, none appears to have read Yegenya Chirikova's many blogs. The few who complain about Khimki are concerned with some form of the balance of the trade-off: "forest vs. highway." Though we know these participants can be very passionate, their discussion of Khimki lacks that emotion and strong personal involvement. They display no empathy and absolutely fail to connect their views to the participants in the protest, many of whom are their age. Khimki, finally, tells us that the 108 very likely place a higher value on their careers than joining demonstrations. They do not appear to consider such mass protest as a means to policy solutions, especially for what they know are complex issues.

THE RIOT OF DECEMBER 2010

While focus-group participants knew about Khimki, they also observed quite a different demonstration around the same time. This nationalist, right-wing uprising, or rather outburst of rage, took place in the heart of Moscow. It was a protest against non-Slavs and left an indelible impression on the group. They regarded the Far Right Nazi-like ideology and violent behavior displayed during the protest with disgust and fear. There was not a single participant who voiced words of solidarity. If this type of mass behavior could happen, anything could punch through the thin crust of order. There were no riot police to speak of and only a few policemen when this hunt for non-Slavs took place. Some of the focus-group participants sounded as though they, themselves, even now, could be threatened by the total breakdown of order and the venomous intent of neo-Nazis to annihilate whomever they wanted—anyone who did not look Slavic. Passersby, accidental pedestrians, it did not matter. This was obviously not a protest-like event the focus-group participants wanted to join; they hated the ideology. Several participants noted the hand the internet had in helping to create this ugly and dangerous neo-Nazi eruption.

What happened? In the southern part of Russia, all across the slopes and valleys of the Caucasian mountains and just north of the Republic of Georgia, lies a whole group of "republics" within Russia. In a relatively small area are found the republics of Chechnya, North Ossetia-Alania, Dagestan, Ingushetia, Kabardino-Balkaria, and Karachay-Cherkessia. Some of them, as the names identify, encompass two or three ethnicities and tribes, and within these republics are yet more ethnic groups and tribes. Most of the inhabitants are Muslim, mixed in in some places with Russian Orthodox. None is homogeneous. Their fierce resistance to the nineteenth-century conquest by the Russian Empire is legendary.

On December 6, 2010, Aslan Cherkesov, a 26-year-old from a Muslim republic in the north Caucasus met Ramazan Utarbiev, a 20-year-old from another north Caucasian republic and some of his friends at a Moscow bar. Yegor Sviridov, who was 28, and four Russian friends got into a drunken fight with the Caucasians just outside the bar. Stories differ as to who started the brawling; at least some were drunk. Cherkesov's side was numerically superior. According to Cherkesov, he saw the drunken Russians beating up his Caucasian friends. When Sviridov and a friend ran toward him, Cherkesov took out his rubber-bullet handgun, fired warning shots in the air and then shot the oncoming Sviridov. The victim's widow and friends have a different story. They contend that the Caucasians misunderstood what the Russians were talking about and took umbrage at what they thought was an ethnic slur. Then one of them shot Sviridov in the head—blowing away the back of his skull—and stomach. The police were called and the suspects taken to the local police precinct. And here the controversy gets tangled, but what happened in that police station was probably really the trigger for the Manezh riot four days later. Five of the six suspects were let go almost immediately after promising to stay in Moscow. Only Cherkesov was detained. Sviridov's widow and friends blamed the deputy chief of the district for a grave miscarriage of justice when the perpetrators just walked away. The police investigator had divided the crimes into two categories: first degree murder and battery. Only Cherkesov was held, because he had committed the murder. Battery has a maximum sentence of two years, which cannot justify pretrial detention. Rumors flew that the Caucasians had bribed the official. Some spoke of shiny black cars appearing. All the young men who were released were rearrested, though it took some time to round them all up. What the Sviridov group and the Russians they contacted immediately after the shooting saw was the release of people who were responsible for the murder of their friend and the denigration of Russians by the Russian judicial system.

On December 11, right-wing extremist soccer fans poured into the central square in Moscow to avenge Sviridov's murder, because the municipal justice authority had treated it so lightly. Moscow is not the only place where this deadly ethnic hatred has been seen. In 2013 nearly 400 were detained in St. Petersburg after a melee in an outdoor market, mainly among North Caucasians. One man was knifed to death. This market is a popular meeting place for migrant workers, and earlier at a nearby mosque more than 270 people were detained for distributing extremist materials.[3] In the Manezh demonstration in 2010, at least 5,000 Russians arrived, many giving the Nazi salute and wearing stylized swastikas, arm bands, and leather belts across their chests. Passersby who appeared to be from the Caucasus or

Central Asia were beaten mercilessly, and a Kyrgyz migrant (among the many) working in Moscow and in nowise related to anti-Russian activity was stabbed to death. The rampaging neo-Nazis also beat non-Slavs so savagely that reportedly at least twenty had to be hospitalized. This time four skinheads were apprehended and sentenced to prison for two and a half to six years. The ringleader, Ilya Kubrakov, was 14 when he killed the Asian migrant; he drew a six-year sentence in a juvenile correction colony. Another underage perpetrator, Mikhail Kuznetsov, was sentenced to three years; he, too, was sent to a juvenile correction colony. In this case out of the 5,000 violent Russian protesters, only 65 were arrested and all were let go within a day.[4]

During the clashes, the police stood by and watched. There were few of them; permission for a march had not been sought and no advance security prepared. The volcanic force was thoroughly unexpected. The bloodshed and beating continued unabated until the arrival of the special riot police. Then the rioters flooded the subway entrance, bashing anyone in the way and left. Subway riders were terrified. The government did not comment on the events for several days.

Then–President Medvedev went on television five days later advocating bringing the guilty to justice. Five days after that came a curious and illuminating action from then–Prime Minister Vladimir Putin. He asked to meet with the representatives of the major soccer fan clubs to discuss Sviridov's murder; he called it a tragedy.[5] That he sought to bring under control the organized sources of violence-for-hire and ethno-nationalist unpredictability is telling. Instead of punishment, he sought a more cooperative stance, for he, too, had possibly benefited from forces they controlled—as at Khimki. Though he used the usual vague platitudes about Russia as a multicultural state, Putin gave the clear impression that he was a supporter of the nationalist cause. With cameras recording, he made an official visit to Sviridov's grave to lay a large and showy bunch of long-stemmed roses. No one paid such public honor to the thoroughly innocent Kyrgyz man, performing his lawful work in Moscow and randomly beaten and killed in the riot because of the color of his skin. On Hitler's birthday, there is a lockdown at universities where foreign students study. They are not allowed to leave the buildings for their own safety.

Vladimir Putin has encouraged nationalism, which can mean many different things: in part, he is guarding his personal power and, in a larger sense, he is protecting what he sees as the inviolable sovereignty of Russia in a predatory world where the United States is bent on dismembering his country. He is against any international projects for "regime change" and was especially concerned with the revolutions to the south: in Georgia and, more strategically important, in Ukraine during its "Orange Revolution" and later when Ukraine overthrew Viktor Yanukovich and sought not ties with Russia, but renewing progress toward future close relations with the European Union. He regards the West's bombing of Serbia and America's hand in regime change in Libya as illegal acts, while the drawn-out international talks about intervention in Syria have further strained fraught relations with the United States. At home, he has been "playing the ethnic card," but this tactic is short-sighted and very likely to backfire. Ethnic groups begin to compete internally over who is "really" ethnically more authentic and who can cause more grief to the enemy ethnos.[6] In December 2010, some of the soccer fans were also thugs for hire, and some were mainly aggressive and anti-social sports fanatics. In the next months, the government started to take serious actions to regulate violent manifestations of ethnic hatred. But, as the Academy of Sciences report concluded, the level of aggression was reaching unheard-of levels in Russian society.

Many of the participants in the focus groups were well aware of that December day and feared that the fanatics could not be contained. The participants did not feel safe, and they did not appear to trust the police and government to put an end to the danger. Everybody knew soccer fans could act like thugs everywhere; they come to games to drink and fight as happens in Russia, Italy, England, and many other countries. But in the Russian case, there was this formidable combination of what appeared to be special latitude given by the state to the rioters, and a stunted and weak judiciary. In those December riots in the center of Moscow, it became clear that skinheads and neo-Nazis would turn against the government as easily as they would beat up non-Slavs. When they later marched in legal demonstrations, some right-wing signs said "Down with Putin!" He had nourished a population of great physical force and no principles; when he tried to restrain them, they turned on him.

DPNI: THE RIGHT EXTREMISTS' UMBRELLA

When we asked the focus-group participants what information source would most likely produce a particular statement, we included DPNI as a possible source. Most of the participants had no idea what the letters stood for: some tried to guess, "let's see...Department of..." One or two participants were able to explain it to the rest; sometimes it was left up to the facilitator. When they did know what the organization was, it was treated as outside the pale; an extreme, violent, and alien presence. Yaroslav understands them this way: "They go and drive out guest workers [from Central Asia and China, mainly]; they beat them up unmercifully; sometimes they wear masks and say 'Moscow for Russians!' [using the ethnic, not the citizenship word] nonsense. Now just a short time ago, this movement was officially prohibited...although earlier they arranged demonstrations and without permits went around Moscow." Dima asks if it was the one in Liublino [district on the outskirts of Moscow] and Yaroslav says depressingly, "There were lots of places where it happened."

One of the statements posed in the section where we asked participants to think about likely internet sources was the following: *"The reason for the extinction of our great Siberian tigers is the inadequacy of border control."*

The Siberian tiger, also called the Ussursiisky Tiger (after the Ussuri River) and the Amur Tiger (another river name) Tiger is the largest species of tiger, weighing up to 700 lbs. It is estimated that only 350–400 are left. They are sacred to the indigenous tribes living in scattered small villages in wild, strange, and often deadly environs. The cold and blinding blizzards suddenly wipe out orientation, and the animals conceal themselves expertly. The gigantic tiger can move silently behind a screen of trees to ambush prey. Whether the tigers will survive at all, where thousands once hunted, is doubtful.

The above statement is interesting because it could be interpreted several different ways: it could be about the poor job the Russian border control is doing to keep out poachers. It could be about bribes and corruption among Russian border guards. It could be about the poachers, who are mainly Chinese and come across the border and kill the animals for their medical preparations. If the focus-group participants choose the first two interpretations, it is criticism of Russian institutions and their likely corruption accepting bribes to let in the poachers. Or, if the third, they could be interpreting it as criticism about a racial group, the Chinese, illegally coming into Russia and despoiling it. When the moderator asked one group who knew what DPNI is, Ivan, Ivan Vladimirovich,[7] and Liza said they did. Vanya decodes the acronym DPNI: Movement Against Illegal Immigration. Ivan wants to make it clear that it is a fiercely nationalist organization not known for any interest in conservation. Andrei in another group thinks that the statement can be attributed to DPNI and puts it this way: "You're not going to believe this, but I put down our [heavy sarcasm in his tone] beloved DPNI...they are very crazy in particular about border control, and it would be a lot like them [DPNI, to want impenetrable borders]." Among the participants there are not very many who can identify DPNI, and the ones who do know about it reject it with contempt. DPNI has become an increasingly important political player. It did not seem so in its early days.

DPNI—Fanning the Flames of Hatred

A 2008 Reuters Institute study of the Russian ethno-nationalist Web presence concluded that "Kept out of the established channels for democratic participation, it would seem natural to turn to the net as a way of putting out propaganda, and above all mobilizing its [DPNI] members for protests marches and demonstrations. But, at best, its Internet presence is patchy: most of all, it speaks to the committed."[8] The key point the authors make—that the organization has been kept out of the "legitimate" mainstream—is, after a dramatic turn of events, no longer true. We shall see below that numbers out on the street are just one dimension in estimating penetration and influence of an outlawed extremist group. There is another far more effective and pernicious strategy and that is to enter the halls where politics is played. This two-front strategy that takes place in the streets and in the council rooms is very tricky. One threatens the effectiveness of the other. The second smacks of compromise and "collaboration" with moderates, while the first yields no ground. Lenin's strategy had it both ways; he was famous for his energetic willingness to appear to compromise and join any group on the Left because in his mind he was merely forging a temporary alliance to further his own unchanged goals. In twenty-first-century Russia the well-known ethno-nationalist internet sites were declared illegal after the Manezh demonstration. So how are the groups to carry the message of often brutal exclusionary ethnic nationalism now? Many are registered elsewhere, beyond Russian jurisdiction; others changed their names slightly and reappeared—hatred intact.

DPNI, to the extent that it is known at all, has been focused mainly on the annual "Russian Marches," or simultaneous national-fascist marches in cities across the country, which it coordinated through its website. Although DPNI claims to have 5,000 members in 30 different regions, there is no way to verify the numbers. DPNI also urged, as early as 2005, that nationalists create small, five-person "mobile units" of fighters armed with legally available weapons. Their marches in Moscow—relegated to a district on the outskirts of the city—have brought out as many as 7,000 marchers. In 2011, buoyed by slowly increasing, but still negligible, public support, DPNI announced that it would broaden its activities to include political and social demonstrations, in addition to those limited to so-called anti-illegal immigration causes.

After the 2010 brutality in the center of Moscow, the Moscow Court declared DPNI illegal in April 2011, and the ruling was upheld on appeal by the higher court. The Duma adopted a law against the display of Nazi symbols or paraphernalia. Banning a name is hardly a spear to the heart, though, as an organization can simply alter its name and that is exactly what happened.

Many who deplored DPNI made the point that marches could take place to persuade the already persuaded, and ugly texts and pictures of hatred could be put up on websites, but the effort resulted only in new echo chambers. The organization had been kept out of the "legitimate" mainstream.

DPNI, Hockey, Skinheads, and Violence

The Right extremists have acted mainly as "accelerators." When an ethnic conflict took place, they went there to add fuel to the fire and make a limited altercation into an uncontrollable outburst of hatred on a larger scale.[9] Alexander Verkhovsky is Russia's greatest expert on encounters with ethnic violence. He gave up a good software job to devote himself to this activity for the civic good. He and his small staff at SOVA, the Center for Information and Analysis, track in great detail xenophobia in Russia. They look at violence, along with ethnic-racist, religious, and other victims across Russia and the judicial treatment of such cases. He says that without question DPNI is the "most important site for them [the violent right]." It is their "basic" site. Verkhovsky notes that the surveys show that Russians are not necessarily filled with more hatred at this time, and most citizens are not activists. What has changed though is that if they said before that "we" should get rid of the non-Russians, now they say I personally hate them and want them gone.[10] In Russia, right-wing fans are organized in each of the soccer clubs into "firms." Within the firms are "hooligans." Firms of some clubs are racist, especially Zenith in St. Petersburg, which refuses to hire black players. Each club has several "firms." Formally, they make up the All-Russian Union of Fans; informally, says Verkhovsky, about half of the people who run it are from the "criminal structure." Sometimes the "fans" are hired out to go beat up people, the likely case in Khimki. In 2010, firms told their fans not to go riot after Sviridov's murder; the fans went rampaging anyway.

DPNI has a history of assisting racist violence. In the past, DPNI's "structure of the whole [was] maintained through internet websites of the central and local branches in different cities and web forums."[11] In DPNI's first act, it mobilized local youth in Krasnoarmeysk in 2002 after a fight between two customers—one Russian and the other from a different ethnic group—grew into a large-scale conflict in the town. In another small town, a Russian woman accused of killing an Armenian taxi-driver she insisted was harassing her was acquitted and Alexander Belov, DPNI leader at the time, awarded her a monetary prize "for courage." One of the most vicious of the ethnic conflicts took place in 2006, in Karelia, in the town of Kondopoga, a Russian region near Finland.[12] There, a small group of ethnic Russians complained to the Azerbaijani owner of a restaurant that their vodka had been watered down. The owner called in his "protectors," Chechens, who randomly attacked Russians. They killed 2, seriously wounded 8, and mutilated 15. The police did not intervene. A Russian mob went after the Chechens, most of whom had left hurriedly. Two days after the beginning of the rioting, DPNI's people came from Moscow to organize and catalyze deadly anger into a generalized fury against peoples from the Caucasian regions.

GAMBLING ON HATRED

DPNI and the smaller groups under its umbrella so far pose no threat to the established parties seeking seats in parliament. I think it important, though, to spend some time on this umbrella organization. We saw the participants in focus groups verbally shudder when they recalled the brutality of right-wing violence in 2010. The organization was proscribed the next year, but no change was made in its "Russian March" and other activities, which activate and multiply incidents of racism and xenophobia. Yet, for all that, its annual March still has not passed the 10,000 mark in Moscow. Their internet presence does not reach out beyond its acolytes. Many of the focus-group participants either did not know the organization's name or had only a vague impression about it.

After 2010 police in Russia have been somewhat more vigilant. They have imprisoned about 2,000 DPNI members. In Nizhny Tagil in 2013, a criminal case was raised for incitement of ethnic hatred on a social network. The Manezh riot in December 2010 did not result in a wider base of adherence or more adherents.[13] If the extreme Right hoped to expand its social base, it was in vain. And even though ethno-nationalism is on the rise, Manezh did not do anything to arouse public support or membership. Then came the 2011 law banning DPNI and some others, and, as we know, names were slightly changed and work went on. But the Far Right split in two basic directions.

Different Strategies Wedging in to the Mass Demonstrations

The report of the Russian Academy of Sciences, which figures so prominently in chapter 2, should be borne in mind when considering the Far Right in Russia. It was a document expressing the urgent need to tamp down the threat of deadly ethnic rampages. Some in extremist right-wing organizations find little progress in the habitual actions and brutality. "Progress" here is used to mean a broadening of adherents. The DPNI's internet site does not accomplish this; the annual Marches do not swell to very large proportions. Likewise, efforts to set off a riot by alleging ill treatment by Russian judges fizzled.

The DPNI and other right-wing fractions are ready to make compromises—or appear to make them—in order to expand their ranks. This strategy is not without risk as the core body of the organization will likely see the move as a betrayal of principle. Some in the Far Right and Left groups say they want to "come in from the cold," that is, move from being always marginal to becoming a real "player" in the political arena. They would curb their openly racist talk and present a "more moderate ethno-nationalism, even with elements of civil nationalism, supporting political opposition and defense of democracy."[14] They also intend to slip into the ranks of the democratic opposition to be more attractive for the "average xenophobically oriented citizen."[15]

This is not a small public: as I noted earlier, surveys in Russia find active xenophobia in the country. Even though some of the Far Right has turned against Vladimir Putin, he persists in supporting a nationalism that must be finely balanced to avoid open conflict in the city. The government has introduced models that exacerbate the xenophobia: for example, in a stark breach of legal procedure, extremists from the "Moscow Defense League" and "Holy Russia" joined the police in Moscow in anti-Tajik (guest-worker migrants) raids in Moscow. The goal was to round up workers for deportation to Tajikistan. Cossacks are patrolling certain neighborhoods together with police. Though, because they are not police, Cossacks are not held to the same standards of conduct as police. A group of muscular young Russians regularly break into apartments where Central Asian migrant workers live. They follow tips to go to cellars to round up others, crowded into narrow spaces. Like the Cossack patrols, Shield has wider latitude than the police themselves on some occasions. A right-wing legend for brutality who goes by the name of "Hatchet" (real name, Maxim Martsinkevich), has started a movement called "Okupai-Pedofiliya" (Occupy Pedophilia), with thirty or so small branches mainly in small cities across Russia, Ukraine, and Moldova. The members get on social networks to lure gay readers to "dates" and when they show up, muscled young men come in groups to beat them.[16] The name of the group is borrowed from a misunderstanding of the American left-liberal protests "Occupy Wall Street." Hatchet's appropriation of "Occupy" for his group's acts of determined cruelty would be absurd, were it not so deeply barbaric. What this Okupai does has nothing whatever to do with the American protests. But, ironically, American protest movements, including "Occupy," had no resonance for the focus-group participants: none made any reference to any demonstrations in the United States, believing them, I think, to take place under such different conditions as to lack any reasonable equivalence. The list of Russian vigilante groups continues to grow: there is "Light Russia" and "Attack," both of which target migrants. Although the police deny working with these groups, videos show the contrary.[17]

DISAGREEMENTS WITHIN THE FAR RIGHT

The extreme Right, until this point, did not benefit much from their internet propaganda; they were too unattractive, as the focus-group participants said after the November 2010 riot. Part of the right wing—the pragmatic right—is seeking a new look: "nationalism with a human face." To have some weight in the move to lessen the marginality of the nationalists, committed participants are needed. New groups and coalitions are forming to represent the Far Right wing. The autonomous ultra-Right is beyond all other groups in its extremist and dangerous commitment to Nazi-inspired acts. In thinking about extremism in Russia today, one must look beyond the various associations and alliances and also consider these smaller freewheeling, very bold, cruel "autonomous" types. The most extreme—from neo-Nazi to anarchists—operate underground, and we know little about them. As we shall see in the next chapter, violence in 2012 in a public gathering was precipitated by the aggressive acts of men clad in black, their faces hidden by balaclavas. Who were they? The presentation in 2013 of a so-called "public report" researched by an impressive list of nongovernmental and oppositionist experts did have an answer, which we shall see in the next chapter. The activities and the threat of the extremist groups has surfaced and multiplied, especially in Moscow. They are considered absolutely unacceptable by the participants.

The wild outburst in the center of Moscow in 2010 was not unique, although it has been treated as an unrepeatable extreme. In 2013, the largest ethnic riot since 2010 broke out in southern Moscow, in the Birulyevo area, after a 25-year-old Russian, Yegor Shcherbakov, was stabbed to death. He was leaving a pool hall with his girlfriend. She described the assailant as having a "non-Slavic appearance." All weekend thousands of young men "took to the streets...overturning cars, breaking windows in street kiosks and attempting to break into the vegetable market that was the target of the violence."[18] The rampaging youth yelled "Russia for Russians" and went after migrants and anyone else they judged to be non-Slavic. When police arrived on Monday, the day after the riots, they took in about 1,200 migrants to check their documents (the migrants had been the target of the violence). Most were gradually released during the day. Migrant workers are continuing to come to Moscow to look for work in lower-level jobs; to some extent the economy depends on them. I found that the video of this ethnic riot revealed something new: the active role taken by women—young and old, with permed gray hair or the long black straight hair of a model. They were in the thick of things, frenzied and screaming. A few days later a man from the southern country of Azerbaijan, a former Soviet republic, confessed to the killing, but said he acted in self-defense after trying to calm an argument between the victim and his girlfriend. (This story is certainly hard to believe.) The girlfriend said the fight broke out because the Azerbaijani man had insulted her.[19]

The members of the focus groups all reject and condemn this kind of behavior. They might have thought 2010 was a frightening but isolated exception. It was not; it was almost matched by 2013.

Part II
One Demonstration and Habits of Democracy

The insultingly open and obvious defrauding of citizens' right to vote in December 2011 brought them into the street. At first, the Russian observers who had seen the fraudulent action first-hand at polling places in Moscow formed a peaceful demonstration just days after the elections. Then, with the help of computer-assisted mobilization, a much larger demonstration followed, and this one brought out tens of thousands of Muscovites. Another demonstration, again massively large, took place on Moscow's Sakharov Prospect, and I concentrate on that demonstration because, in addition to protest, it had a further and much deeper purpose.

Though it was not the first of the huge demonstrations in Moscow, Sakharov Prospect took up a new and specific purpose in inspiring people to protest the 2011 vote fraud. The organizers' intention was to make of the demonstration a real experience in "lived" democracy for voters as well as for the organizing committee. The preceding two very large demonstrations were remarkable in terms of the number of people who came out into the squares; many of them had never before participated in such a move to protest. However, it was the Sakharov Prospect massive demonstration—it attracted about 75,000—that was completely different. People of all sorts came out, as earlier. They included the apolitical, the liberal, and some political extremists. The group was peaceable, throughout the program of music and speakers.

Ultimately, it is not a credo or oath of fidelity that brings democracy into being, but rather democratic habits of mind. A flash mob cannot achieve these goals nor can military-like orders on how to act. I am not at all minimizing the formidable obstacles or the bravery and unceasing devotion to the cause of mass inclusiveness. Those other demonstrations will go down in history, as will this demonstration on Academician Sakharov Prospect, which was, in its preparation and implementation, an extraordinary campaign to spread the experience of democracy in a way that is not possible in a call to gather only. Here, and in the next chapter, we shall get into the details of that demonstration on Sakharov Prospect.

ACADEMICIAN SAKHAROV PROSPECT

Sakharov Prospect was a systematic experiment in the implementation of fully democratic voting procedures through the internet. Within a regime of repression of speech, this complex demonstration put into practice a limited experiment in democracy, with transparency and participation, and the organizers as agents of voters. That meant not only that the "voting public" would be the "principals," but that the organizing committee in Moscow would be their "agents"—making happen what voters wanted. It would not have been possible without an internet-saturated Moscow. It would also be an exercise in acting democratically.

Yury Saprykin, the central figure in this experiment, is modest and, at the same time, a powerful leader. He denies to me that he deserves any more recognition than the group as a whole. Saprykin astutely started up—early in the internet revolution—what became a widely used search engine cum news aggregator. He also started *Afisha* [poster], a glossy magazine and internet site showing what was going on in Moscow. Around 2009, he began injecting more and more (what this Moscow milieu calls hipster) involvement with politics, and the still-popular *Afisha* changed. Saprykin, in several long conversations with me, showed an innate dedication to fairness, balance, inclusiveness, and the strategies to attain them. He does not make fiery speeches or coin slogans. He is serious and lacking in flamboyant displays, but decidedly not weak. It is he who strategized the technologically based, fully democratic internet vote that drove the decisions of the Organizing Committee for the demonstration. In fact, he held the very large public project to strict democratic procedure, which is almost unimaginable within the capital city of an autocracy. In the view of well-known journalist Maxim Trudolubov, Yury Saprykin was "head of the whole thing."[20] He formed an Organizing Committee (orgkom) and worked out ways for ordinary Russians to vote, on Facebook (all over Russia, not just in Moscow), about who should speak to the demonstration and what form it should take.

Saprykin's plan for the first truly open and fair democratic elections recognized that to instill democratic values, you must put them in place for all decisions. The goal was to let people get used to learning that their vote matters and that the Organizing Committee would act as the voters' agent. In most mass demonstrations or flash mobs, there are those who work on the genesis, and sometimes they also carry out the demonstration. This was an entirely different model: carrying it off depended on many computer experts, being able to penetrate the farthest reaches of the country, and a confluence of people with the same values being willing to work for them day and night. The important lesson for citizens would be citizenship: YOUR vote represents YOUR preference. Organizers in Moscow are YOUR agents to be guided entirely by YOUR VOTES. This was a thoroughly non-negotiable principle for Saprykin. It is what makes this demonstration different from the rest and introduces a new way of looking at elections: addressing the issues at hand without unthinking blinders of party and ideology.

So, the orgkom, through Facebook, asked voters to choose who would speak on the stage to the tens of thousands of demonstrators. The next chapter will show how Saprykin and his colleagues took this kernel of democracy-building to an even higher level.

COMPETING ACTIVISTS

Some older activists, formerly in government in some fashion, were attempting to advance themselves and their ideals at this time. Some ethno-nationalists tried to move into Saprykin's planning organization. This was the beginning of the big push to move extremist parties and proto-parties into what would be considered the "acceptable mainstream." Through its website DPNI organized its straggly parade each year, but here was a chance to take on another skin and look quite like other parties for which people were likely to vote. As Alexander Verkhovsky et al. note, "There was an impression formed that the nationalists had become an integral part of the protest movement."[21]

There was no doubt that the orgkom was the main planner, and Yury Saprykin was absolutely central. Looking back, he said that there were "no factions in this collegial organ [the orgkom] as they discussed tactics." But a second nationalist orgkom arose parallel to theirs. Saprykin's conclusion about it was clear: "Their chief obligation was to stake out a place on the stage."[22] Speakers at the demonstration were to be the choice of popular vote on Facebook. Period. Saprykin thought it completely wrong to accept anyone but the choice of the people, who did not, incidentally, choose a single nationalist. Aleksei Navalny and Boris Nemtsov forcefully advocated the participation of right-wing nationalists and left-wing Bolsheviks as members of the organizing committee, and they also argued very forcefully on behalf of the extreme Right and Left for the right to speak on stage.

THE INTERNET STRATEGY TO APPROACH DEMOCRACY

The orgkom was a small group in their mid- to late thirties; Yury Saprykin, the indispensable strategist, who did not seek the limelight, was only 38 at the beginning of the process, and Aleksei Navalny, the compelling speaker, was also in his thirties. Most were, to understate, adept in communication by digital devices in all forms.

The orgkom communicated on Facebook. Every move, every decision was put on Facebook. Decisions were made by the voters on Facebook. The orgkom even devised a simple and effective way to verify the identity of voters, so that one-person one-vote would prevail. The orgkom knew one thing very well: any violence at the demonstration would doom this and probably future public meetings. There were likely to be provocateurs, but every demonstrator had at all costs to avoid violence. The orgkom gave online instructions to the potential demonstrators in order to avoid giving the government any excuses to crack down. The orgkom also put together well organized teams who fanned out among the crowd to prevent provocations. Their aim was accomplished. The peaceful demonstration remained so, as it dispersed and organizers planned follow-up movements.

This successful experiment in participation and voter sovereignty sounds uncomplicated, but it was not. The backstory is a tale of young, extremely computer-savvy entrepreneurs in software and internet sites and massively productive bloggers.

When Saprykin and I talked about the genesis of the demonstration, he declared "I am certain that this movement was born on September 24, 2011," when President Dmitry Medvedev called on United Russia to support Prime Minister Vladimir Putin for president in 2012. Putin in turn suggested that Medvedev should take over the role of prime minister if the party were to win parliamentary elections in December 2011. It was the casual and condescending way both president and prime minister told the country that they had long ago decided on switching jobs in the next election. "For me, it was a decisive day."[23] Saprykin was visibly angry talking about September 24, 2011, and the leaders' self-confident, casual dismissal of human beings as unworthy of dignity and voice.

The first meeting of the orgkom, which was open to any comers, drew about 150 people. The orgkom had not only to plan what they hoped would be a massive demonstration but also make up the list of speakers to mount the stage and speak to the crowd. Every step of the way was to be transparent. A stage was set up at the front, where the winners of the Facebook voting would address the crowd. The vote came in and the speakers the voters wanted, surprisingly, turned out to be veterans of political contests, presenting practiced enthusiasm. I do not mean that the speakers were false in their support of the principles of the demonstration. It is just that they were not new faces with bold new initiatives. Saprykin said to me that he was disappointed; "naturally they [the internet voters] voted for the most famous." But between the tribune speakers, with their lined faces and oft-heard views and the younger, more vital crowd, there was a wide gulf. Restless demonstrators were heard to say "How come they [the speakers] are just old farts?"

There were difficulties in putting together the list of speakers. Thulpan Khamatova, a respected figure who administered a foundation for cancer research, refused to come to the meeting; she supported Putin. There were other platforms, too, not just the main one the orgkom had put together, though it was the biggest. Gorbachev did not speak at this main one but went over to a competing one; there were three different platforms, as it turned out. Only one was considered by the orgkom as "legitimately" the result of popular online voting. Still, figures including Sergei Mavrodi were chosen in the popular internet vote. This man had bilked millions of people out of their rubles in his pyramid scheme early in the Yeltsin period. But his name was familiar; "name recognition" can over time become separated from why the name became familiar in the first place. And because these "over-aged" candidates were famous, they received votes. Boris Akunin, the famous novelist, came from Paris to speak; other speakers were former well-known public figures and liberals, including Boris Nemtsov, politician of past days, Grigory Yavlinsky, and others. One face was young and unique: the striking singer and television host, Ksenia Sobchak, whose gaudy private life and parties were eagerly followed by the public. She was voted in. Anyone who has seen Ksenia Sobchak talk at a strategy meeting or interview a public figure with skill and a tough intelligence knows that she is a woman who can make a political difference, if she chooses to. She has decided to dedicate herself to a fairer and more democratic Russia. Her father, Anatoly Sobchak, was a man of democratic ideals when he was mayor of St. Petersburg. Ksenia was present at many of his critical moments, and now, these experiences seem to have coalesced into making her a fighter for democracy, ready to do whatever it takes—a diva no more. Is this a phase? Her contributions to strategic discussions are serious and important, and she has surprised everyone. When Aleksei Navalny took the stage, it was clear he had grown to be a star of enormous magnitude; not only had he drawn the greatest respect but also the most obvious affection and personal connection with the massed demonstrators.

Then there was the problem of the extremists. The organizers were "liberals," caught in the true liberal dilemma: What do you do when others, from whom you are sharply divided and who do not uphold democratic principles themselves—who are, in sum, extremists—say they want to join in? They may be committed to your destruction. But, if all are equal under democracy, differences in views should only strengthen the society, as citizens of a democracy argue the merits and weaknesses of a diversity of views. The orgkom balked at inviting extremists to speak. All of the speakers had been chosen by vote on Facebook. That was the "contract" with the voters, a promise Saprykin honored. But Navalny and Nemtsov brokered a deal at the last minute to give speakers from the extremist Right and Left tribune time. None of these newly designated speakers had emerged from the Facebook voting. Those from the right wing included Vladimir Tor (called simply Tor) and Konstantin Krylov; on the Left were Aleksei Gaskarov and Ilya Ponomaryev. This arrangement, skirting the wishes of the voters, was repugnant to Saprykin. During the organizational meetings, Saprykin recalled that "they [the newly proposed right- and left-wings] said different things," conciliatory and more centrist; they signed a pledge not to propagandize and incite. When they got up on the tribune to speak to the massed people, several spoke with nationalist and exclusionary language. Aleksei Gaskarov, the "anti-fascist" leader, was the only one of the "added group" who gave a moderate speech, decrying gross inequality in the country. He attacked the extreme Right for their practices and bigotry. They booed and whistled menacingly. Far Leftist Sergei Udaltsov, seeking to move the country back toward the anti-market Left, spoke to the crowd via video from prison. The unexpected and unlikely presence of these extremists made other speakers uncomfortable; former Treasury Minister Aleksei Kudrin began his comments by saying how uncomfortable he was to be next to these types, and his grey-tinged face did look as though he was about to be sick.

The only young face, the only new face, on the speakers' platform was Ksenia Sobchak. Saprykin praised her contributions and told me that he, "wanted very much that next to status politicians would be young activists." That hope was thwarted by the "status politicians" because they "played a role in history and aren't ready to give up this resource in favor of young people with a future."

The orgkom tried hard to bring in popular musicians to whom young Russia was devoted. Disappointing and surprising for Saprykin was the reaction of star performers. He knew the demonstrators would want to hear from their generation in their idiom, which was defined so thoroughly by popular music. Saprykin and his colleagues called seventy top young performers. The majority gave lame excuses for not participating. With heavy irony, Saprykin described the absurd excuses, "sorry I have a performance in Kazan," "I have a Christmas tree in Ryazan." And their common tagline: "Our soul is with you, but we can't manage it that day."

Demonstrators were to enter the sanctioned area in columns. They passed through metal detectors. One can imagine the demonstrators looking askance at each other when the column of the Church stood next to the column of gays and lesbians.

In the impressive public demonstrations, Russians did not turn out as unified protestors. The public gatherings were massive and impressive, but did not bridge the huge gap in values among different groups. On the contrary, the separate "columns" of demonstrators held divergent views, sometimes of great mutual enmity: the column of the Far Right bigoted skinhead types was repulsive to dominant centrists and liberals, as well as to the column of the Church. The extreme Left was partly Stalinist, partly post-Stalinist, and somewhat British Labor.

After the demonstration, Yury Saprykin, looking ahead, said this:

> I must confess. I do not really believe in further increase of the protest action, unlike my colleagues on the organizing committee for meetings "For Fair Elections." If this escalation has not happened already, throughout the previous months, and if the number of participants in meetings are not growing exponentially, but remaining at the level of 60–70 thousand people in Moscow, then there is no reason to believe that this number will grow dramatically over the next few months, unless the government really missteps....If the new opposition leaders designated over the last few months decide that all that remains is to throw themselves on their bayonets, it would be a monstrous mistake. The problem is not that the protest is unraveling and it is not that the protest in its peaceful and agreeable form is dangerous for the government, but that the social basis of the protest, grown sharply in recent months, has gone as far as it can.[24]

Yury Saprykin's understanding of the importance of broadening the social base was vital to building democracy with projects and repeated practice. As we will see in the next chapter, the next venture was more complex. It reached more people and offered deeper election procedures, in which candidates were required to write about their values and programs.

At the end of our first talk, Yury Saprykin offered a speculative alternative, very familiar from Russian history of the nineteenth century: people should work "on concrete projects [including political ones] and organize to solve problems." "Today's Russians," he said, "are new to all this and need a new type of organization, one that is networked, transparent, and technological. The many projects of small groups should be tied to fairness and transparency. People easily and spontaneously come together to put out fires." That could be the next step. It is a picture of individual joint effort guided only by shared interests. It is the basis of civil society and democracy, according to Western tradition. From the repeated interactions shaping their shared virtual "neighborhood" would come more structured bases of acting and, in turn, improvements in the group environment. Political parties are part of the mix, but they may not be the most fruitful way of starting the process.

Everywhere there are limits. It was so at the end of nineteenth-century Russia, as it is now. "Going to the people" had failed in the nineteenth century; Moscow had removed itself from the rest of the country and the result was mutual distrust or worse. After the huge Moscow demonstrations took place and died down, the acknowledged leader, Aleksei Navalny, said their mistake was their failure to reach out to the regions. Young, liberal Muscovites saw no future road blocks preventing their ideals from infusing invisible regions. But obstacles to changing society certainly were there. Increasingly, the demonstrations and online connections were being seen—even by the organizers—as "Moscow tusovki." In many languages, if not English, there is a form of "you" that denotes closeness and the informality born of being in the same circle. One would never use the ty [Russian] or tu [French] or tu [Italian] or du [German] form to your seniors. For formal greetings, it would be the Vy, Vous, Lei or Voi, or Sie forms. So, a tusovka is a colloquial word that immediately calls to mind a group in which everyone knows everyone else and everyone is "in." It also means others are left out. The organizers saw that demonstrations had to go beyond the cozy tusovka and embrace differences and places they had never seen. This they decided to do.

In chapter 2, Lena is quoted as saying with self-satisfaction that "Moscow is a state within a state," and that she has no empathy whatever for victims of floods in southern Russia, because the floods come every year and the inhabitants are unprepared every year. In mid-July 2012 that cynical distancing changed. "Reaching out" to the rest of Russia was the new posture. Aleksei Navalny started a website where people in need of repairs for their homes could get help from volunteers or be connected to the municipal authorities. With housing, plumbing, electricity—the whole infrastructure of living—in such terrible conditions and untouched by governmental regulatory attention—this website is a "small deed" forward. Requests have come mainly from where internet use is high: especially from Muscovites, of course, and from some other regions. I say "small deeds" not to reduce their importance, but to connect them with the conclusions drawn from those disillusioned nineteenth-century returnees from the Russian countryside who turned to a life of "small deeds."[25] When Yury Saprykin says that perhaps after the demonstrations had played themselves out, it was time to turn to some small, concrete projects for the betterment of society, he speaks in the tradition of the nineteenth-century idealists. So, for Saprykin the answer is not more and more demonstrations, each one falling short of the previous one, but each one changing what? Some demonstrations would be necessary, at the very least to keep faith with and support their fallen: their colleagues in prison, termed by them "political prisoners." In the next chapter we examine "another way," but only after understanding the disastrous Bolotnaya demonstration of May 6, 2012, on the eve of Vladimir Putin's return to the presidency. That demonstration was full of violence. There was provocation and harsh policing and frightened, trapped people in between.

Alexander Verkhovsky of SOVA, the organization that keeps track of extremism in Russia finds hockey fans are closely monitored by the police. In the stadiums, it is true, the fans use Hitler symbols and flags of Nazi Germany. But the fans, he believes, are basically apolitical. Both Verkhovsky and others say that there remains an extremist underground of unknown identity. The inclusion of extremist Left and Right speakers in the Sakharov Prospect demonstration, as decided by some organizers but not the Facebook "voters" did have one important consequence for the future. I asked Verkhovsky if the demonstrations had, for the first time, conferred legitimacy on these extremists. Verkhovsky said that they had: before, no one knew them; now their faces were familiar, and their organizations, too

THE GREAT LEGITIMATION

It is probably the case, I conclude, that the appearance of militant ethno-nationalists at public events alongside the accepted parties will do much to counteract their encapsulation, even if they have only done so through political brokering backstage.

What is worrisome, in my view, is not mainly the overt numbers the new right-wing extremist "Russians" organization might attract. In a sense numbers matter much less than legitimacy. In 2011, DPNI and other such parties were included. They gathered in their separate columns, but there they were easily identifiable; they look and act different; they are clad in black leather; they are young, male, and angry, they carry numerous enormous flags and banners appropriating traditional [i.e., Russia as it was before the Soviet Union] nationalist symbols, as well as stylized swastikas. The left-wing extremists also had their banners and enormous flags for the return of Bolshevism. The dilemma is for the parties with liberal values—the eternal problem of upholding constitutive principles in the face of threat that is not imminent, but may be part of a long-term and threatening strategy. One could argue that their inclusion may well tame their goals and methods, while exclusion would only exacerbate them. Or, that being truly liberal and democratic simply does not permit discrimination and exclusion.

A complicating factor we shall treat in the next chapter is the enigmatic figure of Aleksei Navalny. He is a tireless worker for the demonstrations and exposure of corruption; he is also a man with a suspended prison sentence and its limitations hovering over him—there are many Navalnys. But one of them is the Navalny who makes common cause with DPNI and seeks deportation of migrants and strides in the nationalist group's marches. Navalny has many sides, and when he ran for Mayor of Moscow in 2013, his thoughts became clearer. In chapters 2 and 3, we saw some of Navalny; his magnetic presence and intense work make him without any doubt many light years above competitors. We shall see more of this incredible story in the next chapter.

As the reader will have noted, there are many stripes of politics and emotions when groups and movements march. This is a word of caution to the Western press and to photographers in the West: they would be wise to learn symbols, colors, and words on the banners and flags, and certain particular clothing. More than once, I have seen a television reporter, internet video, or newspaper journalist full of excited praise for the new activism, the "new middle class," the awakening of Russians seeking their rights in a demonstration. But the journalist may have made a bad mistake and praised the bigoted and cruel by failing to recognize their symbols and colors.

Looking Toward the Bolotnaya Affair

The demonstration on May 6, 2012, changed the course of the whole movement and halted the wary toleration of the government and, in particular, that of Vladimir Putin. May 6th was a turning point, or rather a steep descent into a resurgent past. This was the second time a demonstration was held in Bolotnaya Square. It was different in every way from the first. Bolotnaya 2 was a catastrophe. Today, political time is figured before and after Bolotnaya. The Bolotnaya Affair was an event that ushered in a new era of repression. In his reaction to Bolotnaya 2, Vladimir Putin has changed the Russia into which the focus-group participants must make their way. It will be much more difficult now for the politically dissatisfied to express their concerns publicly in organized groups.

CHAPTER SIX

GAME-CHANGERS, REPRISALS, AND POLITICAL COMPETITION

Bolotnaya 2 in May 2012 was a turning point. The first Bolotnaya was a success: large numbers of ordinary people gathered peacefully in support of the right to vote in a fair election. The second Bolotnaya demonstration of May 6, 2012, changed everything. The whole environment of politics and punishment changed, and Vladimir Putin speedily signed into law a host of chilling restrictions and punishments. The second Bolotnaya demonstration had such powerful repercussions that it simply cleaved time in two.

In Part I, we will examine what happened in that square on the man-made island in the Moscow River and then, one after the other—the destructive reprisals meted out by the president. We will end Part I with what happened to the concessions granted earlier, after the big peaceful marches of 2011 and 2012.

Part II of this chapter focuses on the politics and mobilization of a transparent coordinating body chosen democratically on the internet. It is a continuing experiment and search for getting to voters to build parties and contest lower-level, local elections.

PART I

TURNING POINT: THE BOLOTNAYA AFFAIR

BOLOTNAYA 2

The most visible leader of the second Bolotnaya, or, "the Bolotnaya Affair," as it came to be called, was Left Front head, Sergei Udaltsov.

He storms barricades; his idea is to march constantly in an unend-
ing string of mass demonstrations, each of which he calls the "March
of Millions." The March of Millions set for May 6, 2012, was to
be at the Bolotnaya Square site. "The Opposition" and the government's deputy director of the department of regional security came
to a formal agreement on the route and place of the demonstration.
This would later be challenged with bloodshed. The document from
the Chief Administration of the Ministry of Internal Affairs of the
Russian Federation shows an agreed route for the procession to the
demonstration.[1]

Bolotnaya Square is bounded on the north by the Moscow River
and on the south, by a wide canal. On the third side, the western
tip of the island—not far from Bolotnaya Square—these two merge
into a wider Moscow River. Bridges over the water are the only way
in and out. In the earlier demonstration at Bolotnaya Square, police
were positioned in a line to cordon off entry from the Square onto
the bridge over the Moscow River and into the city center. As long as
they avoided this human chain, demonstrators were free to come and
go elsewhere. In the first Bolotnaya Square demonstration, marchers
entered the Square as agreed and did not challenge the boundary of
the cordon. That changed on May 6 of the next year. Contrary to
what had been officially agreed to and documented in great detail, the
tough riot police, the Omon, positioned themselves without previous
notice to demonstrators in a manner very different from the earlier
Bolotnaya demonstration. This time, when participants in the demonstration went to Bolshaya Yakimanka Street to get into the square,
they found their way blocked by additional lines of police, who had
put up metal fences. More and more people were building up, squeezed
between lines of guards, unable to get near the speakers' tribune in
the Square. There were no exit points as the way through the crowd
was blocked, and exit was stopped by barriers hemming them in.
In the first Bolotnaya demonstration, protestors could gather on the
asphalt and also in the small park, but this time the grass was off-
limits, guarded by riot police, and there were not enough metal detectors to let protestors through. Jammed in and growing, the crowd had

nowhere to go—and nowhere to exit.[2] Udaltsov was the first to throw a punch and try to strong-arm his way through the line, punching and fighting government forces. That did it; that was the provocation the security forces used for all-out intervention. Then more and more of the pent-up crowd tried to break out by way of the off-limits Moscow River bridge. The melee that followed was bloody. Twenty officers were wounded and ended up in the hospital, enraging the new president. More than 250 demonstrators were arrested, including Udaltsov, Nemtsov, and Navalny.

Was it a "leftist provocation"? Udaltsov admits to provoking the police.[3] The situation had been made impossible for the demonstrators after the unannounced change to this new fencing in. In films of the events, there are mysterious black-clad people in black balaclavas. They distributed themselves among the crowd and intensely fought. No one I have spoken to knows who they were and there has been no public identification, or, apparently, much interest in locating them. When the police moved in, these masked people melted away. Alexander Verkhovsky believes that most of the organized attacks were "from the underground," and that those people were "prepared not to be arrested." Most active, he thinks, were the underground anarchist groups, not the DPNI. Video of the Bolotnaya crowd shows masses of people, squeezed and trapped, with practically no space to turn around. They were pushed and shoved from all sides. Close to two hundred investigators who looked into the identities of the black-clad interlopers arrested some twenty-seven people. In Verkhovsky's words: "[They were] mostly the wrong people—a complete failure."

On April 8, 2013, Mikhail Kasyanov, a former Prime Minister, reported the results of a "public investigation" of what happened: Several hundred witnesses had testified and the many videos were analyzed. Kasyanov, on the internet channel *Rain*, said the report proved that it was the Omon, or riot troops, who provoked the disorder and bloodshed and that they alone bore responsibility for the riot. He also pointed to the government's sudden and illegal change to the agreement governing the demonstration. Instead of planning for 100,000, as had been agreed to, the government, without warning and violating the terms of the agreement, reduced the expected number to 15,000, leaving thousands to be forced into tight crowds with no way out. Kasyanov also announced that the black-clad figures in the crowd, heads covered with balaclavas, were there at the order of the government, who wanted them to egg on protestors and push them into confrontation with the baton-wielding Omon. Whether the mystery of the black figures will ever be solved is unknown. The Omon came out ready to inflict wounds, and masses of innocent people had been pushed into the way of the fighting forces. The report, Kasyanov explained on *Rain*, will be countered, doubtlessly, but it has been officially acknowledged that the rules of the demonstration were changed with no notice.[4]

The Bolotnaya Affair had severe consequences for the leading participants. Aleksei Gaskarov, who was so prominent at Khimki, was one of the protestors at Bolotnaya 2. There is footage showing him being beaten by three Omon police. He undoubtedly also threw punches. But this time, when Gaskarov was tried nearly a year later, he got the harshest punishment yet given. He was charged with beating Omon personnel and with "leading a group participating in mass disorder." These serious charges were issued with the intention of reducing demonstrations; Gaskarov's punishment, announced on April 29, 2013, was two months in prison. Nothing like this had come out of previous mass demonstrations.[5]

The Bolotnaya Affair showed Putin something new and absolutely intolerable: his security troops, his special anti-riot forces had been attacked and bloodied; some were hospitalized. They guarded central Moscow. Now his authority had been targeted not just in words, but in impermissible attack. The first to be blamed were foreigners, whom he accused of trying to destroy Russia in general and his leadership in particular.

BOLOTNAYA AFFAIR AND DEFENSE OF RUSSIA FROM AMERICA

The Bolotnaya Affair sparked responses from the Kremlin, convinced that Russia was in danger of dismemberment from outside, that is, from the United States. In Putin's view the Cold War had never ended, and the destruction of Russia was an active Western policy. He claimed that the Bolotnaya disorders were an act of foreign origin, and that new defensive measures had to be taken. The earlier demonstrations were certainly not welcomed by the Kremlin, but they were civil and peaceful. Even though the Kremlin had suspicions that the United States was stirring up another Ukrainian or Georgian revolution, the excessive distrust was moderated by nonviolent calm. At Bolotnaya 2 the Omon struck back hard; Udaltsov and others sought the confrontation previous demonstrations had been so careful to avoid. The mayor of Moscow changed the rules of the demonstration without warning, so that ten times more people than allowed were attempting to get to the site, only to be caught in a churning mass trying to get in or escape the suffocating masses by breaking through the cordon. Everything was illegal, and pushing, shoving, hitting, and battery followed. The Kremlin saw the plot against Russia more clearly now and the need for harsh new laws to protect Russia.

New Laws, New Restrictions

Penalties for Demonstrations and Public Protests

Fines have risen steeply. All kinds of fines. The new law of June 8, 2012 is aimed at people who organize or take part in unsanctioned marches. For individuals, the fine could be more than the equivalent of $9,000; for organizers, $18,000, and over $30,000 for groups or companies. If a permit has been granted for a demonstration, and the terms violated in any way, these fines apply to the people who take part. If the fine cannot be paid, 200 hours of mandatory work may be substituted for individuals.[6] The sums in question far exceed what most can afford, even in wealthy Moscow. An entire party can even be suspended, which is what happened on April 19, 2013, when Udaltsov's Left Front party was barred from holding meetings and protests, and from using symbols or their frozen bank account for three months.

Slashing Foreign Influences

Involvement of the Republic of Georgia

Bolotnaya brought to mind a larger image of threat for Russia's leaders: the feared Ukrainian Orange Revolution had to be kept from infecting Russia. The rallying cry in previous pro-Putin demonstrations had been "we are the anti-Orange." In chapter 1, the focus-group participants did not see much threat from the Orange Revolution. They belittled the way it petered out. Instead, they see there a "mess" (in their words) and a failure. But not Putin. He located the proximate cause of treason in that impetuous country to the south, Georgia. Russia's government was convinced Georgian agents were assisting opposition movements in Russia. Georgia was accused of holding seminars in Lithuania and financing the training of Russian opposition activists on how to make revolution. One of the three state-controlled Russian television stations ran a "documentary"—a recording of Givi Targamadze, head of Georgia's parliamentary committee on defense, playing what the program called a "concrete role" in organizing Bolotnaya's disorders. In the "documentary," called "Anatomy of a Protest-2," there is purported footage of Targamadze speaking with and handing money to Udaltsov and two others to finance revolution in Russia.[7] Targamadze and opposition leaders Udaltsov and two others have denied the veracity of the video. When Udaltsov was interviewed and asked about this charge, he talked around the question a good deal, calling the documentary faked, slanderous, and based on confusing imprecision. He did say he had never been to Georgia or anywhere out of the country. His voice on the documentary is clearly not his, he says, nor does the face resemble his. The television station that showed it, NTV, has become so well known for photoshopping and gross distortion that Udaltsov's denial has weight. The station's footage and unnamed "witnesses" are said to corroborate the government's charge of "organizing mass disorder." Udaltsov was charged and put under house arrest.

Vladimir Putin in his address to the nation at the end of 2012, spoke angrily against regime change from without, by which he meant by the

United States and its subservient allies. This is how he and the focus-group participants think of America—in the role of puppet-master everywhere in the world. Every incidence of disorder, uprising, and invasion, they see as orchestrated by America in its interests. Putin, in that talk ushering in the year 2013, said that "foreign interference" is absolutely unacceptable. In Bolotnaya, he saw its footprints. The accusations about Udaltsov, Leonid Razvozzhayev, and Konstantin Lebedev—the latter two, associates of Udaltsov—are very serious: plotting with Georgia and being paid by Georgians to overthrow the Russian government. Razvozzhayev fled to Ukraine; he was snatched and jailed, and he later signed a ten-page "confession" accepting guilt for everything he was charged with—about collusion with bankrolling Georgians to foment revolution in Russia. When he was brought back to Russia, he was paraded before the television cameras: his face looked beaten up and his legs did not seem to function normally, as he was dragged along. Razvozzhayev, freed while this case is under investigation, retracted what he said was a coerced confession.

Vladimir Putin sees a whole movement of demonstrations resting on a Georgian plan to destabilize and dismember Russia. That would require money, and the United States had been financing a wide range of democracy assistance projects. Georgia's impetuous move into South Ossetia (which the focus-group participants found, with justification, misreported in the West) added another piece of evidence. Here, in the middle of the "demonstration season's" huge turnouts, already of deep concern to the Kremlin, a new provocation (as it seemed to Putin and other officials) came from the United States. Civil unrest in the streets of Ukraine in 2014 were much more serious and menacing: the Russia-friendly government was overthrown and ties with Europe was the new policy. This, too, was seen by Moscow as a tactic of the United States; aimed at drawing western Ukraine into a new configuration, it could not be merely a paper accession to the organization of the enemy, but also a platform for the placement of missiles targeting Russia. That is how Russia's President saw it; he moved quickly in the early chaos to bring the Crimea back to Russia by annexing it in a lightning strike.

US Embassy Welcome of Anti-Regime Activists

The new and short-term ambassador to Russia, Michael McFaul, took up residence in Moscow on January 10. On January 17, one of the ambassador's first major acts was to invite American-funded activists (many hostile to Vladimir Putin) to the embassy. Among them were Yevgenia Chirikova, the "Save Khimki" leader, funded by the National Endowment for Democracy, and Lilia Shibanova, head of the "Golos" organization for monitoring the integrity of the 2011 parliamentary election, who was funded the same way. Lev Ponomarev, head of the Moscow Helsinki Group (for human rights), who received funding from the National Endowment for Democracy, the Ford Foundation, and George Soros's Open Society foundation, also attended. Boris Nemtsov came, too. Nemtsov, whose name has come up in previous chapters, had been a young wonder when the Soviet Union dissolved. As governor of the major city of Nizhny Novgorod, he was famous for success with attracting direct foreign investment. He was tapped by Boris Yeltsin to be part of his government and then Nemtsov founded a political party and went into the Duma. When the threshold of votes needed to enter the Duma was raised neither his nor any other liberal party was elected. What must have rankled Russian officials was the carnival-like atmosphere outside the Embassy as these excited and thrilled guests entered the grounds. Some bubbled with happiness at official American recognition.

SLANDER CRIMINALIZED AGAIN

In August 2011, just before the demonstrations, defamation was removed from the criminal code and made a civil offense, as it is, for example, in the European Union and the United States, and other countries where freedom of speech is actively protected. Defamation defined as crime chills freedom of speech, especially where the legal environment does not instill an expectation of timely legal redress. After Bolotnaya, in July 2012, defamation was signed back into the Criminal Code as a felony and made punishable by fines up to 5 million rubles (about $153,000 to $170,000) or forced "correctional labor" for up to twelve weeks. Defamation is defined in this Code as "knowing dissemination of false information hurting one's dignity and reputation." The definition is so wide and flexible, that it is practically without boundaries. As a weapon against anti-regime activists, it is open to wide political interpretation—another closing of another door to free speech.[8]

Internet Restrictions

Should the internet be subject to more oversight? It is a constant battle that never lets up in many countries. Russia has had in place a system, SORM and SORM2, requiring internet providers to monitor their own content at their own cost for the internal police (Federalnaya sluzhba bezopasnosti Rossiiskoi Federatsii, FSB).[9] It has not provided what the leadership wants, and, in addition, several Supreme Court decisions have gone against it.[10] One of SORM's biggest problems was that it was implemented regionally and therefore had no assurance of national coverage. The locales differed in their ability to carry out the mission, and surveillance through SORM was spotty at best. The newer system discussed below, Deep Packet Inspection (DPI), is a more powerful and nationally based technology. Post-Bolotnaya, President Putin reasonably argued that no country wants its children to be exposed to pornography targeting and endangering them. Russia, too, would eliminate threats to society's health. On November 1, 2012, the "Single Register" of banned websites went into effect.[11] ROSKOMNADZOR, the agency for supervision of information and technology, communications, and mass media is in charge of the system, but it considers contributions from the Interior Ministry, the Federal Antidrug Agency, and the Federal Service for Consumer Rights and Public Law. It also has the right to change the law. It added a ban on political extremists, another door open to whatever interpretation is politically useful. A Register administered by the Agency for the Supervision of Information Technology compiles court decisions to outlaw sites or pages anywhere in Russia and maintains data submitted by a number of government monitoring agencies, including the internal police. It was begun on a smaller scale to keep track of extremist and terrorist bank accounts, but it is now vastly expanded. It may tell content providers to remove URLs. If no action is taken, host providers must block access to the site within 24 hours. In addition, host providers must constantly check the database of outlawed sites and URLs to see that they are up to date in removing outlawed material. But a far more powerful technology, used commercially in the West for years, has entered the toolbox.

The West has had DPI in place for years, and many very powerful internet companies deny they would ever use it except under court order. The material on the US National Security Agency revealed by the fugitive Edward Snowden tells a story of privacy destruction on an unheard-of scale. Marc Rotenberg, director of the U.S. advocacy organization the Electronic Privacy and Information Center, talked earlier about privacy and DPI in 2009 in his testimony before Congress, stating "advertisers are learning far more about users than the sites that users actually visit or the businesses they actually interact with.... For example, Google recently announced that it would move to 'Interest-based' advertising, which means that the web-based advertising model will be less dependent on the valuable content of web sites and more dependent simply on what Google knows about the users.... But the larger development is the increasing transfer from a customer-business relationship to the user-profile–advertiser model."[12] The sale of personal data to advertising companies is now a more valuable asset than concentrating on product features.

In Russia, the new technology has only recently become available. Though not specifically designated in the new law, the Russian Ministry of Communications has gained approval in the internet industry. "At the end of August, 2012, under the chairmanship of Communications minister Nikolai Nikiforov, a working group was held, drawing representatives of Google, SUP Media (the owner of the Livejournal social network), and of all the other big hitters. They discussed how to ensure that the [filtering] mechanism—they discussed the concrete example of YouTube—can block a specific video without blocking YouTube as a whole. And they reached a conclusion that pleased them all. Ilya

Ponomarev, a member of the State Duma and an ardent supporter of the law, told us. Are we are [sic] talking about DPI technology? 'Yes, precisely.' "[13] They concluded that the new law could be implemented with far more efficiency and coverage nationally, and only with the assistance of DPI nationwide. The technology allows network providers to look into the digital packets "composing a message or transmission over a network." By the end of summer 2012, "all three national mobile operators in Russia already had DPI at their disposal." "IBM's East European Business Development Director Boris Poddubny," was reported as stating that "there may be devices to copy traffic. DPI helps analyze it. And there will be a detailed log: what is downloaded by whom and who looked for what."[14]

Privacy advocates fear that their positions may have been overtaken by increased threats to cyber security. Viruses have become more sophisticated and widespread; data loss has been reported frequently; unknown threats are particularly sensitive for security—not just commercial cyber security but also national security and content manipulation is possible in ways not available before. For these and other reasons, "threat elimination vs. privacy" is becoming more difficult to solve in a world in which crime and terror (including threats of cyber warfare), swarms of severe cyber-attacks, and spreading malware rise to the top of the policy issues in many countries. The notion of privacy as embedded in European Union and American law is a commitment to "net neutrality": that no agency can filter content on the internet. In 2008, the U.S. Federal Communications Commission handed down a ruling against Comcast for "monitoring the content of its customers' internet connections and selectively block[ing] peer-to-peer connections."[15] After Assange and Snowden and revelations about the U.S. National Security Agency's spying at home and abroad, the 2008 ruling seems quaint.

The issues are not straightforward. Privacy activists around the world are concerned about this threat to "net neutrality" and that "general monitoring [is] not acceptable even in preventing crime."[16] It may be, especially with the superior capacity of DPI's follow-on technology, Deep Content Inspection (DCI), to get inside messages to monitor content, that the threats, on the one hand, and the improving capacity of technology, on the other, are overwhelming the principles of privacy, especially in an era of cyber terrorism and globalization of crime on a scale not seen before (and made possible partly by technology). As early as 2008, Virgin Media in the United Kingdom announced it was casting aside net neutrality. The Egyptian government used DPI as early as February 2011. Balancing legal protection of the privacy of individuals and the very large-scale threats on the horizon or already in play is a difficult to impossible task. In 2013, "Dr. Guy Bunker, senior vice president of products at Britain's Clearswift, is concerned that 'governments are at a heightened risk at falling prey to cyber attacks if they do not implement robust security policies and enforce them effectively—and part of a robust policy should be the deep content inspection of communications.' "[17]

What this new, sophisticated filtering and snooping technology will do in Russia is not yet clear and much of it will never be exposed to the public. The situation pits two deeply held and contradictory values against each other in all countries: protection of the country and protection of individual privacy (one could add protection of privacy in terms of proprietary industrial assets). In Russia, protection of privacy has no real standing at all among governmental actors, while foreign private businesses may have different codes.

Maria Zhunich, Director of Google in Russia, is an impressive professional—thoroughly knowledgeable and both graceful and tough.[18] Her job involves shuttling among Ministries and the president's and prime minister's administrations, with a message that technology itself is neutral and serves only to benefit all who use it, including the government. The government would profit from technology; for example, the internet can help policy makers to project their views online. Google Russia tries, she says, to work with policy makers while the discussion is still fluid, so that the outcome is beneficial to all. She also finds that working with the government enables Google to avoid "being misinterpreted by the government." She acknowledges that "sometimes local governments think it [Google] threatens stability and balance." She assures them that the internet is neutral and can be of use to them. Conditions are different now. Since the demonstrations began, she believes the Russian Federal Government perceives the internet as a threat to stability. She insists the internet is not subversive, as many perceive, but rather, provides "tools to promote public government and culture."

The protest movement has contributed to changes toward the internet on the part of the government. Zhunich says: "They have started to take it more seriously. It may result in harsher regulations. There is a law on extremism. It tends to be used by the authorities to remove content." As Zhunich sees it, the pressure on Google Russia is rising rapidly. Gazeta.ru reported that Google said it will cooperate with the FSB "and other judicial organs only within the framework of strict judicial procedures."[19] But judicial procedures are themselves uncertain. Sometimes, the orders for removal are obvious: Facebook took down a page around the world called "Club Suicide." Russia's communications agency for monitoring websites threatened to block Facebook for a page on suicide, and when Facebook complied the threat was withdrawn, avoiding a total ban in Russia. The promotion of suicide is one of the prohibited topics. Twitter has been working with authorities inside Russia to remove tweets that look to be about drug deals and some others thought to be "promoting suicidal thoughts."[20] YouTube faced a more difficult decision with regard to a video showing children applying Halloween makeup; Russian officials saw children painting a cut on a face as an instance of bodily harm. The Halloween video was temporarily blocked.[21] This was the event that sparked the agreement later—and described above—in which commercial entities advocate DPI nationwide. Companies differ: Google issued a statement that its policies are in compliance with Russian law, while its servers (importantly) remain outside the country. Yandex, the Russian search engine, gave up the identities of people who had made donations to Aleksei Navalny.

The Mountain of Revelations and Privacy's Precarious (and Limited) Life

What Edward Snowden revealed dwarfs privacy arguments. Microsoft was revealed to have made mail on its heavily used Outlook and Hotmail accessible to the government. According to the documents,

Microsoft also gave the FBI access to a cloud storage service with millions of users. Skype, owned by Microsoft, "worked with the government to collect both video and audio conversations," and, further, that information the NSA collected was shared with both the FBI and the CIA. Beyond these mail functions, the government had the cooperation of Facebook and other companies under the Prism surveillance program. The Foreign Intelligence Surveillance Court, which secretly rules on the government's data requests, was discovered to be rather casually run, with sometimes a single "judge" available to make decisions. Snowden leaked a Foreign Intelligence Surveillance Act (FISA), court order "telling Verizon to turn over calling data from all of its customers."[22] Two small e-mail services rebelled: Lavabit, based in Texas, and Silent Circle, a rapidly growing start-up based in Maryland, closed their email services and destroyed their servers rather than comply with secret government surveillance orders.[23] Some of the dubious behavior of very large, very rich companies brings them monetary rewards. NSA has "compensated" email providers for the costs incurred in responding to FISA. The NSA "apparently compensated e-mail service providers 'millions of dollars' for costs incurred in the fallout from an October 2011 court ruling that an unrelated aspect of the agency's surveillance operations violated the Constitution," according to a document leaked by Snowden. Prism, the operation which the NSA uses to "collect messages from e-mail providers like Google, required annual certificates and an 'upstream' collection from networks operated by companies like Verizon."[24] The Prism material Snowden released noted that Google rejected reports that "it knowingly participates in Prism...." The [Manchester] Guardian [to whom Snowden supplied a great deal of material] revealed that the NSA gained "direct access to the servers of companies like Google." Google called the material inaccurate, but "declined to answer questions about the fall 2011 episode [see above]."[25] The blockbuster information came in September 2013: The NSA is able to penetrate supercomputers and pass through encryption, and, further, that the NSA has been vacuuming up surveillance information on many countries in the world, listening in on what presidents and prime ministers say wherever they say it. At the meeting of twenty international powers in St. Petersburg in September 2013, a contradictory and embarrassing picture emerged of President Obama's failed attempt to discount eavesdropping on a visibly angry Dilma Rousseff, president of Brazil, and persuade her to join an anti-Assad coalition for military action.[26] Watching President Obama attempt to catch up with and earnestly deal with this doubly difficult task revealed the turnabout in power positions. President Obama did implore, but Brazil went the other way.

We know how important America is for Russian policy makers and for the focus-group participants. What America does resonates there as perhaps nowhere else. When momentous and unrelenting news of the United States trampling on devotion to privacy happens, it is a leading story in the papers and the television news in Russia. When President Putin introduced registration of NGOs as foreign agents because they receive funding from abroad, he cited, among others, American law. He did the same thing when he signed a law outlawing sexually explicit programs on television. That law actually went much further than in the United States, by including wording on curbing "political extremism." The Russian law was written so broadly that it is difficult to interpret what is an infraction, and therefore, the definition becomes a political one. What we should bear in mind is that in this duality of attitude toward the United States, a rationale is often derived from U.S. laws and agencies. Angry at Russia's granting asylum to an American considered dangerous and wanted by American courts and also at Russia's refusal to punish Syria, its ally, President Obama cancelled the summit at short notice. The "table was laid"; the guest declined, and that guest was the most important Russia could host. Not long before this, as we have seen earlier, President Obama made a public statement that Russia was no longer important and should be downgraded while America pivots to the East. Diplomacy generally shuns such public statements, as they reduce room for manoeuver. America's President had received undiplomatic advice, and now unexpectedly, areas of utility have resurfaced.

Yet, in spite of these scenarios of internet snooping, in Russia, access to the internet is far from controlled and what is communicated among most Russians has not been cut down. Most of the participants knew that their identities are probably known, but their behavior is unaffected.

When I first talked to Yury Saprykin, he said, "There is no privacy." He harps on transparency: it is important for accountability of institutions, but it is also a recognition of a fact of life. Russia's belated recognition (by signing the international agreement long after others had done so) that copyright law[27] should actively be protected is still another way the internet can become a likely target for governmental intrusion. There is a new interest in punishing copyright infringement, but it has turned out to be a useful new weapon against freedom of the press, when applied selectively and without determined legal guidance.

Nongovernmental Organizations in Russia

Putin, bent on halting what he saw as American subversion of Russia, signed into law in August 2012, a document stating that nonprofit organizations receiving any funding from foreign sources must register as "Foreign Agents." He said this requirement is unremarkable and is the practice in the West. All nongovernmental organizations, even the ones devoted to health care, were ordered to cease their activity if they were funded by the United States. Some NGOs folded and some hung on for a while. Some American funders moved to Lithuania. As a first step, in the first month of the decree, offices of some 2,000 organizations were searched.[28]

In 2013, the Ministry of Justice clarified the Byzantine procedure for defending foreign funding and nonprofit public advocacy. "Organizations from abroad and engaging in political activity, but not deeming themselves 'agents' will [be able]...to defend themselves in court or alter their activity. Nonprofits can also register as 'foreign agents' voluntarily." Note that the sweep of the law is tightened to "political activity." Immediately after clarification by the Ministry, more than 500 anonymous calls were received to denounce the Levada Center, a well-known survey organization. In the spring of 2013, the Levada Center was told it must register.

Golos, the voting observation NGO, was also the object of complaint. The Ministry disregarded all the calls, observing that they could have been politically motivated.[29] Nonetheless, in April 2013, the Ministry of Justice opened a legal case against Golos and its director, Shibanova.

The United States has its law dealing with individuals and groups financed by foreigners; it is cumbersome, but certainly detailed. The Foreign Agents Registration Act (FARA), which became law in 1938, was passed to deal with the threat of agents spying for Germany in the United States. It was amended in 1966 to focus on lobbyists attempting to affect the operation of the government. Lobbies have since come directly under the Department of Justice. The Act requires every agent of a foreign principal, not otherwise exempted, to register with the Department of Justice, to outline the income from and expenditures on behalf of a foreign "principal." These forms are public records. There are exemptions for diplomats and officials of foreign governments, and for those whose activities are purely commercial or "solely for religious, scholastic, academic, scientific, or fine arts nature." Certain cases of soliciting funds for medical aid or food and clothing are also exempted. Activities and groups with a political purpose are never exempted and in the other categories listed above, the words "certain" and "solely" could provide flexibility.[30] In 2010, when a group of ten Russian "sleeper" spies were apprehended in the United States, the charge was not espionage, but rather, failing to register as foreign agents.

THE MAGNITSKY LAW AND DENIAL OF ENTRY TO UNITED STATES OF HUMAN RIGHTS VIOLATORS

In late 2012, the United States passed the "Magnitsky" law, barring from entry to the United States, Russians who were involved in the abuse of the human rights of Sergei Magnitsky, an auditor at a Moscow law firm and whistle-blower who uncovered massive fraud in collaboration between the police and tax officials. Magnitsky was given inadequate health care and his frequent calls for a doctor were ignored. He died, according to officials, of acute heart failure and toxic shock caused by pancreatitis. Russian officials carried out their own investigation; the head of the Russian federal prison administration was fired, and doctors lightly charged, if at all. Just after this law had been passed, I spoke with Mikhail Fedotov, head of the Presidential Council on Human Rights. Fedotov is a lifelong fighter for human rights—a lawyer who has succeeded in pushing through a number of improvements and who will never give up fighting for his cause. While others may be more dramatic and totalistic, Fedotov works steadily and very often successfully to push ahead the cause of human rights. His successes are not the kind that garners screaming headlines. They are not revolutionary. It is fantasy to think such changes can happen. Instead, Fedotov harbors no illusions and works away at incremental improvement. His honesty and fairness are beyond reproach; he has that rare unsung commitment totally oblivious to external recognition and honors—both of which he deserves. I asked Fedotov about what he thought of the Magnitsky law. His answer should give us pause. He said, "Why not?" Taking the lead in punishing human rights violators would be a good thing. But the law should be directed against all human rights violators, not just Russians. That would be a big step forward.

PROHIBITION OF AMERICAN ADOPTION OF RUSSIAN CHILDREN

Russia swiftly retaliated for the Magnitsky Act with a law prohibiting Americans from adopting Russian orphans. The law does not apply to other countries, but gay couples may not adopt Russian children, anywhere. In a press conference on the matter, Putin recounted the horror stories about mistreatment of some Russian children in the United States and, no less unforgivable, the light punishment or acquittal of the parents.

THE POST-BOLOTNAYA REALITY: RUSSIA BECOMING AN AFTERTHOUGHT FOR AMERICA

The legislation I have summarized above, are laws, hastily drawn up, and immediately moving into force, although it remains to be seen how they can all be implemented. Between Russia and the United States, it has not been all downhill. There were pragmatic gestures of no small importance: conclusion of an arms reduction treaty is one, and much more important for Vladimir Putin is the Americans' decision to cancel part of a Europe-based missile defense program, a missile shield that the Obama administration shifted instead to Alaska and the Western American coast. Repositioning the program made clear its purpose: defense against North Korea. Freed from what Putin considered the anti-Russian object of the missile shield, Russian–American arms talks resumed; Russia's deputy Foreign Minister spoke of new intensity and opportunities in controlling arms.[31] Russia, even before this shift, granted a temporary depot (but not a base, Putin kept insisting; he wants no confusion on this score) in Russia to help America conclude the war in Afghanistan. Russia sent blankets and other aid to America for the victims of Hurricane Sandy. Many Russians study in the United States, most often at the graduate and professional level. Russia is in the World Trade Organization, finally.

When the Boston Marathon bomb exploded, Russia provided robust information about the area, behavior, and conduct of the alleged bombers, originally from the Caucasus. Only a short time later, an officer of the U.S. Embassy in Moscow was apprehended by Moscow police for what appeared to be attempts to recruit Russian spies. Everything about the supposed spy-master was amateurish and incompetent. It prompted the Russian spokesperson to say that this act of enmity was how America repaid their help with the Boston tragedy.

BEFORE THE BOLOTNAYA AFFAIR: CONCESSIONS TO PEACEFUL DEMONSTRATORS

Political Party Formation Rules

When stunning numbers of ordinary Muscovites came to demonstrate peacefully in the first Bolotnaya Square and Sakharov Prospect gatherings, it appeared that the Russian leadership was willing to grant something in return. Two concessions were made. One eased the way political parties could be formed. In chapter 2 Boris says that there are political parties in Russia: "But they were all the same party; there is no one to vote for. They all come from the same source." Future leaders expect little from parliament; many will not vote. The changes made to the party system after the first two demonstrations revert to what was used from 1993 to 2003. It lowers the threshold for percentage of votes needed to get into the Duma. Originally, right after independence, it had been set at 5%. Putin raised it to a crushing 7%, and only four parties were able to reach it. It has now reverted back to 5%. Additionally, to stop fraud, video cameras will be installed by the government in all polling places.

Another barrier to forming a party came down: until 2012, a party could be registered only after gathering 45,000 "valid" signatures. The new law that came into force in April 2013 reduces the requirement for registering a party to only 500 people. Under Yeltsin, half the 450 candidates for the legislature came from lists of political parties, and in those districts voters selected their party of choice. There are different rules for the other half of the candidates, who are elected as individuals. In Yeltsin's time, the single-member districts had an extremely important impact: people who spoke their mind publicly, who had interesting ideas, who had become distinguished in learning or in bravery, people who avidly read newspapers, people with original and interesting ideas, who were on television talk shows, and individual activists of all kinds could run in a district and be voted into parliament. There was a bright pool of heroes, who combatted Soviet repression; they faced down tanks. Television anchors were brave and attractive figures. These young and idealistic new people replaced the dull, dull, dull litany of dusty predecessors. These were the people who provided the most liberal and democratic views when the Duma met.

Will there be time and institutions for the same thing to happen again, under the Putin law? When Aleksei Navalny ran for mayor of Moscow, he was given no exposure on the state-controlled mass media. In spite of an official policy that tried to make him invisible, the opposite happened: he became—without any doubt whatever—the face and voice of the opposition. This electoral contest had far-reaching effects on how the opposition (or multiple oppositions) adapted their strategy to a new reality. We shall return to that contest for Moscow later because its impact spread out rapidly. Navalny's legal troubles constrain his political hopes, even if he did not have to contend with United Russia, the pro-government party, that has ruled many of the Russian regions and small cities for a long time—usually without opposition and often with the close friendship of local industry. But it has grown fat and lazy, scooping up votes for Moscow. Even though it continues to win, its margin of success is declining. If vigorous opponents were to confront it (and not split the vote of their collective followers), United Russia's fortunes would not be so easy to predict. Vladimir Putin, disillusioned with the future of United Russia, inaugurated something new in 2013: the Popular Front. Not exactly a political party, it, with Putin at its apex, would stand above parties and give meaning to the national idea. Obviously, it is not at all clear how these changes will be sorted out and if there will be changes at all. Declarations and ceremonies do not a competitive party make. The focus-group participants say they avoid any site or information involving United Russia—a flaming target of their loathing. Political analyst Grigory Golosov analyzed the fortunes of United Russia after its showing in the 2013 election for governors in the Russian Federation. On the face of it, United Russia appeared to do very well except in Moscow. "[Compared to Navalny,] Sobyanin's [campaign for mayor of Moscow] was as listless and devoid of content as the campaigns of official candidates and governors usually are in today's Russia."[32]

The Disappearing Concession: Direct Election of Governors

The other concession after the first peaceful demonstrations was to return to the public the election of the governors of the regions of Russia—now, with the accession of the Crimea and Sevastopol, their number is eighty-four. Under Boris Yeltsin, governors were popularly elected. That was scrapped for a system of appointment by Vladimir Putin.

The more Vladimir Putin thought about the Chechens and Dagestani putting in their own governors, the more worried he became. He termed the Caucasus an area of instability. Giving them the right to accrue more power could backfire.[33] This concession to the democratic demonstration had lasted a few months; the process of selection was referred back to the Kremlin. A region would receive from the president the names of three candidates and the regional legislature would elect one of them as governor.

WHAT'S NEXT?

Is it time to ask the tens of thousands who held the first large and peaceful demonstrations about concessions? What concessions? The idea of putting pressure on the Kremlin to exact concessions is illusory, a misreading of the real political situation in Russia. Yet that is exactly what many of the planners of the post-Bolotnaya opposition believe their actions will effect. The opposition succeeded in putting on a demonstration on the anniversary of Bolotnaya 2. This time, the security administration of the Moscow Mayor's office prohibited a march or procession to Bolotnaya Square, but it did permit the gathering and speeches. This time, Moscow's government allowed far more space and many more opportunities for getting to Bolotnaya island and, once there, from being jammed into an impossibly small space. The numbers were smaller, estimated anywhere from 20,000 to 30,000. Before the activities began, a two-ton metal piece of scaffolding crushed a worker, killing him instantly. The steel scaffolding was supposed to be the structure supporting a large screen and sound system, and when the demonstration took place, it was virtually impossible for most to hear or see. The organizers' intention was to honor and call attention to political prisoners in Russia. The arrests and terms mounted as security forces closed in on participants and leaders of Bolotnaya 2. Some organizers intended to "make" Putin notice. I think Nikolai Svanidze, a media political commentator, was right when he said that to make any impression on the rulers would take "hundreds of thousands."[34] The thickly toxic and restrictive air of Putin's Moscow was going to make any public act of the opposition very difficult indeed.

PART II

AFTER THE BOLOTNAYA AFFAIR: DEVELOPING A NEW FORM OF DEMOCRATIC CONNECTIONS

AN ONLINE COUNTER-ELECTION

After Bolotnaya 2, the big questions to be answered were just how far, given the watchful and repressive government, on the one side, and the fractious, politically diverse activists, on the other, could demonstrating go? And what role could these mass gatherings have? Would new demonstrations include the regions, left out last time in the Moscow tusovka? What, if anything, would replace demonstrations? The focus-group participants are among the very wary, who calculate personal harm and brakes on their careers, while obsessed with their absent right to govern themselves. The Khimki protests took place while they were preparing to be leaders and yet, no one talked about doing anything. Some spoke in analytic terms about costs and benefits, but only Olga understood from Yevgenia Chirikova's blog what was involved. Olga did not express interest in or intention to join, but she expressed real compassion and respect for the leader of "Save Khimki."

Initiating Digital Democracy

After Bolotnaya 2, Yury Saprykin and other internet organizers of the big Moscow demonstrations agreed to try something entirely new in frozen, politically inhospitable Russia. True, the democratic alternative he had in mind demanded more strategic thinking, more innovative use of the internet, and a vision of what could be done in a continuing project to coach habits of democracy. The Organizing Committee (orgkom) had guided the Sakharov Prospect demonstration, together with internet voters. Those principles would now be put to a much greater and more technologically difficult task: an open, transparent, democratic election held online. Who would qualify as a voter and how would voting fraud be excluded? Could they counter attempts by the authorities to hack, deny service (distributed denial of service, or DDoD), and put up fake messages? And, most important, election to what?

The election was to be for a Coordinating Council (KS) of forty-five representatives. The KS would not rule, issue orders, or present itself as the top of a hierarchy. Avoidance of top-down power was deliberate. Voters would vote for the candidate who best represented their interests; affinity groups in many different fields would be formed. In Moscow, working groups would forward ideas for projects to the full committee. The KS itself had no platform and no strategies: evaluating priorities was to be arrived at democratically.

Leonid Volkov, internet wizard and young software entrepreneur, chaired the KS's first election committee through several stages of voting, quickly recovering from expected cyber-attacks on the site. Thirty were to be elected from a General List and five each from three ideological "blocks"—"leftists," "liberals," and "nationalists." For its designer, Yury Saprykin, it was necessary to retain that "fragile" consensus the demonstrations exhibited. Saprykin conceived of a Coordinating Council voted in not because they were in the competition under the flag of a party. Beginning with party beliefs automatically fashioned a script of divisiveness. Here would be an election that would begin not with parties, but with individuals and their overarching interests, and, if it worked, the meetings, similarly, would address issues not through party blinders, but by discussion of common concerns.

Some 82,108 Russians voted, not only from Moscow, but from distant regions, too. The committee "verified" voters' identity either by asking them to transfer the equivalent of fifty cents from their bank accounts or by sending pictures of themselves holding their passports on or offline. For three months internet-savvy activists and experts worked on how to do it, always rebounding when the police raided an office in one city, overloaded through DDoD on another site, or hacked in to undermine the last stage of the elections. They had not been particularly worried that their system would be destroyed; they had been blocked ten times and each time, their technology expert had been able to restore the site. This has possibly become easier with the cloud and more ways to avoid dangers. *Rain* streamed live all three weeks of the debates and the concluding discussion.

The voting process was complicated. In the first step, 210 candidates ran for the KS; each had to present his or her biography, contact data and social media profiles, and speeches and articles. At this first of three stages, the written contributions were anonymous; proposals and principles could not be judged by name or party. Winners went on to the second round and then the third. These rounds featured a series of debates, with randomly chosen candidates. They were shown on

Rain daily, from midnight to two o'clock in the morning, and a taped version was shown the next day. Voting occurred after each round and narrowed the group of candidates. And then, as the last step—a little later than intended because of an internet attack—the Council came into being. Its first meeting was held in the *Rain* studio. This was a remarkable event, not only for the ambit of the issues they tackled, and the very different views participating, but most of all for the openness of that first meeting of the KS.

KS members were mainly seasoned activists; "compromise" had not really been in their vocabulary. The first meeting of the KS would be crucial. It was aired in its entirety online. This was a meeting to determine priorities—what should they do? Moderator Yury Saprykin was facing an articulate group of activists ranging from Stalinists to neo-Nazis. Between the Far Left and Far Right were liberals, constituting an overwhelming proportion of the group. Several candidates who had been elected were in prison from Bolotnaya 2. Two of them sent representatives.

THE COORDINATING COUNCIL BEGINS: CAN UNITY BE FORGED FROM SUCH DIFFERENCES?

The purpose of this critical first meeting on October 23, 2012, was to draw up an agenda. Yury Saprykin, who ran it, said that the organization was not a protest movement. How could it achieve legitimacy? How could they move ahead without fighting among themselves? He stood at the head of the room, microphone in hand. In a closely packed semi-circle sat the newly elected members.

Although there were large numbers of voters from outside Moscow, only two winners came from the regions. Voting in the regions was complicated, precisely because few had ever heard of many of the candidates and preferred to vote for the more famous ones (a symptom of the continued problem of the hyper-central role Moscow plays), so Muscovites kept winning. The next step after the election was to set priorities for the movement. First priority needed to be to do something for their fellow members who were behind bars because of Bolotnaya.

They all said that the first point on the agenda should be picketing for release of "political prisoners." The group agreed to raise money for the families of prisoners and to hire respected lawyers. They then moved on to suggest the second priority: Why should there be demonstrations? What did they accomplish, and what happened?

Some argued that demonstrations are effective only if frequent. "People should go to a meeting as if they were going to work." They should exhibit steadfastness. Liberal Ilya Yashin said the main thing was to find "what unites us"—that they should represent those who voted for them. When Aleksei Navalny spoke about demonstrations, he said, "What the Kremlin fears most is 'physical people in the street.'" If there were to be demonstrations, he continued, they needed to be planned earlier and done better, and they needed to emphasize the principle of instilling fear. "We need hundreds of thousands on the street." Ksenia Sobchak agreed, but rightly said, that to be effective, each demonstration must be planned and executed when ready. Otherwise they would be straggly collections of the weak.

The third agenda item on the priority list was, in my view, by far the most important and central to the democracy they wish to build, even if the contours of that form of government are unclear and untested in Russia: the simple but fraught question of "How can we get along?" Nikolai Bondarik, head of a small, Far Right nationalist party based in St. Petersburg, spoke up more than once out of concern that the extremist right wing was in the minority. He and the other extremist wings needed protection from the "liberals," so that the "massiveness" of the liberals would not "crush" them. Bondarik went on: "We have to have a system that unites us; we can't prohibit people from participating in the Russian March." In Moscow, liberals may have a massive presence, he said, but outside the city, in the regions, most people lean toward the right wing, and they should be heard. Liberal Ilya Yashin insisted that if they focused on union and found success, the space of agreement would be enlarged. Finally, the right-wing leader, Konstantin Krylov, said what is absolutely vital: that they must prevent divisive argument and concentrate on trust. "We need to trust each other," he said. "We have to make a greater effort to believe each other." Coming from the head of DPNI, it sounded a bit surreal, even if sensible. As chapter 2 showed so vividly, the upcoming leaders in Russia hesitate to bestow trust, because they focus more on the harm trust can generate than on the benefits it confers. These focus-group participants are much more aware of why they should not trust, both on the personal and the broader internet scale. They foresee the harm that trusting can bring and would rather forgo benefits of trust than extend an opening for injury. It is a frame of mind that does not support a move into the unknown: trusting political opposites for the sake of the whole.

The last question Yury Saprykin threw out for discussion was where would Russia be in two years? Vladimir Tor, who has been a vivid figure on the Far Right, said something of great importance. He said one never knows when regimes change. They had to create institutions for new possibilities. Voting is important because it helps to create other new institutions.

To have this meeting at all, to bring together such a crowded political spectrum of Russia is itself an unheard-of achievement. To arrive at an agenda by consensus is even more impressive and surprising. Tor's point about being ready for an election is absolutely essential, and this part of the democracy project has the greatest importance for the country as a whole.

THE KS GETS TO WORK

Many on the Coordinating Council wanted to continue demonstrating in what they thought was a show of people's power. But numbers matter. If demonstrations become thinner and thinner, they fade from the view of the Kremlin. Sergei Udaltsov, on the extreme Left, said continuous demonstrations would "force" the Kremlin to hold talks. Saprykin said that there is no way to start a discussion, except when there are huge numbers, hundreds of thousands in the street. Power reacts only to the numbers, and the numbers are down. Saprykin is building something else: a new way to enter politics. He says that "in 2–3 years, the legislature will be returned to the people."

Perhaps local elections, if they are fair, might be a start in that internet/institution-building strategy, but it is a short timeframe to build up a whole new set of opposition components across the country. In other words, institution-building takes a long time, while activists and their allies want to see change now. How much slack will the KS get? How much time, before the participants and the observers give out grades of passing or failing?

Where Are the Regions?

The organizers received a large number of votes from the regions, but only two candidates from the regions won a place on the KS. Yury Saprykin said that they wanted more from the regions, but the votes from there and everywhere else went to famous people, people they had heard of or seen on television or the internet. I made the point that the trip to the people to help in the flood had the opposite effect. Can anything be done to get outside Moscow and bring in a wider swath of the Russian public? Saprykin said, "We can't do anything with the regions. They have to do it themselves. We can only wait until the first appearance of self-organization in a place and immediately help. Local trade unions and economic organizations have to do it themselves, but the KS can provide organizational and logistical help." He gave the example of a woman in the city of Ivanovo who had gone three years without heat. She went to an unsanctioned demonstration. As a participant in a demonstration held without official permission, she received a "huge fine." Saprykin said the KS would be sending in lawyers and providing subsidies for legal help and the woman's well-being. Saprykin has been at pains to declare that there is no chasm between what he calls the "creative intelligentsia" in Moscow and ordinary people in regional cities and towns. He argues that the Putin administration has stoked the flames of class difference and enmity.

There is not a fundamental difference that would preclude cooperation with anything the KS does in Moscow. He went on to say that they are all living in a constricting human environment and their values are the same and basic. Such engineered enmity is not real and can be dispersed with personal interactions.

Perhaps. But that chasm is there now. It has to do with the standard of life they see on television but cannot have themselves and the over-centralization of Russia in Moscow, which is not traditionally a good neighbor. The smaller places know they have been relegated to a lower level of attention, income, medical and housing assistance, and jobs.

Maxim Trudolubov, the well-known journalist in Moscow, believes that there are such fundamental differences between Moscow and the regions that there is little hope for accord. He called Moscow "almost a developed country within a country." Populations of smaller cities and towns are dependent on the state. New Moscow entrepreneurs are socially and economically independent from the state. "The farther from Moscow, the fewer can dream of independence." Moscow writers, for example, can write in a really free book market. New names can become known in the independent market. Outside it's different. "They depend on the state budget in all kinds of ways and industry depends on the state budget." There are what Maxim calls islands where a governor can be removed. He believes that now Russians, if they had a choice, would vote not just to reject a politician. Maxim Trudolyubov's point is that now, after the creation of the KS, political choices and candidates who came out of that movement would genuinely work on behalf of their constituents. A different kind of candidate could emerge—one who serves the voters and the agenda of broadening democracy. If so, then the narrow choice voters now have: vote against a candidate or don't vote could be replaced by a real election in which people might be able to vote for a candidate. In other words, they, voters, are political and they are more astute than given credit for. As with the future leaders in the focus groups, were this to come about, then there could be real civic activity at the polls, with the internet evening out the chances of a candidate successfully breaking through the television firewall of state-sponsored candidates.

The KS and the Backlash

"Coordinating Committee! Where are your results?" Criticisms like these began when the first big demonstrations were barely a year past and when KS was only months old. All new, altruistic groups face the same dilemma: First, there is great enthusiasm and public support. They recruit more members, raise money, and plan. Within a year come the complaints: Where are your results?

The KS was formed in October 2012, after 82,108 people had voted. On January 6, 2013, Ellen Barry wrote in *The New York Times* an article about Moscow, headlined "In Russia, a Trendy Activism against Putin Loses Its Moment." There is no more "fizz" she said. On the first anniversary of the big, peaceful demonstrations in Moscow, the questioning began: Is this phenomenon a spent force? The organization has been organizing, strategizing, raising funding, and persuading experts and political and cultural figures to smooth the way and also ennoble the effort. The organization is thus constrained to do something to show that the many inputs are producing something tangible and visible.

The fifth meeting of the KS occurred on February 16, 2013. Boris Nemtsov chaired the meeting; Aleksei Navalny, who had been loyal and helpful throughout, was again dedicated and useful; former world chess champion Gary Kasparov spoke at length and emotionally about publicizing the names of the individuals responsible for the death of the lawyer Magnitsky. Another member of the KS described ideas he had not yet put in a proposal: boycotting the Olympics, the draft and other state institutions, like the State Bank or Rosneft (Russian oil).

It surfaced again in the meeting: that suicidal inability to work together for the same cause. Boris Nemtsov, the chair for this KS meeting, said that he, Vladimir Kara-Murza (a respected longtime liberal political commentator) and a few others, would split off from an action the KS proposed in order to be observers at another event. Although Nemtsov insisted that this small group would go together by themselves, it looked to the KS that Nemtsov had created an internal faction. Gary Kasparov shook his head gravely and said it was absolutely not "korrektno" (proper). Ksenia Sobchak said "to tell you the truth…we'd better do something worthwhile than form groups or factions…I mean what's the point?" Another member of the KS called it a "manifestation of personal egos."[35] Nemtsov explained that no, it was just that they were a bunch of friends who agree on everything and he was not backing down, though he said casually, "It's nothing." Typically, in other organizations like this one, the tension between the pressure to produce results and the difficulty of letting organisms grow leads to differences that can gel into factions. Or the slow progress of institution-building can be overtaken by events, as would happen in this case.

COMPLAINTS ABOUT RESULTS

Nothing is off-base in the above complaints. They are all reasonable. Yes, in the KS there are differences on strategy that are particularly hard to iron out because each person is an experienced and well-known activist. There is no reason for deference.

Those strains—call them the "demonstration wing"—are present in the KS. They raise, however, the truth of the fact that numbers in marches are declining, while danger and punishment are escalating because of the new laws. It was agreed to demonstrate on the anniversary of Bolotnaya 2. They received permission to demonstrate in the same place, and this time, the Mayor's office said that there would be more access, but the numbers allowed would be smaller than the previous year. About 20,000 to 25,000 showed up (police put it at 7,000). The Mayor's office did prohibit a march or procession to Bolotnaya.

WHY CAN'T WE ACT TOGETHER?

In my view, this election for the KS, its agenda, its regular meetings, its voting on what should be done, and ability to get losers supporting majority positions as long as minority rights are observed, could be the very fragile initiation of institution-building for democratic government. Institutions are vital to the ability to compete in elections at all levels—a splintered opposition is easily defeated. Local elections for a large number of offices are in play almost all the time; they are ripe targets. Realists know a hostile carapace of power surrounds contenders. Everything that is done is, according to Saprykin, "networked, transparent, and technological." The agenda takes time and outcomes may not appear especially spectacular to the outsider. The real adversary is impatience, lack of discipline, and the fatalistic defeatism the past exerts on the present. The odds are not good. But the odds of mass demonstrations and internet voting were once nil.

The schism can come from anywhere. On May 5, 2013, just a day before the planned Bolotnaya 3 meeting, a group of KS members held their own demonstration, in competition, as it were, with the one the KS had voted on. The Scientific Council, a subgroup of a few dozen failed candidates, insisted that the Bolotnaya meeting be held on May 5, Easter Sunday, the most important holiday in Russian Orthodoxy. The KS discussed the May 5 and 6 options and decided that even though the 5th was not a working day (an advantage), Easter was exactly the wrong time—and, besides, the demonstration would be held in the evening after work. They voted down the 5th and decided on the 6th. Instead of accepting defeat, Mikhail Anshakov, leader of the other body, applied for a permit for the 5th. He held the demonstration, and about 500 protestors showed up. And here is still another problem builders of new systems have to face: the willingness of the losers to accept the decision of the winners. Anshakov wrote a long and bitter blog for *Ekho Moskvy* in which he railed against the "elite club" KS and their dictatorial ways. It was a diatribe intended to break down the KS. He wrote invidiously about individuals in the KS and mixed his acrimony with an overall judgment that the KS did nothing and was self-aggrandizing; and undemocratic. His long blog was called (in English) "Goodbye, KS."[36]

Saprykin described a real scene in which he and Sergei Mitrokhin, deputy chairman of the liberal Yabloko Party, were standing in front of the Duma. Saprykin was picketing to protest a law that was to be passed that day. Nearby, Mitrokhin was picketing the ruling about foreign agents. Saprykin said, "I was saddened that we lacked even minimal coordination."

The KS did not seek to be a political party built on choices, differences, and loyalties. It was not invented as a political organization or a party and should not grow into one, says Saprykin. The point is to overcome differences, to learn to cooperate. To agree on a point may take a long time and much talk, "but that is perfectly satisfactory, because this first step was realized. I think it was absolutely appropriate."[37]

The River of Opposition Takes a Sharp Turn: Aleksei Navalny and the Campaign for Mayor of Moscow

Yury Saprykin's hope for the KS was that it could develop and become a "proto-parliament."[38] What an achievement that would be! And how difficult: a respected political body in which leaders of political parties advance their own ideologies, while at the same time tamp them down in order to work together without the aggressive intrusion of ideological passions. This body, as well as the earlier mass demonstrations, are associated in the popular mind and the press with Aleksei Navalny. He was a central and very public figure, but he was by no means the only creator. Yury Saprykin, who has no particular attraction to public recognition, was central to the "voting" concept of the Sakharov Boulevard demonstration and its continuation as the KS elected by citizen-voters. Even after a year, the pieces of the KS had not really coalesced, and we have seen cracks in the hoped-for unity. As unity was becoming more elusive, a moment of critical significance was coming up fast: in October 2013, the mandate of the first KS was to run out and a new election was coming up. It was at this point that the powerful tsunami of Aleksei Navalny's run for mayor took place. At what was the last meeting of the KS, there were too few in attendance to form a quorum. The KS had successfully led the way to continuing the mobilization democratically after the mass demonstrations. If we call Navalny's run for mayor the second stage of mobilization, it is clear he accomplished something unexpected and remarkable: he received 27%

of the vote. The KS had brought in over roughly 80,000 votes; Navalny had attracted about 600,000. Lesser candidates had negligible numbers. He did not win, by a longshot, but registered a remarkable showing under circumstances of rank discrimination.

Navalny and his excellent campaign team were led by Leonid Volkov, so important to the birth of the KS. Now the most talented and thoughtful liberal members of the KS resigned to work with Navalny, who, himself, left to try to continue his political future. This part was not clear: he had been convicted and sentenced for an alleged crime in Rostov. The penalty had been suspended, but not the verdict. He was still a convicted felon, a category that imposed limits on running for political office. What was foggy was whether that restriction applied to the whole period of the conviction or to his whole life. Or to something much shorter? If that wasn't clear, what was clear is that his suspended sentence was also a kind of probation, and he had to be careful about free-wheeling aggression in protests. To add to the confusion, charges of embezzlement from long ago were being brought forward slowly, against Navalny and his brother. Navalny and his talented team wanted to build a party, called "Popular Alliance" (it could also be translated as People's Alliance). And there were local offices to contest: elections to the Moscow City Council were in the offing. In Yury Saprykin's words, Navalny "created the effective and successful campaign—reaching the people who didn't know about him, and spreading his influence far beyond the circle of his internet supporters—without any TV coverage, confronting the constant stream of bad PR…from the state media. He's got the biggest percentage of votes than any opposition politician on any elections in years. He left far behind all the 'system opposition' parties. And, of course now he became the most influential and popular opposition leader."[39]

The Coordinating Council aimed high and hoped to instill the habits of compromise, cooperation, and mutual understanding, for without a deliberative body of this sort, democracy cannot function. After the mass demonstration on Sakharov Prospect these goals looked possible with the help of the internet and the participation of elected representatives. But compromise was foreign, even if, ultimately, their aims coincided. They were, after all, the combined opposition. Even if factions and arguments were many at the end, the KS had built the bridge from demonstration—usually an evanescent impulse—to real political deliberation, fairness, and the inclusion of some 80,000 people in civic action. If even some of those achievements remain in attenuated form, it was a herculean civic effort.

Creation of a proto-parliament and a de-ideologized discussion of the most serious issues of the future, were Saprykin's most optimistic plan. If it could be realized, then at the local and then, perhaps, moving up the political scale, some real elements of democracy could push through, but it requires time. In Russia, unaware of the complexity and necessity of institution building, there would never have been enough time. Saprykin still thinks those outcomes could be achieved, if only the traditional divisiveness and aversion to compromise had not broken into pieces the fledgling institution. Tellingly, Aleksei Navalny no longer even acknowledges such a thing as the KS.

CHAPTER SEVEN
FUTURE TENSE

Before my visits to Russia, I often e-mail or call the people with whom I'd like to talk. As Americans typically do, I might begin this process a few months in advance. Well, I hear, that would be wonderful, but it's so far away. Let's get in touch just before you leave. During that call, I hear the same enthusiasm, but also a request to call when I arrive. Then, during the next call, it's let's make dinner plans for, say, Thursday this week and we'll call each other the night before. Is this a cultural difference: Americans make arrangements six or eight months or more in advance, while Russians are uncertain up to the last minute? Perhaps culture has something to do with it, but much more, I think, the difference I illustrate above is about time horizons. I have long ones; Russians I talk to have very short ones. Short time horizons show that uncertainty is a critical part of life. Short time horizons in the Russian case seriously impede economic growth, personal plans, and overall confidence that life is more a matter of continuity and confidence than tension and uncertainty. The future leaders who speak in this book are confident about their professional futures. They are also very tense about it: defensive about trust, dissatisfied, but normally not speaking about it, threatened about the uncertainty of the continuation of life itself in a world where the most hostile and powerful state (the United States) is unpredictable, lethal, and anti-Russian.

And if we look beyond Moscow for a sketch of Russia—the vast country? It is something of a depressing sight. Alexander Oslon is founder and head of the large and established Public Opinion Foundation (FOM) in Moscow. The agency conducts polls for the Russian president, for the public, and also market research for all sorts of products, foreign and domestic. One morning, as we both sat in his office, he presented a sociological analysis of today's Russia.

ALEXANDER OSLON'S PORTRAIT OF RUSSIA: THE BIG PICTURE

Oslon dismisses the big Moscow demonstrations as retreads jostling for the limelight. Many of their leaders are hangers-on, attempting to show up everywhere in the hope of seizing the prize of a public position, any position. He counts among them Boris Nemtsov and Aleksei Navalny, whose only goal, Oslon thinks, is to become president. We will return to these ideas later.

Russia is a country of deep-seated and widespread problems. Oslon drew for me this overview of the country.[1] He divides the country into halves. Fifty percent do not work. They are students, pensioners, invalids, street sweepers, house attendants; in short, he says, they live "pointless lives." They depend wholly on the state for their existence and receive either whole or partial assistance. They live day-to-day and have no interest in technology, business, or any conception of "success or achievement." They are not interested in demonstrations and opposition rallies.

The other half of the population has work. Of this half, Oslon says that 35% of them have duties to perform, but have no ambition, no aspirations for success, no purpose for which they have demands. As he put it, they have no project, something that is their personal passion or interest, something for which they want to work, want to progress, to realize an idea, a plan, a movement toward the success of what they want to create. The remaining 15% do have a project. They are some of the young students, businessmen, and entrepreneurs. They want to do well. They have a purpose and are ready to work toward it and expend the energy to achieve it. And, no less important, they have money from previous stages of success, or, possibly, access to some of their parents' resources. The term "project" does not exclude the project of corruption. This 15% are people Oslon calls "people of the 21st Century."

By the time of the 2011 elections, these people had their own equipment and resources and wanted to engage in competition, but considered themselves too hemmed in by State organs and all the red tape. Oslon here refers to the people who actually create, for society, as opposed to the supervisors of natural resource companies who gobble up income and store it in secret offshore havens. The new young businessmen want to throw off the vestiges of the post-Soviet state's constricting rules. At this time, Vladimir Putin returned to the presidency.

If the visitor goes out into the country beyond the comfortable two biggest cities, it will be immediately apparent that, as Oslon says, the vast majority of Russians are still dependent on the state. The tremendous proportion of this dependent population means that confining one's ideas and protests to the capital is a losing strategy. The demonstrators are woefully myopic. Besides, Oslon sees no common ideology among Moscow's demonstrators and no "glue" to hold them together. He mentions the online voting of over 82,000 for the KS. It is, he says, the thinnest of slivers. He is wholly unimpressed by and critical of the demonstrations and motivations.

It is true that the KS was created to try to harness the momentum of the demonstrations and prolong their commitment to expression. It is also true, that the organizers sought to do this by overcoming the historical divisions in Russia among people who do not agree and would rather drown than catch a life-saver thrown from a different deck. Besides, liberal or democratically inclined political parties in the post-Soviet time were tiny and weak. So, by focusing on obvious problems to overcome, the KS members could bring their followers together to the front of the stage and, discarding cant, unite to solve problems everyone agreed were hurting them all. At first, it did have some success (just sitting in the same room and addressing the same subject with civility was the first), but there is a reason for political divisions: different value systems and different ideologies are not anesthetized because problems must be solved. Ideologies are activated in their different goals, approaches, and methods.[2]

Can we really discount the 50% who are not working? It is true that technology comes in many flavors now and has become so owing to user-friendly devices. Mobile devices of all sorts and Twitter have swept Russia. Because of significant regional differences in Russia, not all will have the same degree of technological sophistication and resources. But students of all ages are deeply involved with the internet at different levels of complexity. These students are in state-run schools, but the importance of the internet for a productive labor force has pushed its training and use in the earliest grades. In the focus groups, many, especially from Moscow State University, study at the state's expense. They are not outside the limits of society and cannot be compared to the aging street sweepers and doormen, sad vestiges of the past. Russia is depopulating; any skilled contribution students can make—and the internet will be critical—will make the society stronger. They are not part of a weak half of Russia, but preparing to be something quite different, if there are incentives to shun gangs and ethnic violence. Theirs may not be a pointless life if the limitless internet can inform and inspire. I am not here making an argument that using the internet is transformative in a positive way for all who use it, or a deterministic claim that only good comes from a technology that is fundamentally indifferent to its use. I should also add that the decline in Russia's birth rate (even if signs of slight growth are appearing) means labor force numbers and military will still reflect serious contraction for decades, and paired with the much-too-early mortality rate among adult men, makes us see this 50% in a different light: the demographic realities of aging and poverty. This is a reality that does not turn around quickly and when most needed. Vladimir Putin in his address at the end of 2012 asked for Russian émigrés to return.

The 35% who make a living do depend strongly on the state and do not look to the future. They live blinkered lives of constant repetition. When the Soviet Union dissolved, neither of the presidents who followed allocated sufficient attention and funding to help those just getting by at the lowest level. The state has failed many in its population, and the birth and death rates show it. There is no adequate safety net and funding for those in need. Recall then-president Dmitry Medvedev's blog that took up the problem of adolescent alcoholism with United Russia deputies, and then turned it back to them to solve in their own regions, when it was patently clear that more support from the center is vitally needed—support that does not feed corruption.

The future is in flux. When we look back at the warnings of the Academy of Sciences and the long data series underlying their conclusions, Russia seems certain to fall victim to hostilities among the many ethnicities grasping for a decent future. We know that policing has improved to some extent, from sheer passivity or collaboration, to something more orderly. The taking of the Crimea and "bringing it back home" was treated as a great national victory. It has been a long time since a stunning exploit from Russia astonished the world. The admonishments, sanctions, ejection from the group of industrial giants—what are these in comparison with Russian-made glory for Russia? We know the future leaders are not nationalists, but they are patriots. They are deeply attached to Russia, even though they do not praise the leaders. We also know that Russia has no powerful allies, practically none at all. At the same time, 50,000 people marched in Moscow to protest the president's disregard of Ukrainian sovereignty and, they thought, his extreme, even imperial, nationalism.

Such a sudden raid can be powerfully distracting and satisfying domestically. Whatever one's station in life, Russian television's thrillingly biased and skillfully delivered images of the great victory and the restoration of Russia gripped even Putin's foes. They thought the dismemberment of Ukraine an unlawful act that trod on international norms, another example of their President's hunger for power and adulation. For others concerned about their material well-being, it is likely that personal grievances and desire for material well-being were superseded. For how long? The warranty wears out in time; the need for heating fuel and proper living space come up again. A powerful economy delivering basic needs to all its citizens is vital to the stability of the country. What we know of dependence on oil and failure to diversify, suggests that the "curse" of oil usually stunts development of less immediately wealth-producing sectors, and it is rare for the purest honesty to keep owners from diverting natural resource riches to private pockets. There are examples all over the world and through history. In Russia "Friends of Vladimir" are well positioned in the energy sector.

DIGNITY AND DISSATISFACTION

The future leaders think about the society they will enter after university. They watch keenly what is going on and do so with a wide range of sources. They see the palliatives distributed as solutions and, most of all, they are tired of being treated as naïve, undiscerning fools by their own government. As Misha said so vividly, the government treats them as unthinking animals, "yapping dogs" to whom the rulers toss some raw meat to keep them quiet. They are insulted by the way their government tramples on their dignity.

Josiah Ober has described dignity as a core value of democracy. He observes, "…indignity is bad in itself. Indignity entails suffering harms, or being liable to suffer harms, as a consequence of falsely attributed inferiority or immaturity.…Humiliation is incompatible with the sort of liberty necessary to sustain democracy because the individual who suffers or is subject to humiliation is not in a position to employ free speech or free association in the robust manner demanded of participatory citizens.…Likewise infantilism is incompatible with the sort of equality necessary to sustain democracy."[3] Yury Saprykin was thoroughly changed by the casual announcement that Vladimir Putin and then-president Medvedev had agreed on the double switch long before elections: Putin to prime minister and Putin back to president, vice versa for Medvedev. It was an intolerable wound to a citizen's dignity. The focus-group participants are being taught daily that they merit dignity. They have been chosen as the best nationwide; they receive the best education and are full of anger at attempts to infantilize them: the news on television; Medvedev's blog. "Everything is fine," said about every one of the numerous disasters and misshapen plans of the government; the pantomime election performed with witless party and government stumbling while defrauding voters. It is this destruction of their dignity in a government that brooks no serious opposition, that most infuriates participants in the focus groups.

ELECTORAL COMPETITION

The focus-group participants are very negative about United Russia, the government's puppet-party that excludes democratic decision making from the legislature. The participants favor contestation, competing views, real content in party programs, and independence of legislators. This has been a theme running through all of the sessions. The future leaders show no interest in sham voting or serving autocratic masters whose rule is personal and apt to change for unknown reasons and at unpredictable times. Instead, they will serve professions. They want new faces and fellow leaders who will communicate in meaningful ways.

Competition among real, as opposed to manipulated, crony parties is possibly in flux. The new party reforms encouraging formation of parties may well split the vote and waste the votes going to parties that cannot meet the 5% threshold requirement. The next parliamentary and presidential elections are still some time ahead. But hosts of local elections are on the docket. They have not meant much in the past—the Moscow City Council, for example—but if suddenly contested and competitive, their stature could quickly change. Traditionally, proto-parties, parties, and their leaders take pride in their refusal to compromise and join with others, diluting the purity of their absolutist political views. An insuperable obstacle, apparently for a long time to come, is that any elected candidate for federal legislative office and the presidency would have to face a Constitution made to protect Boris Yeltsin's reforms by lodging power in the office of the presidency and reducing the legislature in a tremendously unbalanced contrast in power. Gradual advancement in regional and local elections is a likely strategy for the future, if it is permitted. But all of these very difficult steps may be models and hopes; they are far from the frozen heights.

TOLERANCE

Tolerance is a learned virtue.[4] Toddlers and young schoolchildren are not tolerant, because it is not natural. Tolerance in practice relies on the belief that although you may be well off and well placed now, you grant tolerance to those who are not, because you believe that some day, the positions can switch—and switch back and forth. When you are no longer on top, you would want the same tolerance you had extended when you had the upper hand. It is difficult to learn, because it assumes that, when weighing future potential, there will be alternation in power and that your own situation can change significantly.

The habit of tolerance in practically all focus groups excludes Caucasian ethnic groups. In the focus groups, trust, which is hard won, begins with being a Slav. This is the first sign that the person can be trusted (though it is not sufficient). The participants rationalize it by saying that it is easier this way; you already know that your thinking is similar and you have much in common in your upbringing. They resemble me; the "other," less so. What resembles me reassures me. What is different is more difficult to trust and takes longer. Artemy hesitates to speak about his intolerance, his intense dislike of Caucasian citizens of Russia. He recognizes his racism. There are migrant workers from Central Asia who are forced to live in poverty. In a different category are the Chechens, Dagestani, and other Caucasian people, who are also workers but much more in evidence as bosses of open-air markets and outdoor flower selling; they divide the city into zones for collection of protection money. Russian gangs do the same. At home in the Caucasus, some of these people are fighting for independence and have become terrorists. One who bombed the Boston Marathon in 2013 returned to his Caucasian birthplace to be indoctrinated in terrorism. Russia's Caucasian republics desperately need relief from a life of poverty and brute force. When funds are allocated to them, any progress is undermined by bribery, on the one hand, and massively brutal Russian military actions, on the other. Most in the focus groups speak about white Western European countries as people and places with whom they have much greater affinity.

Under Vladimir Putin, an already unbalanced state became even more Moscow-centric and Russo-centric. He has encouraged nationalism. The Russian Federation is heavily Russian but not homogeneous. There are rapidly growing numbers of Muslims, and much smaller numbers of many different ethnic groups and languages. Church and State are separate in the Constitution, yet television carries services for major Orthodox holidays and Sunday mass, and the Patriarch of the Church is often at the president's side, a practice that harks back to pre-Soviet Russia, when the country had a national religion. So, almost everything in the environment reinforces the notion that the "we" is so huge and that the "they" is so small and not respected. It is not surprising that in terms of ethnicity and religion, the focus-group participants reproduce the intolerance of their society and their childhood education. It does not appear that feelings of tolerance of all ethnicities within Russia should be assumed for the future leaders.

A significant increase in the instances of ethnic or racially motivated brawls and killing also points to increased feelings of ethno-nationalism. On July 10, 2013, in Pugachov, a town of 40,000 near the city of Saratov on the Volga River, a 20-year-old former paratrooper and a 16-year-old ethnic Chechen fought over a girl; the Chechen stabbed and killed his opponent. For days after the fight, hundreds of local citizens marched through the streets shouting for the deportation of the people from the North Caucasus. The head of an extremist group rushed from Moscow to help accelerate the violence, but well before he reached the fighting, police forced him off the train.

In the second chapter of this book, we discussed a disheartening and thorough report of the first twenty years of the Russian Federation by the Russian Academy of Sciences and the Ebert Foundation of Germany. It is a comprehensive study of many facets of Russian life. The most urgent and serious part of it dealt with inter-ethnic relations within the Russian Federation. On September 16, 2013, the Russian Center for Information and Analysis, headed by analyst Alexander Verkhovsky, published its own analysis. Based on a survey conducted by a Moscow survey organization, ROMIR, and commissioned by the Norwegian Research Council, it is entitled *Nation Building and Nationalism in Contemporary Russia: Overview of a Sociological Survey.* In the sample of 1,000 people, 90% considered themselves ethnic Russian; of 600 people in the regions, 94% to 97% of the respondents regarded themselves as Russians. The main subject of the poll was inter-ethnic relations. The survey analysts found that more than a third of the respondents consider inter-ethnic relations "bad or very bad" and in Moscow, it was 47%. When considering particular ethnic groups, such as Roma, Chechens, Central Asians, and Chinese, Moscow, again, was the most "against" these nationalities—between 63% and 66% of respondents consider it inappropriate to have a relative from one of these groups.

Although more than half of all the respondents considered migrants necessary to the economy, 43% want to send them all home and, once again, Moscow is most xenophobic of all: 82% want limits on migrants allowed in for work, and more than 60% of the respondents in Moscow do not want migrants and their children to have permits for living quarters. At the same time, the respondents are not attracted by skinheads and Far Right extremist organizations. But a fifth of the respondents say that migrants beaten up by Russians deserve it, and that figure rises to 27% among the group aged 29–34. These latter groups, it hardly needs repeating, are able-bodied and usually well able to administer punishment, though it should be noted—always—that these responses are just that; they are not evidence of previous or future behavior, unpleasant though they may be.

More worrisome is that in Moscow, more than 80% support the use of armed Cossack and other patrols of young nationalists, none of whom is subject to the same constraints of the law as are, presumably, the police. Xenophobia is expressed in all kinds of ways, but clearly remains very high and multi-ideological. Everywhere, it is Moscow that leads on the particular expressions of hate among respondents.[5]

In 2013, there was another mass race riot: thousands of people in West Biriulovo (a section of Moscow) flooded the streets, beating up migrant laborers. Local residents came out infuriated and vengeful and soon became a mob. But, they might not have done so, or behaved so viciously, had they not been sure that organized neo-Nazis were there in force, and they expanded the pogrom to an uncontrollable mass action. It was this combination of the viciousness of ordinary people spilling into the street to harm their prey and the organized activist right wing that made this event so dangerous.[6]

THE CONUNDRUM OF ALEKSEI NAVALNY

Even though Aleksei Navalny stands out as the best hope of the opposition, it is precisely his ethnic nationalism that worries many—many who will, *faute di mieux* support him wholeheartedly. Though legal constraints may prevent him for running for an office, and even though his right to use a computer has temporarily been taken away because he violated the terms of his house arrest, these are only restraints to act with ingenuity. In a handwritten blog placed by others in LiveJournal, Navalny writes, "you can call me a Slavic chauvinist, but I think that the most important strategic advantage of Russia in this world will be not oil, not gas and not nuclear bombs, but friendly (even brotherly, and so on) relations of Russians with Ukrainians and Belorusians. Look I sat [in prison] *7 days and nights in a special [harsh] regime,* [and] in the room was a Belorusian, who came to earn money, an Azeri and an Uzbek. They were all good guys and we all were friends eating the potato with sprats…[Ukrainian and Belorusian] each of us instantly feels a togetherness and shared cultural codes. I don't exactly know how to describe it more precisely. If you have formed close bonds with fellow countrymen and experienced deep connections you go against other ethnic groups, simply everything is immediately understood: they are the same as I." I understand that this is rather a politically incorrect thought, but I wanted to formulate it.

Navalny goes on to say that anyone under 40 in the former Soviet countries of Central Asia "hasn't read the same things, and they barely know Russian. We look at things differently, we have different sayings, values, and our inner compass is different. ***Friendly and brotherly relations with this country [Ukraine] and its people is the most important geopolitical advantage of Russia and all people living in Russia [emphasis in the original].*** Putin, is destroying this advantage, right now, in front of our eyes…."[7]

When Aleksei Navalny ran for mayor of Moscow in 2013, the extremist right-wing Russian March was about to put on its annual parade, replete with brown leather, stylized swastikas and flags with symbols of imperial Russia, and pre-Soviet religious images. At a press conference, Ksenia Sobchak, was in the audience. Navalny had just finished saying that illegal migrants (from elsewhere in the former Soviet Union) should be sent back, that the narcotics trade had increased enormously, and that children brought to Moscow are exploited for money (though they are paid far below the wages of others doing the same work). He charged that, as a result, the migrants are uneducated and the situation contributes to inter-ethnic conflict. Ksenia Sobchak spoke from the audience: "I'd like to know under what conditions, in connection with what, will Aleksei Navalny, candidate for mayor of the city of Moscow, go on the 'Russian March'? Or will he not go?"

She continued, "I [asked] about limits; you don't consider that the 'Russian March' is a marginal action?" (Marginal is used here to mean outside the system. The extremist parties are called *marginaly*.)

Maxim Kats, a professional poker player, added that the question about the "Russian March" remained unanswered by Navalny. He asked, "You didn't go to the last march—you said you were sick. And will you go to the next one?"

Navalny answered the questioner, saying that "the 'Russian March' is a spontaneous political action in which you and everybody else act the same...."

Vera Krichevskaya, a documentary filmmaker and one of the founders of *Rain* TV, said, "and if there's a protest movement by Muslims in Moscow, because they live badly, are you ready to go on a march to enlighten Muslim masses...?"[8]

The Russian March for 2013 took place on November 4. What would Navalny do? The marchers were again put in the distant Liublino area of southwest Moscow. The organizers said 20,000 marchers had participated; they said they based this number on marchers going through metal detectors. The police had their figure: 6,000 participants. Aleksei Navalny did not march. He announced that while he supported the march, he would not be joining them "for a number of reasons."[9] This was probably one of the most important decisions of his political life. How much could this ambitious, dedicated power-seeker emerge as leader for all? Had he really moved away from an exclusionary nationalist ideology? Right up until the mayoral campaign—just weeks before—though his rhetoric softened—he was still standing on a platform that many of his followers found intolerant. The litmus test was the Russian March, and he repeatedly and publicly said he would march. And then he did not. It was the buzz of the blogosphere. And a very wise move for his future—whatever it might turn out to be.

Do the future leaders tolerate positions, including political positions, different from their own? In the groups there are different points of view, but no ad hominem attacks; they question each other and listen to the answers. They reject unanimously the position of DPNI, "ultras," and nationalists of all kinds. There is one unspoken taboo on the internet. They agree to keep away from talk about religion, calling it a recognized taboo.

Participants have also learned democratic procedure. They do not dominate discussions and prevent others from speaking; they are apologetic if once in a while they interrupt the discussion to bring up a point relating to the subject just gone by. They do not scoff at others' views, although they often cannot resist an injection of sardonic humor. In short, they respect equality of contributions to conversations, and if some do not know a word or organization, the ones who do know, explain with no condescension. They are all in their own community, with peers. How much these habits carry over to interactions with other social strata and other occasions we cannot be certain.

Is Mutual Trust Possible?

Mutual trust is central to the successful working of society. Trust lowers transaction costs in very important ways, but it involves two elements—the benefits conferred upon one and the self-disclosure one must make for true trust. In self-disclosing, there is risk. This group of future leaders are not, as we have seen in so many forms, at home with risk. In the tension between the risks and benefits of trust, some want very much to commit to trust, only to end up on the side of watchful prudence. In the offline world, they stress not just the risk of trusting, but the likely betrayal that self-disclosure can generate. Avoiding harm to their professional future is a concern, and the more they talk about trust, the more tests and observations and time they claim must be expended in order to safeguard their own futures and suppress rumors and stains on their reputations. Such pervasive wariness and distrust, which we have seen repeatedly under different conditions, may seem intolerant, but they are a much more real fear. They all live in an undemocratic system, coupled with intense competition without rules.

At the first meeting of the Coordinating Council of the Opposition (KS), with all the hues of political beliefs around a table, an almost desperate question was taken up: How can we trust each other? The grand design of the KS sought to minimize the anguish of trust and the divisiveness of political or ethno-national ideologies by building cooperation based entirely on issues of mutual concern and leading to cooperative work to fix the issues. In Soviet times, the state coopted the space for association, rendering illegal spontaneous groups and filling the free time of young people, by coercing them into official organizations. This KS is an attempt to sustain fairness, transparency, and activity within the outer shell of governmental control of political life.

The Anxiety of Betrayal

Masha, in chapter 3, has considerable self-knowledge. She speaks of splintering: this young woman is afraid that the stress required in today's Russia will be unbearable—defining each required "persona" as required by the context. What she is talking about is the tension between who she is and the conforming "splinters" of the persona inside her head. These young people speak of "rebellions in their heads"; they are savvy about avoiding sites and public rituals that continually underestimate their intelligence. They are different inside and this dissonance is especially worrisome, as they face the future and enter a world in which conformity will exact too high a price on their evident love of life and the internet-assisted ability to use their intellect and roam far and wide, free of boundaries, both geographic and political.

They have shifted to living online. They are almost wholly in that world, and because of it, have absorbed profoundly important new ways of thinking: one is that on the net there is a tendency toward lev-eling. Offline status means little in the online world. A self-important claim of importance is vacuous. That is why, when then-President Medvedev's blog was inaugurated, it did not matter to the focus-group participants that he was president and therefore should be com-mended on the excellence of the blog and his advanced technology culture. They thought the blog insipid, old-fashioned, and generally amateurish. After all, he was a latecomer to the net; that did not earn him any compassion points. The fact is that for these participants the internet forces content to matter more than status and even denigrates the powerful whose claim to be heard rests on their power alone.

They want to develop and expand and seek different viewpoints. They do not, with only a few exceptions, seek people just like them-selves, but seek contradictions and are determined to resolve them. This applies to professional matters, but also, to news. As leaders, it is likely that the spectrum of views to which they will expose themselves will be closer to the dictum of John Stuart Mill than many citizens in established democracies where the "echo chamber" or just distraction pulls citizens away from knowledge and meaningful participation.

The Significance of Demonstrations

The series of demonstrations protesting the destruction of the last for-est bordering Moscow were political, but not directly anti-Kremlin. The demonstrations were happening in the suburbs as well as in the center of Moscow, all around the future leaders, and it was about something important to them: the environment. It was present on the internet; the leader wrote blogs continually. Neo-Nazis attacked the environmentalists; "anti-fascists" went after them, since there was no sign that police would restore order. In fact, police arrested left-wing anti-fascists and not others. This, then, was a demonstration that was far from trivial and attempted to uphold the same values the partici-pants hold: disgust at violent neo-Nazis and support of the environ-ment (many of the future leaders will be working in some area of the environment, including environmental law).

As shown earlier, in all the sessions, there was hardly a mention of the demonstration. It was on the minds of a handful of participants and then only in comments about costs and benefits of the proposed construction; granted, a greater weight was assigned to the environment, and justification for degrading the environment, they say, should have to be at a more critical level. Future leaders, we can conclude, will be unlikely to transform their democratic values and ideals—the anger we see in chapter 2, for example—into actions against the very leadership administration they will likely join. Still, inside the heads of many of these future leaders resides a remarkably different world from the society around them. Misha says that there is an ongoing revolution; all the time, rebellion boils. It will stay there. The participants who talk of this inner insurgence deliberately never speak of action to follow. I think we are not talking about physical cowardice (though the demonstrations grow increasingly violent) or careerism only. They would have no careers as leaders if the photographs of demonstrations identified them; that is true. I think, rather, that though both of these observations are true, they are studying hard to make a difference. They do much more than they have to, even though their course of study is exceptionally difficult. Their stance appears to be oriented toward attaining the best profession possible and doing the best job, which may be in Russia or partly in another country. They do not expect to initiate political change, but would welcome it. They are dissatisfied with government economic initiatives, foreign policy, legislative activity, political party "representation," crippled mass media mouthing platitudes with no credibility, and, most of all, lack of choice to speak about their preferences and support a "real" party for a real legislature. Though critical of the behavior of their leaders, they remain deeply attached to their country and want it to benefit from their expertise and experience.

The first demonstration at Bolotnaya Square was a protest against vote fraud, but included anybody who came for any reason, even a lot of people who did not know why they joined. Moscow was safe; other marchers were well dressed; why not? It is not a misnomer to call them "flash mobs." They were reached by the social media to which they are attached, and they converged in astonishing numbers. The next demonstration, the even larger one at Sakharov Prospect, was different. I shall return to it below.

In 1999, a flash mob jammed the streets of Seattle during a meeting of the World Trade Organization. They objected to what they regarded as exploitation of poor nations. The shock of this instant creation of a mob has become legend, but it was not quite like that. What Jennifer A. Peeples and Bentley Mitchell in their study call "an almost mythic understanding of the Direct Action Network in the Seattle *demonstrations* has developed." That myth portrays the demonstration as "structureless, fully liberated and liberating..." One observer described it as "no hierarchy, no membership, nobody belongs and everybody belongs....No one owns the name; nobody makes decisions for anyone else."[10] The authors call this an "engaging description," but one that is inaccurate:

> We maintain that the problems of the organization were structural and tactical differences which grew out of the Network coming together in preparation for a campaign. These strategic choices were profitable for a demonstration, but did not function to maintain a social movement organization—one that had a general purpose but no longer had a specific, material, time-dependent goal....Affinity groups that coalesced for the protest did not appear to have the lasting power of the interpersonal connections which were formed prior to the demonstration....
>
> Finally, under crisis-situations, most notably the short amount of time needed to put together a mass protest, leader-dominated decision-making took the place of consensus government.[11]

The flash mobs of Tahrir Square in Egypt protested the rule of the Mubarak regime and their own lack of rights, work, and adequate housing in a country where the leader's wife sported chunky gold adornments. The spontaneous crowd was mainly unorganized. Only one institution, other than the army and government bureaucracy, was still alive, but it was careful to stay away from the demonstrations until it was safe to join. The Muslim Brotherhood had existed since the 1920s;

it had started as an adversarial, often violent, activist group, until it was declared illegal and routed massively and violently. It then chose another strategy; the members forswore violence and instead patiently worked among the rural and urban poor providing food and looking after health—both badly needed and badly neglected by the government.

At first the Brotherhood remained on the perimeter of the Tahrir demonstrations, but when it joined, and when Constitution-writing and elections were at issue, the Brotherhood was in the fray. For the poor demonstrating for jobs, the educated young with no prospects at all for economic sufficiency, for minorities hoping to keep from being overridden, significant power in government was not to be theirs. Instead, it was the experienced institution of the Muslim Brotherhood that could best convert the "after-protest" into power. The only other solid organization was, of course, what was left of the old regime and the powerful military.

When employment did not materialize, there was another protest. But very soon the leader's intolerance and political extremism became obvious and nothing improved in material life. When workers at Port Said went on strike, another protest occurred at Tahrir in support; another toppled the leader and returned the military to power, ousting, imprisoning, and declaring the entire Brotherhood organization illegal.

Flash mobs were not themselves an instrument to convert disparate discontent into more sustainable institutions that could effect change, *providing that their disparate views come together for the common good.*

Yury Saprykin, Aleksei Navalny, Leonid Volkov, and their colleagues were obviously aware of the upside of flash mobs: people could be inspired to get together in huge numbers and in this way capture the attention of the Kremlin. They were also aware that people with many divergent and mutually incompatible political views (including extremists beyond the law) could come together for the demonstration on Sakharov Prospect. That is why Saprykin insisted on transparency—every organizational meeting was open. He insisted on building a habit of electoral democracy under which every individual voter could register a preference for a speaker at the demonstration, and only winners could speak to the crowd (this last condition being modified at the behest of Boris Nemtsov and Aleksei Navalny, over Saprykin's objection). Saprykin and his colleagues were only too aware that the police were hoping for a provocation to discredit and stop this, the largest demonstration of all. Therefore, in advance, the organizers made sure to keep in constant touch on Facebook, issuing advice for avoiding violence at all cost and behaviors to practice or avoid. The organizers were present at various places in the demonstration to stop incipient violence, should it occur.

Was this a flash mob? Consider the inclusiveness of ordinary citizens in each step of the planning, the way formal votes determined the choice of speakers through Facebook in real elections, the continuous discussion about avoiding violence: it was, I think, the beginning of a hybrid form, in which participation was defined by more than showing up and protesting. Participation began to be a kind of (embryonic) co-management. This way of bringing people together over agreement on common issues was the basis for the larger elections for the Coordinating Council and constitutes an attempt to convert the demonstration into institutions without hierarchies: transparent, networked, and democratic. The KS was at the apex, true, but considered itself the agent of voters and voting on proposals—all of which could be watched on the internet. The KS declined as the political success of Aleksei Navalny and his party rose to prominence and success. Shifting into the real world was a change of great magnitude.

Jensen, Jorba, and Anduiza write that "by themselves, technologies do not do anything, nor do the opportunities and agency they afford compel people to act, and so their implications are felt as people take them up and incorporate them into their practices. In this sense digital media do not create civil society or introduce new practices of citizenship. But where these are incipient or contested, use of technology can support, reinforce, or amplify trends."[12]

NOT EVERY DEMOCRACY IS ALIKE

Some of the participants who seem most interested in democracy are at the same time opposed to the imposition of "American democracy."

Artyom and Misha think deeply about this conundrum: America is the home of democracy; a worldwide revolution of ideas began there. Artyom and Misha do not like the emphasis on the market and the greed, lying, fraud, and distrust it engendered. Although they do not blame American programs for all of it, they know full well that home-grown corruption vigorously moved in. When several focus-group participants wrote about America in their thumbnail sketches, they may have noted virtuous and effective attributes, but they also wrote disdainfully or even with animosity of the "excessive materialism" of America. For all that America has done in the past, it is not the current American democracy most of them respect and like. None wants the old Russian autocracy or empire, and all want to be treated like citizens, not subjects. They want a democracy in which citizens can live their lives in peace, without the constant fear that they will be swallowed up by an economic or political maneuver. They want to be able to trust, but they know they cannot trust—"not here and not now." In the form of democracy they do not want—extreme materialism, as they call it—their fellow citizens must always hide their cards; play them close to the chest; never give up information in this zero-sum game. One might think that they are simply describing today's Russia and rejecting it. That is not true; they are Russian patriots, understood as having affection for the history and culture, the beauty and vastness of the land. In sessions, they often wish to offer an illustration for the point they are making, and often it is something from a nineteenth-century novel; they rarely refer to the Soviet period. When they are critical of American democracy, it is the excessive inhumanity of an all-powerful and secretive market they have in mind.

They believe there are other forms of democracy more humane and still democratic and this is what they want. Michael Coppedge, in his exhaustive work on democratization and methodologies, writes that the major democracies exhibit differences in emphasis on economic equalization of wealth and status, participation, representation, and the degree to which citizens vote on more matters than holding public office. Coppedge notes that democracy is a "contested concept."[13] In the focus groups, only a third or fewer, believe America—at present—is the most attractive model of democracy; the rest think mainly of Scandinavian countries, even if in idealized form. They do think this type of democracy can happen in Russia. They do not minimize the long haul and do not know what it would take to effect these changes, since society is so immobilized and the system so frozen. But in saying, as they do, about fundamental changes in trust and participation, "not now" and "not yet," they acknowledge that a different future is possible. All the variants are seen on the internet; they know how different kinds of democracies arrange their value systems and allocate their resources. They will continue to make comparisons; it is their most important way to comprehend and influence future policy.

PROFILES OF THE THREE ELITE UNIVERSITIES IN RUSSIA

Moscow State University (MSU)

Moscow State University (MSU) was established in 1735. It has thirty-nine faculties (equivalent to schools, e.g., faculty of law).

It grants a B.A., which takes four years to complete and an M.A., which takes two years.

The total number of students is somewhat more than 40,000.

The government grants stipends for study to all but 15% of the students. This 15% pay their fees themselves.

Admission is determined by competitive standing on the Unified State Examination and by examinations by the university itself.

Moscow State Institute of Foreign Affairs— University (MGIMO)

Founded in 1944, MGIMO began as the diplomatic academy for the Ministry of Foreign Affairs.

In 1994, MGIMO was granted the status of university in recognition of its much expanded programs of study, faculty, and students. It has twelve schools and four institutes and within them, twenty-five departments of study. Some fifty-three languages are taught.

Admission is determined by competitive standing on the Unified State Examination and by examinations by the university itself.

It grants a B.A. normally after four years of study and an M.A. after two years. It requires all students to take several foreign languages, of which English must be one.

There are about 6,000 students at MGIMO.

Some students' stipends are granted by the state, and some pay their own fees.

THE HIGHER ECONOMIC SCHOOL (HES)—NATIONAL RESEARCH UNIVERSITY

HES was founded in 1992 by a group of reform-minded economists "for production and dissemination of modern economic knowledge."

Its website states: "HES is ranked among the top three most prestigious universities in Russia (MSU, MGIMO, HES)."

It now offers a wide range of disciplines to about 2,700 students (non-M.A.).

Of the prospective students somewhat less than half are from Moscow.

Some students receive stipends.

The Unified State Examination is mandatory for entrance. HES may choose not to supplement it with further examinations.

CHARACTERIZING THE COUNTRIES

THREE WORDS FOR TWO COUNTRIES YOU ARE MOST INTERESTED IN READING ABOUT ON THE INTERNET

THREE WORDS FOR TWO COUNTRIES YOU ARE LEAST INTERESTED IN READING ABOUT ON THE INTERNET

Note: Author's clarifications are in brackets; parentheses come from participants' questionnaires. Some words come up fairly frequently on several questionnaires, but are given only once here; for example for Japan, Fukushima and radiation are mentioned by all participants. I have not included city names, landmark names (e.g., Eiffel Tower), leaders' names (e.g., Obama, Sarkozy), unless they were modified by some kind of evaluation or sentiment. Such words as hamburger, sausage, beer (if not part of a point of view or attitude toward the country) were also omitted. When an entire category, such as military/threat or any of the others was not referred to at all by the participants for a given country, I eliminated the category, rather than leaving it empty.

MOST INTERESTED

UNITED STATES OF AMERICA

Economy: life on credit, consumption, Silicon Valley, technology, economic development, progress, science, CNN, new technology, prosperity, comfort, budget crisis, opportunities, development of medicine, qualified specialists, iPad, standard of living, competitor, "a lot of everything"

Political System: democracy, freedom of speech, arrogant actions of government, Westernization

Military/Threat: aggression, air strikes, nuclear war, war in Iraq, Libya, U.S. Army, Pentagon, military might, expansionist

Character Traits: benevolent, stupid, self-assured, hostile

Culture: study, modernism, films, "weighty role of homosexualism," Masons

GERMANY

Economy: goods, shopping, modern city, economic problems, economic boom, technology, well-being, success, possible place to work, science, stability, energy-saving (conservation)

Military/Threat: Bundeswehr

Character Traits: long-range work, reliability, industriousness, punctuality, discipline

Culture: education, literature

FRANCE

Economy: comfort, wine, strikes

Political System: social policies

Culture: latest trends in fashion, boutiques, romance, culture, Louvre, good art, Bohème, educational system, perfume

TURKEY

Economy: close to Russia in economic development

Culture: sweets, Bedouins, Islam, bazaar, study, culture, incompatibility

UKRAINE

Economy: gas, technology, poverty of people

Political System: political instability

Military/Threat: confrontation, Black Sea Fleet

Character Traits: brotherly, friendly, funny, absurd, senseless

Culture: salo [salted pork fat]

CHINA

Economy: fastest developing economy in the world, interesting economic model, construction, production, overpopulation, everything is interesting in economic policy, export, import, labor force, success of socialism
Military/Threat: army
Character Traits: uniformity, industriousness, self-denial
Culture: philosophy, culture, traditions

JAPAN

Economy: resources, work, computers, robot technology, development of science, innovation, progress, economy
Political System: Kurile Islands
Character Traits: exactness, slanted eyes, decency, wisdom
Culture: Murakami, rich culture, anime, martial arts

UNITED STATES OF AMERICA

Economy: Consumer society, money

LEAST INTERESTED

GERMANY

Economy: production, unemployment, (social) help, industry
Political System: Hitler, Nazis
Character Traits: strictness, punctuality, animosity
Culture: art, culture, movie festivals

FRANCE

Economy: wine
Political System: governmental ranting
Character Traits: snobbery
Culture: perfume, fashion, romantic city, not interesting, boredom, museums

TURKEY

Economy: spices, poverty, "hole" [figuratively], many Russian visitors, filth, cheap things, machine industry, negative conditions

Political System: vassal of US, mutual friendship with RF, "I don't like their government; I don't like their politics; I just don't see any sense in them."

Military/Threat: war

Culture: Russian–Turkish War, sweets, Bedouins, Islam, bazaar, study, culture, religious incompatibility

UKRAINE

Economy: Donbas mines, poverty, bad roads, cheap, lack of gas, coal

Political System: Orange Revolution, parliamentary elections, violation of law, mess, gossip, rumors, collapsing autocracy, instability, nationalism, political situation, "now everything is stable," "not worth worrying about," falling apart, collapse, totalitarianism, chaos

Character Traits: arrogance

Culture: salo, moonshine, Taras Bulba, Ukrainian history, university

CHINA

Economy: production, resources, work, progress, internet, mass consumption, planned economy, cheap technology

Political System: dictatorship, different political system, USSR, Tibet

Culture: culture

JAPAN

Economy: poverty, computers

Culture: anime

NOTES

INTRODUCTION

1   Quoted in David M. Herszenhorn and Andrew Kramer, "Another Reset of Relations with Russia in Obama's Second Term," *The New York Times*, February 2, 2013, p. A4.

2   Natalia Antonova, "Russian Nationalists Feed the Fires of Moscow's Race Riots," *The Guardian*, October 14, 2013. http://www.theguardian.com/commentisfree/2013/oct/14/russian-nationalists-moscow-race-riots.

3   Mark Blumenthal, "Do Pollsters Need Random Samples? Fundamental Assumptions about Representative Polling Are at Issue in the Debate over Internet Surveys," *NationalJournal.com*, October 13, 2009. http://www.nationaljournal.com/njonline/do-pollsters-need-random-samples--20091013.

4   W. Gamson, *Talking Politics* (Cambridge: Cambridge University Press, 1992), p. 192.

5   James H. Kuklinski and Paul J. Quirk, "Reconsidering the Rational Public: Cognition, Heuristics, and Mass Opinion," in *Elements of Reason*, edited by Arthur Lupia, Matthew D. McCubbins, and Samuel L. Popkin (Cambridge: Cambridge University Press, 2000), p. 163.

CHAPTER 1

1   In a study published in 1988, I and my research team meticulously coded and analyzed over 100 hours of Soviet and American television in 1984 and 1985. We compared the official Soviet television news with "World News Tonight" on ABC. From the Soviet news we found that "Only two genuinely global powers inhabit the earth: the United States and the Soviet Union, and they are inextricably bound by the nuclear threat...[but] the United States is so central and looms so large, that it is not far off the mark to call it an obsession." Their closest neighbors and fellow Communist countries of Eastern Europe "are of far less interest than the distant adversary."Ellen Mickiewicz, *Split Signals: Television and Politics in the Soviet Union* (Oxford and New York: Oxford University Press, 1988), p. 223.

2   Zbigniew Brzezinski, *Second Chance: Three Presidents and the Crisis of American Superpower* (New York: Basic Books, 2007), p. 23.

3   President Boris Yeltsin strongly objected at the time and warned of military consequences. It was not until December 1999 that Yeltsin resigned in favor of his new protégé, Vladimir Putin. It was not, therefore, tough talk from what would be an increasingly nationalistic Putin that was at play at this point. It was his predecessor.

4   At the time, a housing development in Long Island, NY, that would be "affordable" to all strata of the middle class.

5   Ellen Mickiewicz, "Efficacy and Evidence: Evaluating U.S. Goals at the American National Exhibition in Moscow in 1959," *Journal of Cold War Studies* 13, no. 4 (Fall 2011): 142–143.

6   "Education," http://countrystudies.us/russia/52.htm, Library of Congress.

7   "Country Note: Education at a Glance 2012: OECD Indicators," Russian Federation, Questions can be directed to: Andreas Schleicher, Advisor to the Secretary-General on Education Policy, Deputy Director for Education. http://www.oecd.org/education/EAG2012%20-%20Country%20note%20 -%20Russian%20Federation.pdf; "Education," http://countrystudies.us/ russia/52.htm, Library of Congress.

8   See "Internet v Rossii: dinamika proniknovenie" Oslon, 2013. Monthly users in Russia = 57% of population, while 46% are at this time daily users. http://fom.ru/SMI-i-internet/11288 This applies to the country as a whole.

9   Sarah Oates, *Revolution Stalled: The Political Limits of the Internet in the Post-Soviet Sphere* (New York: Oxford University Press, 2013), p. 57.

10   http://www.newmediawatch.com/markets-by-country/10-e

11   To explore these attitudes, during the course of the session, each participant received a list of seven countries in a column on the left of the page. In each university, in each group, the order of countries was changed. The United States was never at the top of the column, to avoid an unthinking, quick check-off. There were three columns: (1) very interested in reading about this country on the internet, (2) little or no interest in reading about this country on the internet, and (3) a middling category of some, but limited interest. Finally, for two countries in category 1 and two in category 2, participants were asked to jot down off the top of their heads three words about the country. There were seven countries to consider. In each university, different groups received lists with countries in completely different order.

12   Cf. full list for all countries in Appendix A.

13   Craig R. Whitney, "Memo from Standards Editor on Coverage of South Ossetia," *The New York Times*, April 2, 2009, http://www.nytimes .com/2009/04/02/business/media/03whitneymemo.html/>sq=who started war in south ossetia&st=cse&scp=164&pageswanted=print

14 From "CNN reports," reprinted in *Transatlantic Relations*, August 8, 2008, at website, *Atlantic Review*.

15 On April 2, 2009, the distinguished *New York Times* ombudsman (called there the "standards editor") made a thorough analysis of the paper's coverage of the war, beginning with the context on February 18, 2008, and ending with a piece on November 7, 2008. In this long article, Whitney includes all of the key coverage in full and comments on the internal dynamics of the newspaper that helped or hindered coverage. For example, when the war broke out there was no one from the paper in the area. The next day, a reporter from the Moscow bureau was sent to the region of hostilities to begin the process of trying to find out what, exactly, was going on. Whitney's dissection of the development of coverage, from near-total bewilderment to more informed analysis, is a model of journalistic responsibility on his part. He was particularly suited to the task, having spent 1977–1980 as correspondent in the paper's Soviet bureau. This and following quotations are taken from his study. Craig R. Whitney, "Memo from Standards Editor on Coverage of South Ossetia," *The New York Times*, April 2, 2009, http://www.nytimes.com/2009/04/02/business/media/03whitneymemo.html/>sq=who started war in south ossetia&st=cse&scp=164&pageswanted=print

16 Reproduced in the Whitney report: C. J. Chivers and Ellen Barry, "Accounts Undercut Claims by Georgia on Russia War," *The New York Times*, November 7, 2008.

17 Spiegel Staff, "Did Saakashvili Lie? The West Begins to Doubt Georgian Leader," *Der* Spiegel, September 15, 2008. Reprinted in #8, *Johnson's Russia List* 2014-#47, March 5, 2014. JRL Homepage: www:russialist.org

18 Jay Newtown-Small, "Senator John McCain: "We Are All Ukrainians"", February 28, 2014. http://time.com/10829/ukraine-john-mccain-putin-crimea/

19 Donald Horowitz, *The Deadly Ethnic Riot* (Berkeley and Los Angeles: University of California Press, 2001).

20 I have not included in this comparison the category of middling interest. The middle position is used so often in polls to avoid any position, that I reproduced the plus and the minus, not the in-between. Since participants were asked to write about two in the most interested category and two in the least interested, a country could fall in either. If there were more than two in each category, the participants were asked to choose two.

21 Ronald Chasser, Mikhail Bondarkov, Robert J. Baker, Jeffrey Wickliffe, and Brenda E. Rodgers, "Reconstruction of Radioactive Plume Characteristics along Chernobyl's Western Trace," *Journal of Environmental Radioactivity*, September 22, 2009.

22   Keith Beverstock and Dillwyn Williams, "The Chernobyl Accident 20 Years On: An Assessment of the Health Consequences and the International Response," *Environmental Health Perspectives* 114, no. 9 (September 2006).

23   "Cloud Seeding," *New World Encyclopedia*, April 2, 2008, http://www.neworldencyclopedia.org/entry/Cloud_seeding

24   Igor Elkov, "Chernobylsky 'Tsiklon.'" *Rossiiskaya gazeta*, April 21, 2006, http://www.rg.ru/2006/04/21/ciklon.html

25   Ibid.

CHAPTER 2

1   Pavel Lebedev, "Zatylkom k TV, litsom kompiutery: tak rossiyane vosprinimaiut informatsiu," *Fond Obshchestvennoe Mnenie*, February 6, 2010.

2   Of interest here is Timur Kuran's book, *Private Truths, Public Lies* (Cambridge, MA: Harvard University Press, 1995).

3   Ellen Mickiewicz, *Television, Power, and the Public in Russia* (Cambridge: Cambridge University Press, 2008), pp. 22–23.

4   Ellen Barry, "Though One More Rally is Set, a Protest Movement Wanes in Post-Election Russia," *The New York Times*, March 10, 2012, p. A7.

5   Michael Schwirtz, "What? I Won? Opposition is Surprised by Its Success in Moscow Vote," *The New York Times*, March 9, 2012, p. A4.

6   David Stern, "Svoboda: The Rise of Ukraine's Ultra-Nationalists," *BBC News Magazine*, December 26, 2012.

7   Andrei Kolesnikov, "Vse dorogi veli v Krym," *Kommersant*, March 19, 2014.

8   *National Interest*, Rossia I, December 10, 2011, 6:05–6:50 p.m., Moscow time.

9   Maxim Kononenko, blog, "Idiot," March 13, 2012. A month earlier on February 23, 2012, Kononenko contributed http://kononenkome.livejournal.com/635330.html

10   Multitasking, it is increasingly evident, does not produce efficient and high-level results. Marcel Just and his colleagues, in looking at the architecture of human thought, find worrisome results in overlapping, simple tasks involving different areas of the brain: when just two tasks are involved, doing them separately is twice as efficient as when they are done at the same time. In addition, it takes longer when they are done simultaneously rather than separately. These are extremely simple tasks, I should emphasize. Marcel Adam Just, Patricia A. Carpenter, Timothy A. Keller, Lisa Emery, Holly Zajac, and Keith R. Thulborn, "Interdependence in Nonoverlapping Cortical Systems in Dual Cognitive Tasks," *Neuroimage* 14 (2001): 417–426. http://www.idealibrary.com on IDEAL.

Just is Director of the Center for Cognitive Brain Imaging at Carnegie Mellon University, Psychology Department.

11   Ellen Mickiewicz, *Changing Channels: Television and the Struggle for Power in Russia*, rev. and expanded edn. (Durham, NC: Duke University Press, 1999).

12   Ibid., p. 141.

13   Ibid., p. 142.

14   Victor Pelevin, *Homo Zapiens*, trans. Andrew Bromfield (New York: Viking, 2000).

15   He had one other portfolio: eliminating corruption. The sheer scale of corruption in Russia from policemen on the street to money-laundering corporate chiefs was and remains beyond repair under today's power structure. See the work of Janine R. Wedel, *Collision and Collusion* (New York: St. Martin's Press, 1998); and *Shadow Elite* (New York: Basic Books, 2009).

16   Simon Shuster, "Occupy the Kremlin: Russia's Election Lets Loose Public Rage," December 5, 2011. http://www.time.com/time/printout/0,8816,2101569,00 .html#

17   Government funds that are disbursed to reform public utilities, for example, including housing, "continue to be stolen." "Russians' expenditures on housing and utility services are significantly higher than the average European level,...the services' quality remains far worse....Experts believe that such a sharp increase in tariffs [as planned] could have been avoided had the authorities not bowed to the interests of the natural monopolies." Lyudmila Alexandrova, "Prices of Housing, Utility Services in Russia—Bad and Expensive to Rise Further," ITAR-TASS, September 20, 2011. Reprinted in *Johnson's Russia List*, 2011-#168, 20 September 2011.http://www://archive .constantcontact.com/fs053//1102820649387/archive/1102911694293.html

Ellen Barry's descriptions add still more observations about the desperate lives of Russia's very large population of the suffering poor. "At the edge of Russia's two great cities [Moscow and St. Petersburg] another Russia begins....people are struggling with choices that belong to past centuries: to heat their homes with a wood stove, which must be fed by hand every three hours, or burn diesel fuel, which costs half a month's salary." "Between the Big Cities, a Road Passes the Russia Left Behind," *The New York Times*, October 15, 2013, p. A1.

18   *Dvadtsat let reform glazami rossian (opyt mnogoletnikh sotsiologicheskikh zamerov), Analitichesky doklad* (Twenty years of reform through the eyes of Russians, Findings of multi-year sociological studies: Analytic Report) (Moscow: Institute of Sociology of the Russian Academy of Sciences, 2011), p. 66.

This is a major project by eleven sociologists responsible for different parts of the study: the "science consultant" was the head of the Friedrich

Ebert Foundation, R. Krumm. The study is drawn primarily from national surveys carried out by the Institute of Sociology from 2001 to 2011.

The Academy of Sciences study points to substandard and increasingly expensive housing as the first dissatisfaction of Russians in 2011 and the sentiment that "the whole weight of the crisis has been put on ordinary citizens...the sacrifices are not spread around equally." They (respondents in the survey) have also heard official statements about ending the crisis as meaning that the "'long term' 'eradication of the effects' means their income will be falling...and it will not be temporary." The feeling of helplessness is growing, together with a belief that social mobility, including acquiring good education and being able to rise in professions, is gone (p. 92).

19 Ibid., p. 66.

20 Ibid., pp. 72–76.

21 I. Denisova, "Income Distribution and Poverty in Russia," *OECD Social, Employment and Migration Working Papers*, No. 132 (Paris: OECD Publishing, 2012). http://www.oecd-ilibrary.org/docserver/download/5k9csf9zcz7c.pdf?expires=1395324586&id=id&accname=guest&checksum=BBB8E421946F7F5C27143407A32C4191

22 Ibid., p. 11. It should be noted, as always, when analyzing Russia, that there are significant regional disparities.

23 Ibid., pp. 37–38.

24 W. Bruce Lincoln, *Between Heaven and Hell: The Story of a Thousand Years of Artistic Life in Russia* (New York: Viking, 1998), p. 227.

25 Alessandro Orsini, *Anatomy of the Red Brigades: The Religious Mind-Set of Modern Terrorists*, trans. Sarah J. Nodes (Ithaca, NY: Cornell University Press, 2011), p. 32.

26 Ellen Barry, "Russia, Shifting from Soviet Ways, Hesitantly Welcomes Volunteers in Flood Zone," *The New York Times*, July 15, 2012, p. A6.

27 Ibid.

28 Peter Lekarev, "Press Review—Krymsk: Volunteers vs. Authorities?" *The Voice of Russia Radio*, http://voiceofrussia.com/radio_broadcast/25950828/82014072/

29 Ellen Barry, "Russia: 4 are Jailed as Tolerance for Flood Volunteers Wears Thin," *The New York Times*, July 18, 2012, p. A6.

CHAPTER 3

1 Luis V. Casalo, Carlos Flavian, and Miguel Guinliu, "Understanding the Intention to Follow the Advice Obtained in an Online Travel Community," *Computers in Human Behavior* 27 (2011): 622–633.

2   Diana C. Mutz, "Effects of Internet Commerce on Social Trust," *Political Opinion Quarterly* 73, no. 3 (Fall 2009): 439–461, 440.

3   Robert Putnam, Robert Leonardi, and Raffaele Y. Nanetti, *Making Democracy Work: Civic Traditions in Modern Italy* (Princeton: Princeton University Press, 1994).

4   Ardion Beldad, Menno de Jong, and Michael Steehouder, " 'How Shall I Trust the Faceless and the Intangible': A Literature Review on the Antecedents of Online Trust," *Computers in Human Behavior* 26 (2010): 857–869.

5   Mutz, "Effects of Internet Commerce on Social Trust," p. 440. See also-Paul J. Zak, "The Neuroeconomics of Trust," in *Renaissance in Behavioral Economics*, edited by Roger Frantz (New York: Routledge, 2007);Paul J. Zak and Stephen Knack, "Trust and Growth," *The Economic Journal* 111 (2001): 295–321;Stephen Knack and Philip Keefer, "Does Social Capital Have an Economic Payoff? A Cross-Country Investigation," *Quarterly Journal of Economics* 112 (1997): 1251–1288.

6   Research in the United States has shown that friendship groups have less diversity of points of view than any other source of points of view, such as media. It is logical: one picks one's friends, but not completely other sources of views. The next note provides a citation for the larger research project.

7   Matthew Gentzkow and Jesse M. Shapiro, "Ideological Segregation Online and Offline," April 13, 2010. Chicago Booth Research Paper No. 10–19, Chicago Booth initiative on Global Markets Working Paper No. 55, Social Science Research Network. http://faculty.chicagobooth.edu/jesse.shapiro/research/echo_chambers.pdf.

8   Howard Raiffa, *The Art and Science of Negotiation* (Cambridge, MA: Harvard University Press, 1982).

9   Annette Bolte and Thomas Goschke, "On the Speed of Intuition: Intuitive Judgments of Semantic Coherence under Different Response Deadlines," *Memory & Cognition* 33, no. 7 (2005): 1248–1255, 1248.

10 D. Kahneman and G. Klein, "Conditions for Intuitive Expertise: A Failure to Disagree," *The American Psychologist* 64 (2009): 515–526. This and several other citations on which this discussion is based may be found in Akinci Cinla and Eugene Sadler-Smith, "Intuition in Management Research: A Historical Review," *International Journal of Management Reviews* 14, no. 1 (June 14, 2011): 104–122.

11 For a look at this process in the case of Russian television viewers, see Ellen Mickiewicz, *Television, Power, and the Russian Public* (Cambridge: Cambridge University Press, 2008).

12 Katelyn Y. A. McKenna, Amie S. Green, and Marci E. J. Gleason, "Relationship Formation on the Internet: What's the Big Attraction?" *Journal of Social Issues* 58, no. 1 (2002): 9–31. This discussion of the passenger effect is based mainly on their study.

13 Sherry Turkle, *Alone Together: Why We Expect More from Technology and Less from Each Other* (New York: Basic Books, 2011), p. 288.

14 Ibid., p. 10

15 Ibid., p. 11.

Chapter 4

1   *Internet World Stats* defines a user as anyone who currently "has the capacity to use the internet." Two conditions are necessary: the person must have access to an internet connection and the person must have basic knowledge to make use of the internet. There are no age or frequency variables. Nielsen Online has a category called active Internet User: this is the number of people who viewed the internet "at least once during the last month." I do not think we will get a true picture of Russia's future leaders by including in the study users who occasionally drop in to a site or two once or twice a month. We will not be using these data. We concentrate on the true inhabitants of the internet: going there every day or every other day, and unless specifically stated, we confine the study to these real, not casual, users. Information produced by Universal McCann and ComScore is very helpful. Spring 2011 data from the Foundation for Public Opinion in Moscow, by 2011, found 53% of Russians 18 and over were monthly visitors. Daily users in the winter of 2012–13 poll results from the Public Opinion Foundation were fewer, 43% of the population of the country.

2   ComScore, "Russia has Fastest Growing Internet Population in Europe," November 7, 2007. http://www.comscore.com/Insights/Press_Releases/2007/11/Russia_Fastest_Growing_European_Internet_Population

3   A very large study of Twitter convincingly concluded that the skewed distribution of followers and the low rate of reciprocity suggest that Twitter is closer to an information-sharing network than a social network.

4   Matthew Gentzkow and Jesse M. Shapiro, "Ideological Segregation Online and Offline," April 13, 2010. Chicago Booth Research Paper No. 10-19, Chicago Booth Initiative on Global Markets Working Paper No. 55, Social Science Research Network. http://www.nber.org/papers/w15916

5   These data and those that follow, unless otherwise noted, are based on "Top 20 Most Popular Russian Websites." http://topsitesblog.com/russian-websites/

6   "Facebook is Nr. 1 Social Network in 15 of 18 European Markets," March 2, 2011. http://www.comscoredatamine.com/2011/03/facebook-is-nr-1- social -network-in-15-of-18-european-markets/

7   http://en.wikipedia.org/wiki/VK_%28social_network%29

8   For a detailed provision of data for additional sites, see Sarah Oates, *Revolution Stalled: The Political Limits of the Internet in the Post-Soviet Sphere* (New York: Oxford University Press, 2013).

9   William Evans, citation from David Remnick, "Letter from Moscow," *The New Yorker*, September 22, 2011. See n. 14 for information on Evans's excellent thesis.

10 Evans, citation from Alina Rebel, "Russia: Ekho Moskvy Chief Editor Comments on New Format, Freedom of Speech," Gazeta.ru, October 27, 2006.

11 Much of the above, about Venediktov and his practices over time, is based on a fine M.A. thesis by William Evans, "The Anomaly of Ekho Moskvy: Adaptation Strategies for the Survival of Diversity of Viewpoints in Russian Media during the Putin Era," Slavic Studies Department, Duke University, Spring 2012. His massive dataset included name, position, topic addressed, date, and other pertinent information for every guest on an *Ekho* program personally hosted by Venediktov, as well as other information, such as the business model devised by Venediktov to reduce or eliminate economic reliance on the owner.

12 Paul Goble, "Five New Statistics about Russia that Say More than a Glance Might Suggest," *Window on Eurasia*, Johnson's Russia List, 2013, #41, March 1, 2013. http://windowoneurasia2.blogspot.com/2013/03/window-on-eurasia-five-new-statistics.html

13 http://tns-global.ru/

14 New restricted areas may be handed down by new CEO, Yekaterina Pavlova. Oleg Sukhov, "More Pressure on Liberal Media, as Ekho Moskvy gets new CEO," *Johnson's Russia List*, 2014, #15, February 24, 2014.

15 Ellen Mickiewicz, *Television, Power, and the Russian Public* (Cambridge: Cambridge University Press, 2008).

16 Stephen Hutchings and Vera Tolz, "Fault Lines in Russia's Discourse of Nation: Television Coverage of the December 2010 Moscow Riots," *Slavic Review* 71, no. 4 (Winter 2012): 873–899.

17 The suggested sources are: DPNI, a right-wing nationalist site, Alexei Navalny's site on LiveJournal, Lenta.ru (a news aggregator and interactive news commentator), LiveJournal, Channel One, Other.

CHAPTER 5

1   An extremist nationalist organization: Movement Against Illegal Immigration. It will come up in greater detail later in the chapter.

2   A popular news aggregator and discussion site.

3   Keith Bradsher, "Russia: Nearly 400 Are Detained in Immigration Raid," *The New York Times*, April 12, 2013, p. A9.

4   This material is largely based on: Simon Shuster, "Russia's Race Riots: Are Police Turning a Blind Eye?" *Time*, December 15. 2010. http://content.time.com/time/world/article/0,8599,2036936,00.html

5 Andrew Roth, "Ethnic Tension Drives Russian Crackdown on Rubber-Bullet Guns," *The New York Times*, November 6, 2012, p. A8.

6 Donald L. Horowitz, *Ethnic Groups in Conflict*, 2nd edn. (Berkeley and Los Angeles: University of California Press, 2000).

7 In this focus group there were three Ivans, so one was Ivan; one was the short-form Vanya; and the third was the full name plus the patronymic: Ivan Vladimirovich.

8 Floriana Fossato and John Lloyd, with Alexander Verkhovsky, "The Web that Failed: How Opposition Politics and Independent Initiatives Are Failing on the Internet in Russia," Reuters Institute for the Study of Journalism, University of Oxford, Oxford, 2008, p. 23.

9 Donald L. Horowitz, *The Deadly Ethnic Riot* (Berkeley and Los Angeles: University of California Press, 2001). In this important work, Horowitz examines how "specialists" enter nonviolent ethnic riots, converting them to broader, more deadly and less controllable events, often with the collusion or deliberate inattention of the institutions of law and order.

10 This and the following discussion are from an interview the author had with Alexander Verkhovsky on October 21, 2011.

11 Dennis Zuev, "The Movement against Illegal Immigration: Analysis of the Central Node in the Russian Extreme-Right Movement," *Nations and Nationalism* 16, no. 2 (March 11, 2010): 261–284. Published online.

12 I thank Svetlana Pasti for local sources about this incident.

13 Much of the discussion that follows is drawn from parts of Ksenofobia, svoboda sovesti, i antiekstremizm v Rossii v 2011 gody, Doklady informatsionno-analiticheskogo tsentra 'SOVA', Moscow, 2012.

14 The Nationalists and the Protest Movement," SOVA (Center for information and analysis], August 23, 2012, no author listed.http://www.sova-center.ru/en/xenophobia/conference-papers/2012/08/d25143/

15 Ibid., p. 16.

16 Police in the small town of Kamensk-Uralsk suspect that at least eleven beatings of different victims were carried out between April and June 2013. The footage of one beating is a display of as many as half a dozen young men repeatedly beating, stomping on a helpless young man held down on the ground by the "Occupy" members. "Nazi-Linked Russian Vigilantes Busted in Bullying Footage Probe," *RT*, August 8, 2013.

17 Andrew Roth, "Russian Youth Group with a Mission: Sniffing Out Illegal Movements," *The New York Times*, September 4, 2013, p. A6.

18 Sergei L. Loiko, "Russian Police Detain Migrants Who Were Targets of Riot," *latimes.com*, October 14, 2013. http://articles.latimes.com/2013/oct/14/world/la-fg-wn-russian-police-migrants-riot-20131014

19 David Herszenhorn, "Russia: Self-Defense Claim in Killing," *The New York Times*, October 17, 2013, p. A16.

20 Trudolubov interview.

21 Ibid., p. 33.

22 Interview with Yury Saprykin, May 2012.

23 Interview with Yury Saprykin, May 2012.

24 James Kimer, "Yury Saprykin: Quo Vadis, Opposition?" Robert Amsterdam .com: Perspectives on Global Politics and Business, March 7, 2012. http:// robertamsterdam.com/2012/03/yury-sprykin-quo-vadis-opposition/

25 Andrew E. Kramer, "Fixing Leaky Pipes with Opposition Help," The Global Edition of *The New York Times*, December 14, 2012, p. 5.

CHAPTER 6

1 "Ofitsialny sait Glavnogo upravlenia Ministerstva vnutrennikh del Rossiiskoi Federatsii po g. Moskve. Press Service of the CD [Chief Directorate] MVD [Ministry of Internal Affairs] po g. Moskve [for the city of Moscow].

2 Ekaterina Vinokurova, "Occupy!"www.gazeta.ru, October 23, 2012.

3 Michael, Schwirtz, "A Russian Protest Leader Takes Center State," *The New York Times*, May 12, 2012, p. A6.

4 TV-*Rain*, April 18, 2013, interview with Mikhail Kasyanov and video of Bolotnaya 2. The most detailed examination of the events was a 66-page report presented by the non-governmental "International Expert Commission." May 6, 2012 Events in Bolotnaya Square in Moscow: Expert Evaluation , Moscow 2013. http://6maycommission.org/sites/default/files/ iec_report_eng.pdf

5 tvrain.ru/articles/alekseja_gaskarov_ostavili_v_sizo_do_28_ijunja-342384

6 David M. Herszenhorn, "New Russian Law Assesses Heavy Fine on Protestors," *The New York Times*, June 9, 2012, p. A5.

7 Jonathan Earle and Alec Luhn, "Georgian Organized Clashes, Investigators Say," *The Moscow Times*, December 14–16, 2012, pp. 1 and 2.

8 Russian Duma Passes Controversial Defamation, NGO Bills, RFE/RL, July 12, 2012.http://www.rferl.org/content/russia-duma-to-vote-on-controversial-bills/24643937.html

9 Andrei Soldatov and Irina Borogan, "The Kremlin's New Internet Surveillance Plan Goes Live Today" http://www.wired.com/danger-room/2012/11/russia-surveillance/all/. I thank Andrei Richter for bringing this source to my attention.

10 Sarah Oates, *Revolution Stalled: The Political Limits of the Internet in the Post-Soviet Sphere* (New York: Oxford University Press, 2013), pp. 93–103.

11 The following discussion is based partly on Soldatov and Borogan, "The Kremlin's New Internet Surveillance Plan."

12 Marc Rotenberg, "Communications Networks and Consumer Privacy," testimony before the House Committee and Energy and Commerce Subcommittee on Communications, Technology and the Internet, April 23, 2009. I thank Marc Rotenberg for sending me his testimony.

13 Soldatov and Borogan, "The Kremlin's New Internet Surveillance Plan."

14 Ibid.

15 Art Reisman, "What is Deep Packet Inspection and Why the Controversy?" NetEqualizer News Blog, February 8, 2011. http://netequalizernews .com/2011/02/08/what-is-deep-packet-inspection-and-why-the-controversy/

16 "Forgoing Deep Content Inspection Leaves Doors Open to Criminals," Reed Exhibitions Ltd., January 30, 2013. http://www .infosecurity-magazine.com/view/30478/forgoing-deep-content-inspecti on-leaves-doors-open-to-cyber-criminals/

17 Ibid.

18 Interview with Maria Zhunich, November 25, 2011.

19 Alisa Shtykina, "Chislo polzovatelei Google, zainteresovavshikh rossiiskikh silovikov, vyroslo za dva goda v tri raza (Russian internal police interested in Google users trebled in two years), Gazeta.ru, January 24, 2013.

20 Liat Clark, "Facebook, Twitter, YouTube Complying with Russia Blocking Requests," Wired.co.uk, April 2, 1013. http://www.wired.co.uk/news/ archive/2013-04/2/russia-internet-censorship?oo=o

21 Ilya Khrennikov, "Russia Withdraws Threat to Block Facebook After Content Expunged," Bloomberg, April 1, 2013. http://www.bloomberg .com/news/2013-04-01/russia-withdraws-threat-to-block-facebook-after- content-expunged.html

22 James Risen, "Report Indicates More Extensive Cooperation by Microsoft on Surveillance," *The New York Times*, July 12, 2013, p. A14.

23 Somini Gupta, "2 E-Mail Services Close and Destroy Data Rather Than Reveal Files," *The New York Times*, August 10, 2013, pp. B1–B2.

24 Charlie Savage, "N.S.A. Said to Have Paid E-Mail Providers Millions to Cover Costs from Court Ruling," *The New York Times*, p. A14.

25 Ibid.

26 Nicole Perlroth, Jeff Larson, and Scott Shane, "N.S.A. Able to Foil Basic Safeguards of Privacy on Web," *The New York Times*, pp. 1, 12.

27 Although Russia agreed to the worldwide copyright protection, it has not been active.

28 "Russia: Hundreds of Groups Searched," AP, reprinted in *The New York Times*, March 22, p. A6.

29 Valeriya Khamrayeva, "The Justice Ministry Surprised Rights Advocates: The Department Has Settled on the Procedure of Definition of 'Foreign Agents,'" *Nezavisimaya gazeta*, February 17, 2013. Translated and Reprinted in Johnson's Russia List, 2013-#41, 2 March 2013, http://www.russialist.org

30 FARA.gov

31 David Herszenhorn, "Progress is Reported in Arms Talks with Russia," *The New York Times*, March 22, 2013, p. A12.

32 Grigory Golosov, "Have the September Elections Changed Anything?" published in http://www.opendemocracy.net, September 17 2013, Reprinted by Johnson's Russia List, 18 September 2013, #2013-#170.

33 Henry Meyer and Stepan Kravchenko, "Russian Lawmakers Back Bill Abolishing Direct Regional Elections," Bloomberg.com, January 24, 2013.

34 Nikolai Svanidze interviewed by Evgenia Samsonova on streaming video station, *Rain*, May 6, 2013.

35 Editorial: "Coordination Council's False Start. Why Politicians Have Been Forced to Leave the Opposition Structure." *Nezavisamaya Gazeta*, February 7, 2013. Reprinted and translated in Johnson's Russia List, 2013#7. February 8, 2013.

36 Mikhail Anshakov, "Goodbye, KS," Radio *Ekho Moskvy*, May 7, 2013.

37 Ibid.

38 Communication to the author, September 20, 2013.

39 Ibid.

CHAPTER 7

1   Interview with Alexander Oslon, December 22, 2012.

2   John Aldrich, *Why Parties? The Origin and Transformation of Political Parties in America* (Chicago: University of Chicago Press, 1995) and his later *Why Parties? A Second Look* (Chicago: University of Chicago Press, 2011). Aldrich's works are essential studies showing the roles political parties play in the United States. Henry E. Hale, *Why Not Parties in Russia? Democracy, Federalism and the State* (Cambridge: Cambridge University Press, 2006), is a valuable source for thinking about the "older" parties as well as United Russia, difficult to label easily as a "normal" political party. The group of parties and groupings outside the mainstream (called by Russians "non-system") differ in their genesis and leadership. The broadening of lists of parties and individuals able to overcome a lower threshold may make of the party landscape in Russia, something substantially different, but the time this process may take to alter the political system may be glacial, in the sense that considerable agreement expressed in voting coalitions may be the key to the success of the liberal agenda, should fragmentation be the result of a proliferation of parties.

3   Josiah Ober, "Democracy's Dignity," *American Political Science Review* 106, no. 4 (November 2012): 827–846, citation is on 831.

4   For studies of America and tolerance, see David O. Sears, James Sidanius, and Lawrence Bobo, *Racialized Politics: The Debate about Racism in*

America (Chicago: Chicago University Press, 2000). See also works by James L. Gibson, John L. Sullivan, George E. Marcus, David Kinder, and many others.

5   "Natsionalnoe stroitelstvo i natsionalizm v sovremennoi Rossii. Obzor sotsiologicheskogo oprosa," www.sova-center/racism-xenophobia/publications 2013/09

    See also Paul Goble, "Window on Eurasia: Russians Deeply Conflicted on Ethnic Issues, Poll Shows," *Johnson's Russia List*, 2013-#171, September 19, 2013. http://archive.constantcontact.com/fs156/1102820649387/archive/1114980559317.html

6   Alexander Verkhovsky, "O Biriulevskom fronte," Blog in *Svobodnoe mesto*, October 23, 2013.

7   Aleksei Navalny, "Razvyornutaya positsia po Ukraine i Krymu," navalny. livejournao.com/914090.html March 12, 2014.

8   "Dopros s pristrastiem dlya Alekseya Navalnovo," *The New Times*, no. 23(291), July 1, 2013.

9   "Politsija i organizatory razoshlis v otsenke chislennosti 'Russkogo marsha' "/tvrain.ru/articles/November 4, 2013.

10   Jennifer A. Peeples and Bentley Mitchell, " 'No Mobs—No Confusions—No Tumult': Networking and Civil Disobedience," *The Electronic Journal of Communication*, 17, nos. 1 and 2, 2007. http://www.cios.org/EJCPUBLIC/017/1/01714.HTML

11   Ibid.

12   Michael J. Jensen, Laia Jorba, and Eva Anduiza, *Digital Media and Political Engagement Worldwide* (Cambridge: University of Cambridge Press, 2012), p. 17.

13   Michael Coppedge, *Democratization and Research Methods* (Strategies for Social Inquiry (UK: Cambridge University Press, 2012).

INDEX

adoption, 190
advertisements, 116
Afghanistan, 12
Afisha (magazine and internet site), 162
Agence France Presse, 39
Akunin, Boris, 165
Aldrich, John, 247n2
Alexander II, Tsar of Russia, 73–74
American National Exhibition (Moscow, 1959), 15–16
Anduiza, Eva, 226
Anshakov, Mikhail, 204
appearance, 84, 86–91
Assange, Julian, 183

Bandera, Stepan, 54
Barnard, Anne, 34
Barry, Ellen, 202, 239n17
BBC (British Broadcasting Corporation), 39
Beketov, Mikhail, 142
Belov, Alexander, 156
Bezugly, Ivan, 78
Black Panthers, 74
blogs
    Chirikova and, 147
    Kononenko and, 59
    Medvedev and, 2, 47, 59, 60, 62, 65–70, 135, 211, 213, 222
    Navalny and, 3–4, 45–46, 62, 113
    politics and, 111–12
    social networks and, 61–62
Blumfield, Mark, 6

Bolotnaya demonstration (2011)
    events of, 76–77, 174, 191, 223–24
    media and, 58–59, 73
    Putin and, 38
Bolotnaya demonstration (2012)
    events of, 173–76
    responses to, 172, 176–91
Bolotnaya demonstration (2013), 194
Bondarik, Nikolai, 198
Bono, 143
Boston Marathon bombing (2013), 191, 215
broadband access, 20–21
Brzezinski, Zbigniew, 14

Cameron, David, 11
Catechism of a Revolutionary (Sergei Nechaev), 74
Chechnya, 46
Cherkesov, Aslan, 148–49
Chernobyl nuclear disaster, 40–42
China
    internet in, 76
    Putin and, 58
Chirikova, Yevgenia, 141–42, 143–44, 146, 147, 180, 195
Chivers, C. J., 34
Classmates, 114
cloud-seeding, 40–41
CNN, 34
cognitive dissonance, 9
Cold War, 27–28, 30
Collins, James F. , 1

Communist Party of the Soviet Union, 11
Coordinating Council (Koordinatsionny
    Sovet, KS), 195–207, 210, 221
Coppedge, Michael, 227–28
copyright law, 188
corruption, 43, 49
Cossacks, 77–78
Crimea
    McCain and, 36
    nationalism and, 212
    Putin and, 50, 54–56, 57–58, 179
    Ukraine and, 53–56
Czechoslovakia, 12

Dagestan Republic, 46
Deep Content Inspection (DCI), 183–84
Deep Packet Inspection (DPI), 181–84
defamation, 180–81
democracy, 226–28
demonstrations
    penalties and fines for, 177
    significance of, 222–26
    in Soviet Union, 51–52
demonstrations in Moscow
    Bolotnaya demonstration (2011), 38,
        58–59, 73, 76–77, 174, 191, 223–24
    Bolotnaya demonstration (2012), 172,
        173–91
    Bolotnaya demonstration (2013), 194
    gay rights and, 52
    Khimki Forest protests, 2, 140–47, 195
    media and, 123
    Sakharov Prospect
        demonstration, 3, 160–71, 191,
        195, 205–6, 224–26
Deutsche Welle, 39
Dickens, Charles, 83
dignity, 213
disclosure, 94–96
DPNI (Movement Against Illegal
    Immigration), 152–57, 163, 170–71
Ebert Foundation (Germany), 216–17
echo chamber, 108, 111
The Economist (periodical), 39

Egypt, 24, 184, 224–25
Eisenhower, Dwight D., 15
Ekho Moskvy ("Echo of Moscow,"
    internet radio and blog), 56–57,
    120–23, 127, 204
environmental demonstrations. *See*
    Khimki Forest protests
ethnicity, 107–8
Euronews, 39
Evans, William, 243n11

Facebook
    demonstrations and, 226
    internet restrictions and, 185, 186
    Organizing Committee and, 163,
        164–66, 170
    in Russia, 112, 113–14
family, 134–36, 137–38
Fedotov, Mikhail, 190
fines, 177, 180–81
First Channel (Russian television
    channel), 124–27
flash mobs, 161, 224–25
Ford Foundation, 180
Foreign Agents Registration Act
    (FARA), 189
France, 21, 39, 232, 233–34
freedom of speech, 180–81

Gagarin, Yury, 67
Gamson, William, 8
Gaskarov, Aleksei, 166, 176
gay rights, 52
Gazaryan, Suren, 78
Gazprom, 59, 121
Georgia, 24, 151, 178–79
Georgian–South Ossetian–Russian conflict
    (2008), 31–36, 121, 179
Germany, 12, 21, 232, 233
Goddard, Ben, 63
"Going to the people" movement, 73–74,
    75, 79, 169
Golos (organization), 40, 180, 189
Golosov, Grigory, 193

Google, 38, 112, 184–85, 186
Gorbachev, Mikhail, 14, 52, 165
governors, 50–51, 193
Great Expectations (Dickens), 83
Grushin, Aleksei, 41–42
The Guardian (newspaper), 39

Higher Economic School Research
   University (HES), 7, 17, 230
higher education
   leadership and, 6–7, 17
   in Russia, 6–7, 18
Homo Zapiens (Victor Pelevin), 64
hooliganism, 78–79
Horowitz, Donald L., 244n9
Human Rights Watch, 35

India, 58
inequality, 72–73
Institution of Higher Education (Vysshee
   Uchebnoe Zavedenie, VUZ), 18
internet
   access to, 20–21, 110, 210–11
   in China, 76
   favorite sites in Russia, 112–13
   leadership and, 44
   personality and, 103–4
   politicians' sites and, 118–19
   research on, 6
   research participants and, 2, 26,
      58–60, 110–11, 113–20, 136,
      138–39
   restrictions on, 181–88
   social networks and, 61–62, 64–65, 97,
      111, 113–15
   trust and, 96–109
   See also blogs
internships, 7
intuition, 97–98
Iraq, 24
Izvestia (Russian newspaper), 73

Japan, 21–22, 27, 233, 234
Jensen, Michael J. , 226

Jorba, Laia, 226
Just, Marcel, 238–39n10

Kagan, Robert, 35
Kahneman, Daniel, 98
Kara-Murza, Vladimir, 202
Kashin, Oleg, 143
Kasparov, Gary, 202–3
Kasyanov, Mikhail, 175–75
Kats, Maxim, 219
Khamatova, Thulpan, 165
Khimki Forest protests, 2, 140–47, 195
Khrushchev, Nikita, 13, 53, 57
Kommersant (Russian newspaper), 143
Kononenko, Maxim, 58–59
Kozyrev, Andrei, 14
Krichevskaya, Vera, 219
Krumm, R., 240n18
Krylov, Konstantin, 166, 198–99
Krymsk flood (2012), 77–79
Kubrakov, Ilya, 150
Kudrin, Aleksei, 167
Kuznetsov, Mikhail, 150
Kyrgyzstan, 24

Latvia, 51
Lavabit, 186
leadership
   education and, 6–7, 17
   internet and, 44
Lebedev, Konstantin, 179
Lebedev, Pavel, 44
Left Front (party), 177. *See also* Udaltsov,
   Sergei
Lenta.ru, 56
Levada Center, 188
Libya, 24, 27, 151
Lithuania, 51
LiveJournal (ZhZh, Russian social
   network), 112–13, 133

Magnitsky, Sergei, 189–90, 202
Magnitsky law, 189–90
Martsinkevic, Maxim ("Hatchet"), 158

mass public opinion survey, 8

Mavrodi, Sergei, 165

McCain, John, 35, 36

McFaul, Michael, 180

media and news sources
  Georgian-South Ossetian-Russian
    conflict and, 30–35
  race riots in Moscow (2010)
    and, 36–38
  research participants and, 9, 38–39,
    128–29
  restrictions on, 56–57

Medvedev, Dmitry
  blog and, 2, 47, 59, 60, 62, 65–70, 135,
    211, 213, 222
  Bolotnaya demonstration and, 38
  Khimki Forest protests and, 141
  Putin and, 49–50, 164
  race riots in Moscow (2010) and, 150

microblogging, 111

Microsoft, 185–86

Mill, John Stuart, 222

Mitchell, Bentley, 224

Mitrokhin, Sergei, 204–5

Moscow
  race riots (2010), 5–6, 36–38, 147–52,
    159
  race riots (2013), 5–6, 159–60, 217
  as separated from the rest of
    Russia, 52–53, 134, 169, 200–201
  See also demonstrations in Moscow

Moscow Helsinki Group, 180

Moscow State Institute of Foreign Affairs
  (MGIMO), 7, 17, 229–30

Moscow State University (MSU), 7, 17,
  61, 229

Muslim Brotherhood, 224–25

National Endowment for Democracy, 180

National Security Agency (NSA), 182,
  183, 186–87

nationalism
  Crimea and, 212
  Navalny and, 218–20
  Putin and, 151, 158, 215–16

NATO, 35

Navalny, Aleksei
  blog and, 3–4, 45–46, 62, 113
  Bolotnaya demonstration and, 175
  campaign for mayor of Moscow
    and, 3–4, 45, 113, 192–93, 205–7,
    218–19
  Coordinating Council and, 198, 202
  corruption and, 3–4
  DPNI and, 171
  internet and, 169
  on Moscow and Russia, 53
  nationalism and, 218–20
  Organizing Committee and, 163–64,
    166
  Oslon on, 209
  research participants views of, 46–47,
    48, 145
  Sakharov Prospect demonstration
    and, 169, 225–26
  Yandex and, 185

Nechaev, Sergei, 74

Nemtsov, Boris
  Bolotnaya demonstration and, 175
  Coordinating Council and, 202, 209
  Organizing Committee and, 163, 165,
    166
  Sakharov Prospect demonstration
    and, 226
  Yeltsin and, 180

net neutrality, 183–84

The New York Times (newspaper), 12, 34,
  53, 202

news sources. See media and news sources

nongovernmental organizations, 187,
  188–89

North Korea, 191

NTV (Russian national television
  channel), 58–59, 121, 124, 126, 178

Obama, Barack, 187

Obama administration, 191

Ober, Josiah, 213

Occupy Wall Street, 158

Okupai-Pedofiliya, 158
Open Society foundation, 180
Orange Revolution (Ukraine), 22, 23, 24,
    151, 178
Organization for Economic Cooperation
    and Development (OECD), 72
Organizing Committee (orgkom), 162–68,
    170, 195
Oslon, Alexander, 208–12

parents and family, 134–36, 137–38
passenger effect, 99, 102–3
patronage, 134–36
Peeples, Jennifer A., 224
Pelevin, Victor, 64
performance, 84
political parties, 191–93
Ponomarev, Lev, 180
Ponomaryev, Ilya, 166
Popular Front, 193
poverty, 72
Prism (surveillance program), 186
privacy, 183–84, 188
Public Opinion Foundation
    (FOM), 208–12
public relations, 62–65
Pussy Riot (punk band), 59, 78
Putin, Vladimir
    "Address to the Nation" (2012), 76
    Bolotnaya demonstration and, 38, 173,
        176–79, 181
    Chernobyl nuclear disaster and, 41, 42
    Crimea and, 50, 54–56, 57–58, 179
    governors and, 193
    internet restrictions and, 181
    media and, 60, 123
    Medvedev and, 164
    nationalism and, 151, 158, 215–16
    NTV and, 121
    political parties formation rules
        and, 192
    Popular Front and, 193
    as president and prime minister, 49–50
    presidential campaign (2012), 66

race riots in Moscow (2010) and, 150–51
registration of NGOs as foreign agents
    and, 187, 188–89
Russian émigrés and, 211
Sarkozy and, 11, 21
Ukraine and, 22, 151
on United States, 24, 40
Putnam, Robert, 83
race riots
    in Moscow (2010), 5–6, 36–38,
        147–152, 159
    in Moscow (2013), 5–6, 159–60, 217
    in Pugachov, 216
    in St. Petersburg, 149

Rain (internet channel), 56, 123–24, 127,
    175–76, 196–97
Ramazan Utarbiev, 148
Razvozzhayev, Leonid, 179
Red Brigades (Italy), 74
religion, 107, 220
reputation, 84, 91–93, 117
research participants
    authority and, 60–62
    characteristics of, 3–4, 9–10, 16–19
    on democracy, 226–28
    on demonstrations, 223–24
    focus groups and, 2–3, 8–11, 25, 220
    as future leaders, 19–20
    future plans of, 135–37
    on important countries in the
        world, 21–23, 23, 39–40, 231–34
    intention to vote and, 10, 48
    internet and, 2, 26, 58–60, 110–11,
        113–20, 136, 138–39
    media and, 127–29
    moderator and, 8–9, 10, 32
    news sources and, 9, 38–39, 128–29
    patronage and, 134–36
    on people as source of
        information, 129–32, 133–34
    questionnaires and, 10–11, 132–34
    on race riots, 160
    recruitment of, 7–8

research participants (*Cont.*)
  on trust, 42–43, 80–82, 215
  on United Russia, 213–14
right-wing extremist groups, 5–6
Rotenberg, Marc, 182
Rousseff, Dilma, 187
Russia Channel, 58
Russian Academy of Sciences, 14, 157,
  212, 216–17
Russian Center for Information and
  Analysis, 216
Russian March (2013), 219–20
Russian political system, 49–51
Rybchinsky, Vitaly, 42

Saakashvili, Mikheil, 31, 33
Sakharov Prospect demonstration, 3,
  160–71, 191, 195, 205–6, 224–26
Saprykin, Yury
  Coordinating Council and, 195–200,
    204–5, 206–7
  on flash mobs, 225
  on internet restrictions, 188
  on Navalny, 206
  Putin and, 213
  Sakharov Prospect demonstration
    and, 161–70, 205, 225–26
Sarkozy, Nicolas, 11, 21
Schwirtz, Michael, 34, 53
Seattle, 224
Segalovsky, Ilya, 135
self-segregation, 110–11
Serbia, 14, 24, 25, 151
Shcherbakov, Yegor, 159
Shevchuk, Yury, 143
Shibanova, Lilia, 180, 189
Siberian tiger, 152–53
Silent Circle, 186
Skype, 96, 97, 186
Slavophiles, 75
Snowden, Edward, 3, 182, 183, 185, 186
Sobchak, Anatoly, 165–66
Sobchak, Ksenia
  Coordinating Council and, 198, 203

Navalny and, 218–19
Sakharov Prospect demonstration
  and, 165–66, 167
Sobyanin, Sergei, 113
soccer clubs, 155
social networks, 61–62, 64–65, 97, 111,
  113–15
social tension, 67–73. *See also*
  demonstrations
SORM and SORM2, 181
SOVA (Center for Information and
  Analysis), 155, 170
Soviet Union, 12–13, 42, 51
Der Spiegel (German newspaper), 35
St. Petersburg, 149
suicide, 185
Svanidze, Nikolai, 194
Sviridov, Yegor, 148–49
Syria, 151

Taliban, 12
Targamadze, Givi, 178
terrorism, 74–75
tolerance, 214–17
Tor, Vladimir, 166, 199
transparency, 188
Trudolubov, Maxim, 162, 201
trust
  criteria of, 84, 86–94
  disclosure and, 94–96
  internet and, 96–109, 220–21
  market and, 84–85
  political system and, 49
  research participants' views of, 42–43,
    80–82, 215
  risk and, 82–83
Turkey, 232, 234
Turkle, Sherry, 102
Tversky, Amos, 98
Twitter, 62, 185
Tyahnybok, Oleh, 54

U2, 143
Udaltsov, Sergei

Bolotnaya demonstration and, 173–75, 177, 178, 179
  Coordinating Council and, 199
  Sakharov Prospect demonstration and, 166–67
Ukraine
  civil unrest in (2014), 179
  Crimea and, 53–56
  Orange Revolution in, 22, 23, 24, 151, 178
  Putin and, 151
  research participants' views of, 22, 23, 39, 232–33, 234
United Nations (UN), 24
United Russia, 213–14
United States of America (USA)
  foreign policy of, 1
  research participants views of, 1–2, 22, 24–31, 39–40, 178–79, 187, 227, 231–32, 233
  Russian policy makers and, 187
  Russian views of, 13–16, 14
USAID, 40

Venediktov, Aleksei, 56, 121
Verkhovsky, Alexander, 155, 163, 170, 175, 216–17
Virgin Media, 184

virtual friendship, 100–1, 108
VKontakte (VK, Russian social network), 97, 112, 113–14, 133
Volkov, Leonid, 196, 206, 225
vote fraud, 44, 160–61. See also Sakharov Prospect demonstration
Vremya (tv news program), 124–25

Whitney, Craig, 34–35, 237n15
women
  in focus groups, 18
  race riots and, 160
  trust and, 87
World Trade Organization, 191, 224

Xi Jinping, 21

Yandex, 112, 135, 185
Yanukovich, Viktor, 22, 54, 151
Yashin, Ilya, 198
Yavlinsky, Grigory, 165
Yeltsin, Boris, 49, 62–63, 126, 180, 236n3
YouTube, 185
Yugoslavia, 12
Yushchenko, Victor, 54

Zhunich, Maria, 184–85
Ziuganov, Gennady, 135